THE
EVERYTHING.
HEALTHY COLLEGE COOKBOOK

Nicole Cormier, RD

Avon, Massachusetts

An Everything® Series Book.
Everything® and everything.com® are registered trademarks of F+W Media, Inc.

Published by Adams Media, a division of F+W Media, Inc.
57 Littlefield Street, Avon, MA 02322 U.S.A.
www.adamsmedia.com

ISBN 10: 1-4405-0411-3
ISBN 13: 978-1-4405-0411-2

Printed in the United States of America.

10 9 8 7 6 5 4 3 2 1

Library of Congress Cataloging-in-Publication Data
is available from the publisher.

This publication is designed to provide accurate and authoritative information with regard to the subject matter covered. It is sold with the understanding that the publisher is not engaged in rendering legal, accounting, or other professional advice. If legal advice or other expert assistance is required, the services of a competent professional person should be sought.

—From a *Declaration of Principles* jointly adopted by a Committee of the American Bar Association and a Committee of Publishers and Associations

Many of the designations used by manufacturers and sellers to distinguish their products are claimed as trademarks. Where those designations appear in this book and Adams Media was aware of a trademark claim, the designations have been printed with initial capital letters.

Contains material adapted and abridged from:
The Everything® College Cookbook, by Rhonda Lauret Parkinson, copyright © 2005 by F+W Media, Inc.,
ISBN 10: 1-59337-303-1, ISBN 13: 978-1-59337-303-0.
The Everything® Glycemic Index Cookbook, by Nancy T. Maar, copyright © 2006 by F+W Media, Inc.,
ISBN 10: 1-59337-581-6, ISBN 13: 978-1-59337-581-2.
The Everything® Calorie Counting Cookbook, by Paula Conway, copyright © 2008 by F+W Media, Inc.,
ISBN 10: 1-59869-416-2, ISBN 13: 978-1-59869-416-1.
The Everything® Low-Fat, High Flavor Cookbook, 2nd Edition, by Linda Larsen, copyright © 2008 by F+W Media, Inc.,
ISBN 10: 1-59869-604-1, ISBN 13: 978-1-59869-604-2.
The Everything® Whole-Grain, High-Fiber Cookbook, by Lynette Rhorer Shirk, copyright © 2008 by F+W Media, Inc.,
ISBN 10: 1-59869-507-X, ISBN 13: 978-1-59869-507-6.
The Everything® Guide to Being Vegetarian, by Alexandra Greely, copyright © 2009 by F+W Media, Inc.,
ISBN 10: 1-60550-051-8, ISBN 13: 978-1-60550-051-5.
The Everything® Flat Belly Cookbook, by Fitz Koehler, copyright © 2009 by F+W Media, Inc.,
ISBN 10: 1-60550-676-1, ISBN 13: 978-1-60550-676-0.
The Everything® Vegan Cookbook, by Jolinda Hackett with Lorena Novak Bull, copyright © 2010 by F+W Media, Inc.,
ISBN 10: 1-4405-0216-1, ISBN 13: 978-1-4405-0216-3.
The Everything® Guide to Macrobiotics, by Julie S. Ong with Lorena Novak Bull, copyright © 2010 by F+W Media, Inc.,
ISBN 10: 1-4405-0371-0, ISBN 13: 978-1-4405-0371-9.

This book is available at quantity discounts for bulk purchases.
For information, please call 1-800-289-0963.

THE
EVERYTHING
HEALTHY COLLEGE COOKBOOK

Dear Reader,

Throughout my experience as a registered dietitian, certified in adult weight management and owner of Delicious Living Nutrition, I have discovered there is a strong need for nutritional guidance, especially among the student population. College life brings challenges: between class schedules, independent meals, and having a social life, it can be difficult to think of eating for energy. After seeing many of my teenaged patients getting ready to head off to college within the next year and seeing their parents' looks of fright, it was clear there should be more simple tools to give students about surviving, from a nutritional standpoint, while at college.

Looking back on my college days at the University of Massachusetts at Amherst, I wish there had been more guidance around nutrition for me and my friends to follow. I remember trying many new fad diets we heard about instead of learning more about basic nutrition. I now know I would have felt better, had more energy, my weight wouldn't have fluctuated, and my studying would have been improved if I had just learned to eat healthy. Basically your typical should-have, could-have, would-have scenario!

My hope for this book is that it will give you an abundance of ideas for meals to eat that are delicious, easy to make, and give you the energy you need. As you read through the recipes, you'll be able to understand small changes you can apply everyday that will improve your college experience.

Yours in good health,

Nicole Cormier, RD

Welcome to the EVERYTHING® Series!

These handy, accessible books give you all you need to tackle a difficult project, gain a new hobby, comprehend a fascinating topic, prepare for an exam, or even brush up on something you learned back in school but have since forgotten.

You can choose to read an Everything® book from cover to cover or just pick out the information you want from our four useful boxes: e-questions, e-facts, e-alerts, and e-ssentials.

We give you everything you need to know on the subject, but throw in a lot of fun stuff along the way, too.

We now have more than 400 Everything® books in print, spanning such wide-ranging categories as weddings, pregnancy, cooking, music instruction, foreign language, crafts, pets, New Age, and so much more. When you're done reading them all, you can finally say you know Everything®!

FOOD LANGUAGE 101

Important terms for
eating healthy

THINK OUTSIDE THE BOX

New and creative ways
to stay healthy

BARGAINS FOR YOUR BUDGET

Ideas for stocking a
kitchen on the cheap

PUBLISHER Karen Cooper

DIRECTOR OF ACQUISITIONS AND INNOVATION Paula Munier

MANAGING EDITOR, EVERYTHING® SERIES Lisa Laing

COPY CHIEF Casey Ebert

ACQUISITIONS EDITOR Katrina Schroeder

SENIOR DEVELOPMENT EDITOR Brett Palana-Shanahan

ASSOCIATE DEVELOPMENT EDITOR Elizabeth Kassab

EVERYTHING® SERIES COVER DESIGNER Erin Alexander

LAYOUT DESIGNERS Colleen Cunningham, Elisabeth Lariviere, Ashley Vierra, Denise Wallace

Visit the entire Everything® series at *www.everything.com*

THE FOLLOWING TERMS ARE SHOWN ACCORDING TO EACH RECIPE:

Low-calorie: Less than 250 calories.

Low-fat: Less than 3 g.

Gluten-free: Food brands contain different ingredients, so be sure to read labels to ensure the item does not contain gluten.

Vegetarian: Some recipes may have eggs or egg beaters.

Vegan: Some recipes may still contain items that may have come in contact with animals.

Lactose-free: Does not contain lactose, but this depends on which brands you use.

Low-carb: Less than 15 g.

High-fiber: More than 5 g.

Contents

Introduction

Why Cook in College?

EVERY FALL, HORDES OF students just like you leave the familiarity of their parents' houses and hometowns and arrive on college campuses, ready to move away from their high school days and transition into the adult world. For most, this means living away from home for the first time, meeting new people from different places, and beginning to consider what kind of a career they might want. Very few, however, consider the fact that their new dorms do not come complete with personal chefs. Now your family's kitchen at home has been reduced to, at worst, a lone hot pot that plugs into the wall, or, at best, a communal kitchenette that may only contain appliances as sophisticated as a two-burner stove and a toaster oven.

No matter what your background, college is going to be a learning experience for you. You might find yourself learning to do logarithms, or learning to do laundry. But whatever you're studying, you'll have to eat, and that's where this book comes in. While you may think cooking belongs at the bottom of your college to-do list, think again. First of all, cooking is cheaper than eating out. If you're now responsible for paying your own way (or part of your own way), you know that your money is better spent on tuition than expensive restaurant checks. And don't think you're off the hook if you live at home and attend a local college. You'll probably find that your hectic schedule doesn't align with your family's mealtimes, and your parents will likely be unable or unwilling to go on kitchen duty at midnight.

Another advantage to cooking is that it's healthier than dining out. Why is eating healthy so important, you ask? A balanced diet increases your ability to handle the stresses of college life. Eating nutritious meals at regular times helps you sleep better, gives you more stamina, and makes it easier to resist sugar-loaded snacks that temporarily raise your blood sugar levels but leave you feeling more tired than ever an hour later. Cooking healthier meals at home will also help you avoid the weight gain many students experience in their first year of college: the dreaded freshman fifteen.

Finally, don't forget that cooking is fun! Spending Sunday afternoon in the kitchen is a great way to unwind after a hectic week of studying, and mastering new skills gives you a sense of accomplishment. Besides, what better way to win new friends than to invite them over for some homemade French Bread Pizza (page 211) or Fried Chicken with Cornmeal Crust (page 230)? Heck, you might even get a date out of it!

CHAPTER 1

Staying Healthy in College 101

Leaving home for college presents challenges as well as opportunities. If you're someone whose kitchen know-how doesn't extend beyond the reheat setting on the micro-wave, the idea of having to learn basic cooking skills along with calculus can seem overwhelming. It's all too conve-nient to give in to the lure of the dining hall or food court. However, the basic tips in this chapter will help transform cooking from a chore into a creative, stress-free break from studying.

The Infamous Freshman Fifteen

Statistics show that approximately half of all students put on between ten and fifteen pounds during their first year of college. Yikes, right? It's easy to fall victim to the freshman fifteen when you're trying to adjust to a busy schedule and there's fast food at your fingertips everywhere you look. However, putting on weight will just increase the stress that you're already feeling from academic pressures, and it can be hard to take off later. Luckily, there are ways to keep the pounds away, and they don't include limiting yourself to a bowl of plain oatmeal for breakfast, lunch, and dinner.

First and foremost, stick to a regular meal schedule. If you are planning a lengthy study session away from the dorm, prepare healthy snacks to take with you. Simple snacks such as Peanutty Bananas (page 182) and Trail Mix (page 183) provide energy without the fat and calories in potato chips and chocolate. Also, try to plan your meals about a week in advance. One option is to cook ahead, making all your weekly meals over the weekend. It's much easier to stick to a healthy meal plan on a busy weeknight when all you need to do is heat up dinner instead of preparing it from scratch. Finally, take time to exercise. Many colleges have excellent exercise facilities right on campus that are free for students. With a little planning, you can fit an exercise session into your daily schedule. A daily swim or aerobic workout makes it easier to control your weight, and it also lifts your spirits by releasing endorphins, giving you a much-needed boost of energy.

Flintstones Vitamins Don't Cut It Anymore

Obviously, avoiding the freshman fifteen is a good reason to eat well and take care of your body while you're in college, but it's not the only reason. Food isn't just about how your body looks on the outside; in fact, it's how your body looks on the inside that's most important. For this reason, it's a good idea to get acquainted with the basics of nutrition in order to understand the fuel aspect of the food you eat. In other words, things like vitamins, minerals, protein, calcium, and all that jazz.

First of all, it's very important to try to avoid eating processed foods whenever you can. College is perhaps the most difficult environment in which to do this, but it is possible—and the benefits are many. Try to always choose the whole foods that are complete as nature intended them. Processed foods such as grains, sugars, and flours are often stripped of their natural nutrients. Even when vitamins and minerals are added back in later—a process called "enriching," which means that the nutrients lost during refining are added back in to enrich the product—the total effect is never the same.

Take the example of rice: White rice may cook faster and have a more adaptable taste, but when the outer bran layer is stripped away, the rice grains lose much of their beneficial fiber and minerals. As proof, 1 cup of brown rice contains 3.5 grams of fiber. One cup of white rice contains less than 1 gram. Even enriching white rice doesn't make up the difference in the loss of fiber and minerals.

Now that you know to avoid processed foods that have all the good stuff stripped out of them, it's time to cover what you *do* want in your food. Key nutrients that your body needs include protein, iron, calcium, zinc, and vitamins A, D, and B12. You will also need a source of omega-3 fatty acids, important for preventing heart disease.

Your body's nerves, tissues, and bones are all made up of proteins, so proteins are necessary for growth and repair. Protein is found plentifully in meats and other animal-based foods, but that doesn't mean you should eat a cheeseburger every day to get your protein. Meats and other animal-based foods contain a lot of fat and cholesterol, so you'll want to find other sources of protein as well. Dairy foods such as milk, cheese, and yogurt are excellent protein sources. Such nondairy sources as eggs, beans, and soy products contain enough protein to round out even a vegetarian diet.

Your body needs iron for the red blood cells carrying oxygen throughout the body. While iron is found plentifully in red meats, eggs, and seafood, and in lesser quantities in white meats, you can also get your daily allowance of iron from foods like spinach, kidney beans, lentils, and whole-wheat baked goods.

Calcium is the key mineral needed for forming and maintaining strong bones and teeth, but it also helps with other body functions. To get enough calcium, make sure to eat plenty of dairy products as well as calcium-rich vegetables like leafy greens.

You've heard about taking a zinc supplement if you begin to feel sick? That's because the mineral zinc helps bolster the immune system, assists in healing wounds, and helps sustain the senses of smell and taste. Zinc occurs naturally in red meat and poultry, in some seafood, and in beans, nuts, whole grains, and dairy products.

Vitamin A prevents eye problems, promotes a healthy immune system, is essential for the growth and development of cells, and keeps skin healthy. Good sources of vitamin A are milk, eggs, darkly colored orange or green vegetables (such as carrots, sweet potatoes, pumpkin, and kale), and orange fruits (such as cantaloupe, apricots, peaches, papayas, and mangos).

FOOD LANGUAGE 101

In the 1930s, a vitamin-D deficiency disease called rickets was a major public health concern in the United States. However, a national milk fortification program has nearly eliminated this disorder. Currently, about 98 percent of the milk supply in the United States is fortified with 400 International Units (IU) of vitamin D per quart. Although milk is fortified with vitamin D, dairy products such as cheese and ice cream are generally not.

Your body may need only small amounts of vitamin B12, but it is essential for the proper growth of red blood cells and for the health of some nerve tissues. Signs of a B12 deficiency include numbness and tingling in hands and legs, weakness, disorientation, and depression, among others. Vitamin B12 occurs in animal proteins, but you can also get plenty in your daily diet by eating eggs and dairy products.

The most abundant natural sources of omega-3 fatty acids, which help prevent heart disease, are fish and fish oils. Other good sources include flax-seed oil and such vegetable oils as olive oil and canola.

Get Active: Food Is Only Half the Battle

By this point, you've read about the evils of processed foods and what nutrients your body needs, but there's another very big piece to the college health puzzle: exercise. Having read a little about the freshman fifteen, you already know that the idea of weight gain in college is a scary thing—and totally avoidable. You're in your late teens or early twenties; this is your prime! You'll need all your brain cells to do well in your classes, so don't spare any worrying about your weight. What's the secret? It's simple: Get moving.

In addition to eating well and on a regular schedule while you're in school, you also need to make sure you get regular exercise. Most colleges have fitness centers right on campus that are free or inexpensive for enrolled students. Go join! Depending on what your school's fitness center offers, you can stick to machines like treadmills, ellipticals, and weight machines, or you can get in on classes, such as yoga, kickboxing, and step aerobics. Get yourself a cute new fitness outfit, drag your friends along with you to make it more fun, and generally do whatever it takes to ensure that you make time to work out.

THINK OUTSIDE THE BOX

Trapped inside on a rainy or cold day? Whether you want to admit it or not, you can still get a workout in. Buy yourself a yoga mat (they generally sell for around $15) and hit the floor for some stretches, yoga poses, sit-ups, and push-ups. You can also invest in some small hand weights and do a series of exercises such as bicep curls and tricep extensions. As long as you get your body moving in some way, it's always better than no exercise at all.

But don't tell yourself that indoor options are the only ways to stay in shape. In nice weather, hit the pavement and go out for a brisk walk or a jog. This is something else you can do with a friend, and it's a great way to get out in the sunshine and breathe the fresh air. You may even pass by that cute guy from Spanish I, who will be very impressed by your athletic abilities. Another option is to arrange a casual soccer or basketball game with friends. Grab a ball and hit the field or the court on a nice day. As long as you get your heart rate up and your blood pumping, you're getting much-needed exercise.

The Perks of Good Health: You Might Get a Date!

Let's get serious. You're a young adult, you're living away from your parents for the first time, and your life is yours for the making. Are nutrition and exercise really the biggest things on your mind? Probably not, and that's okay. College is about a lot of things, including getting an education, meeting new people, trying new activities, and learning who you are as a person. But here's the thing about good health: It comes into play in every area of your life, and it always will.

FOOD LANGUAGE 101

You've heard the phrase "brain food"? Well, that's because foods that are good for you actually do help your brain and the rest of your body function at maximum capacity. That means having more energy to go out for an intramural field hockey league, having more stamina to get through late-night study sessions, and generally looking and feeling your best. Remember, getting an A in life is just as important as getting an A in class.

When you look and feel good, other people will be attracted to you, and not just in a romantic way. Your professors will show more interest in your work, your classmates will want to team up with you for projects, and the people you live with will be more likely to become new friends. And of course, health and confidence are great turn-ons to those you may be interested in dating. A healthy lifestyle may also help you find someone who has similar interests, such as cooking or running. You might even start a weekly potluck dinner party or a weekend running club. See? A healthy college life can also be fun! In short, there's no limit to the benefits of good health in college, so why not get started and discover them for yourself?

Setting Up Your College Kitchen

You can't cook so much as a can of soup without the right equipment, so the first step in your quest to become a great college cook is to take inventory of what you have already and make a list of what you need. Of course, what you ultimately decide to bring with you to college will vary according to your own personal circumstances. For example, residences with communal kitchens often provide pots, pans, and other cooking essentials for residents. Some college kitchens, on the other hand, are only equipped with the more basic appliances, such as a toaster oven, in which case there would be no point in spending money on a heavy-duty frying pan. So, taking into account your own kitchen situation, review the following lists of basic items and mix and match according to your needs:

BOWLS, POTS, AND PANS

- A few mixing bowls for combining ingredients and serving noodle and salad dishes
- A few good pots and pans of various sizes
- A plastic or metal colander for draining washed, blanched, and boiled food
- One metal cookie sheet for baking cookies or warming up rolls
- One or two glass baking dishes for use in the oven

UTENSILS AND TOOLS

- One or two wooden spoons for stirring and mixing
- A heatproof rubber spatula for mixing ingredients and turning food during cooking
- A few good knives, including a serrated bread knife, a sharp chopping knife, and a small paring knife
- A plastic or wooden cutting board for cutting, chopping, and mincing food
- A vegetable peeler
- A can opener

- A grater for grating, shredding, and slicing cheese and other foods
- A wire whisk for whisking eggs and sauces
- A set of measuring spoons
- A set of measuring cups

Some college residences allow students to keep small electrical appliances in the dorm or the residence kitchen. A coffeemaker allows you to have a cup of java ready as soon as you wake up in the morning. Tea drinkers will want a kettle for boiling water. Along with a toaster or toaster oven, these items will help make your living quarters seem more like home. When it comes to larger appliances, definitely consider a microwave if your budget and college regulations permit it. Although it can't completely replace a standard electric oven, a microwave can be used for everything from making popcorn to preparing an entire meal. Compact microwave and refrigerator combinations, designed specifically for dormitories, are also available. Some even come with a small freezer attached.

BARGAINS FOR YOUR BUDGET

If you're like many college students, you probably don't have all kinds of extra cash to spend on kitchen gadgets. No problem! Before you go away to school, ask friends and family members if they have any older mixing bowls, utensils, or other kitchen items that they don't use anymore. Hand-me-downs may not be as pretty to look at, but they'll work just as well as expensive new ones. Also, hit up discount home goods stores and even garage sales before you head back to school. Someone's old but perfectly good $5 blender could be your gain!

Many recipes call for food to be beaten, blended, whipped, processed, or crushed. If your budget is limited, hand tools can perform many of these functions; for example, a manual hand mixer is fine for beating eggs. And nothing beats a mortar and pestle for grinding and crushing nuts, herbs, spices, crackers, soft fruit, and almost any food that will fit into the mortar (that's the bowl-shaped part). However, if your budget permits, you may want to explore some higher-tech options. For example, a blender is perfect for harried but health-conscious students. Compact, inexpensive, and easy to clean, a blender will do everything from liquefy smoothie ingredients to purée vegetables.

Your Hot Pot and You

All this talk of blenders and other electrical kitchen gadgets leads us to the most quintessential college appliance of all: the hot pot. Let's say you don't have access to a kitchen of any kind while you're in college. Worry not—that's what your hot pot is for! A hot pot is just what it sounds like: a small plastic pot with a heating element in the bottom and an attached lid on top that plugs into the wall and acts as a stovetop and a pot all in one. All you have to do is plug it in, turn it on, and fill it with anything that needs to be heated up. You can boil water to make coffee or tea, or to cook pasta or steam vegetables. Alternatively, you can use it to heat up leftovers or pre-pared foods, such as soup and chili.

The beloved cousin to the hot pot is the hot plate. Basically, a hot plate performs all the functions of a burner on a stovetop, while taking up con-siderably less space than a conventional stove. A hot plate can be used for everything from making pancakes to frying pork chops.

THINK OUTSIDE THE BOX

Another handy device for dorm cooking is a rice cooker/steamer combination. Compact and inexpensive, this appliance steams meat, seafood, and vegetables, and it cooks rice and beans more quickly than the standard stovetop heating element. As an added bonus, it has a plastic surface that makes cleaning easy. For students who have a microwave, the addition of a rice cooker/steamer can provide some of the advantages of stovetop cooking, making it unnecessary to pur-chase a hot plate.

Now before you get all excited about how easy it will be to cook cans of soup and heat up frozen chicken nuggets with your new hot pot and hot plate, take note that quick cooking is not always healthy cooking. While your hectic schedule will have you tempted to heat up ramen noodles for dinner every night, remember that there's a whole lot more you can do with your college kitchen appliances than make soup from a package. Fresh, natural ingredients such as vegetables and whole-grain pastas will always make more nutritious (and believe it or not, more delicious) meals than you can buy wrapped in plastic at the local 7-Eleven. Let's get started!

CHAPTER 2

Make Time for a Healthy Breakfast

Eggs Benedict

This is a high-protein breakfast that will give you energy throughout the morning. This recipe serves 4, so be sure to invite a few friends over to join you.

INGREDIENTS | SERVES 4

3 tablespoons skim milk

½ cup low-fat mayonnaise

4 eggs

4 slices bacon

4 slices whole-wheat bread or 2 whole-wheat English muffins

Incredible Edible Eggs

Eggs provide a tremendous amount of protein and very little carbohydrate, and they make you feel full. You should have one egg a day, but remember that so many things we consume daily already contain eggs. Before you have your daily dose of egg, make sure your other meals and snacks do not contain too much egg or you could overdo it.

1. Mix the skim milk with the mayonnaise and heat in the microwave for about 40 seconds to warm.

2. Crack each egg into individual microwaveable bowls, being careful not to break the yolks.

3. Cover each bowl with plastic wrap and microwave on high until the whites are cooked and yolks firm, about 2 minutes.

4. In a skillet, cook the bacon.

5. Toast the whole-wheat bread slices and place the bacon on top.

6. Add the eggs on the bacon and top each egg with 2 tablespoons of mayonnaise mixture.

PER SERVING Calories: 295 | Fat: 20 g | Protein: 13 g | Sodium: 739 mg | Carbohydrates: 16 g | Fiber: 2.8 g

Egg White Bruschetta

This is a great breakfast to share at a morning gathering or to enjoy by yourself. Add two more slices of bread to spread out the bruschetta if you want to serve more people.

High-fiber, Vegetarian

INGREDIENTS | SERVES 2

7 egg whites
4 whole eggs
1 chopped tomato
½ cup chopped mushrooms
1 small onion
¼ cup fresh basil
½ teaspoon salt
½ teaspoon pepper
4 slices whole-grain bread

1. Beat egg whites and eggs together.

2. Heat chopped tomato, mushrooms, and onion in a large skillet. Add egg mixture and scramble. Add basil, salt, and pepper as you scramble.

3. Toast bread and top with the egg mixture.

PER SERVING Calories: 395 | Fat: 13 g | Protein: 34 g | Sodium: 1192 mg | Carbohydrates: 39 g | Fiber: 6.6 g

Spinach and Ricotta Mini Quiches

Top these mini quiches with a slice of tomato and sprinkle on some shredded cheese to add a nice touch of color and great flavor.

Low-calorie, Gluten-free, Vegetarian, Low-carb

INGREDIENTS | SERVES 5

10 ounces chopped frozen spinach
2 eggs
1 cup skim ricotta cheese
1 cup low-fat shredded mozzarella cheese

1. Preheat oven to 350°F. Place cupcake liners in 12-hole cupcake tin.

2. Heat spinach in microwave according to package directions, until soft and warm.

3. Whip the eggs and add the spinach. Blend together. Fold in the ricotta and shredded mozzarella cheese.

4. Fill each cup with egg-spinach mixture, about ½" per cup. Bake 30 to 35 minutes.

PER SERVING Calories: 175 | Fat: 10 g | Protein: 16 g | Sodium: 273 mg | Carbohydrates: 5 g | Fiber: 1.8 g

Eggs Florentine

*You can replace the mayonnaise with nonfat yogurt. This
recipe is particularly good with nonfat vanilla yogurt.*

Vegetarian

INGREDIENTS | SERVES 2

2 English muffins

2 eggs

5 ounces chopped frozen spinach

1 tablespoon low-fat mayonnaise

1 teaspoon salt

1 teaspoon pepper

2 teaspoons shredded low-fat cheese

Frozen Spinach to the Rescue!

Frozen spinach is a great item to have on hand. Just buy a couple of packages at a time and pull them out whenever you're in a bind. It heats up quickly in the microwave or in a frying pan, and then you have an easy, nutritious ingredient for omelets, sandwiches, side dishes, and more. Keep an eye out for more recipes in this book that call for frozen spinach, such as Spinach and Ricotta Mini Quiches (page 13) and Cannellini Minestrone (page 67).

1. Preheat oven to 350°F. Place muffins on a baking sheet.

2. Crack an egg onto each muffin. Bake for 10 minutes.

3. Meanwhile, heat the spinach in the microwave until soft and warm, about 2 minutes.

4. Add low-fat mayonnaise, salt, and pepper to spinach. Blend together.

5. Remove muffins and top with the spinach mixture. Add a teaspoon of shredded cheese and serve.

PER SERVING Calories: 260 | Fat: 10 g | Protein: 15 g | Sodium: 1621 mg | Carbohydrates: 31 g | Fiber: 4.3 g

Chive and Cheddar Omelet

Chives are an excellent herb because they can be purchased year-round and will keep in the freezer for long periods of time.

Vegetarian, Low-calorie, Gluten-free, Low-carb

INGREDIENTS | SERVES 2

4 large egg whites

1 large whole egg

¼ teaspoon salt

1 tablespoon olive oil

¼ cup reduced-fat shredded cheddar cheese

2 tablespoons chopped fresh chives

Awesome Omelets

The fantastic thing about omelets is that you can stuff them with all kinds of things. Various veggies, fruits, and cheeses make delicious combinations. Brie cheese and sliced turkey, or mushrooms and onions with Swiss cheese, are a couple of combinations you might try for your next omelet.

1. Beat the egg whites and egg in a small bowl. Mix in the salt.

2. Heat the olive oil in a small skillet on low heat.

3. Pour the egg mixture in to coat the surface.

4. Cook egg mixture until edges show firmness.

5. Sprinkle the cheese evenly over the egg mixture, and then do the same with the chives. Fold one side over the other.

6. Flip the half-moon omelet so both sides are evenly cooked.

PER SERVING Calories: 156 | Fat: 11 g | Protein: 14 g | Sodium: 1392 mg | Carbohydrates: 1.5 g | Fiber: 0.075 g

Very Veggie Omelet

Vary this recipe by chopping up any vegetable you like and adding it or substituting it for the peppers.

Low-calorie, Gluten-free, Vegetarian, Lactose-free, Low-carb

INGREDIENTS | SERVES 2

4 large egg whites
1 large whole egg
¼ teaspoon salt
½ cup chopped red peppers
½ cup chopped green peppers
¼ cup chopped onions
½ cup chopped mushrooms
1 tablespoon olive oil

1. Beat the egg whites and egg in a small bowl. Mix in the salt.

2. Mix the vegetables together in a small bowl.

3. Heat the olive oil in a small skillet on low heat.

4. Pour the egg mixture in to coat the surface. Cook until edges show firmness.

5. Add the vegetable mixture so that it covers the entire egg mixture evenly. Fold one side over the other.

6. Flip the half-moon omelet so both sides are evenly cooked.

PER SERVING Calories: 159 | Fat: 10 g | Protein: 12 g | Sodium: 442 mg | Carbohydrates: 8 g | Fiber: 7 g

Sausage and Mushroom Omelet

If you like a little spice, add a dash of Tabasco sauce to kick up the flavor.

Low-carb, Lactose-free

INGREDIENTS | SERVES 2

4 large egg whites
1 large whole egg
¼ teaspoon salt
1 tablespoon olive oil
½ cup chopped cooked turkey sausage
½ cup chopped mushrooms

Turkey Sausage

Never heard of turkey sausage? Well, it's time you did! Turkey sausage is a great, healthy alternative to the standard variety. Turkey is leaner and less greasy than beef or pork, but it still has all the great meaty goodness that you want in a warm breakfast or hearty sandwich. Use cooked turkey sausage in lots of varieties of omelets, sandwiches, casseroles, stuffings, and more!

1. Beat the egg whites and egg in a small bowl. Mix in the salt.

2. Heat the olive oil in a small skillet on low heat.

3. Pour the egg mixture in to coat the surface. Cook until edges show firmness.

4. Add the sausage and mushrooms so that they cover the entire mixture evenly. Fold one side over the other.

5. Flip the half-moon omelet so both sides are evenly cooked.

PER SERVING Calories: 266 | Fat: 20 g | Protein: 20 g | Sodium: 631 mg | Carbohydrates: 2.5 g | Fiber: 0.34 g

Fruit and Cheese Quesadillas

Bland mozzarella is a perfect backdrop for fruit, and you can vary the fruit and jam according to what's seasonally available. These are knife-and-fork quesadillas, too gooey for finger food.

Vegetarian

INGREDIENTS | SERVES 4

4 tablespoons strawberry jam

4 (6" to 8") whole-wheat flour tortillas

2 cups shredded mozzarella cheese

1 cup diced fresh strawberries plus extra for sprinkling

4 tablespoons strawberry yogurt for garnish

Confectioners' sugar for dusting

Marvelous Quesadillas

Much like omelets, quesadillas are one of those foods that can come in a wide variety of flavors. This breakfast quesadilla includes fruit and cheese, and you can swap out the mozzarella cheese and strawberry jam for any other types that you prefer. A great lunch quesadilla might have sautéed vegetables and hummus, and you can also make a dinner quesadilla with Tex-Mex fillings such as grilled chicken, black beans, salsa, and cheddar cheese. When quesadillas are on the menu, let your imagination run wild!

1. Spread 1 tablespoon jam on a tortilla and sprinkle it with ½ cup mozzarella cheese and ¼ cup diced strawberries. Fold over the tortilla to enclose the filling. Repeat with the remaining tortillas, mozzarella, jam, and strawberries.

2. Spray the skillet with nonstick cooking spray and heat it over medium heat. Cook the quesadillas, one or two at a time, until golden on the bottom, about 3 minutes. Flip over and cook the second side until golden and the cheese has melted.

3. Top each quesadilla with a dollop of yogurt, a sprinkling of strawberries, and a dusting of confectioners' sugar. Serve hot.

PER SERVING Calories: 380 | Fat: 16 g | Protein: 17 g | Sodium: 530 mg | Carbohydrates: 42 g | Fiber: 3 g

Baked French Toast

This dish is great when served with sliced pears or peaches on the side. To sweeten it further you can drizzle a tablespoon of sugar-free maple syrup across the top.

Vegetarian

INGREDIENTS | SERVES 2

2 eggs
½ cup skim milk
½ teaspoon ground cinnamon
½ teaspoon vanilla extract
1 tablespoon powdered sugar
4 slices bread

1. Preheat oven to 400°F.

2. Beat eggs and skim milk lightly in a bowl. Add the cinnamon, vanilla, and sugar.

3. Soak the bread in the egg mixture and place on a nonstick baking sheet.

4. Bake for about 10 minutes or until golden.

PER SERVING Calories: 253 | Fat: 8 g | Protein: 14 g | Sodium: 360 mg | Carbohydrates: 34 g | Fiber: 2.8 g

Oatmeal Buttermilk Pancakes

To make these pancakes sugar-free, substitute Splenda for the sugar.

Low-calorie, Low-fat, Vegetarian

INGREDIENTS | SERVES 6

1 cup uncooked oatmeal
½ cup flour
¼ cup sugar
1 teaspoon baking powder
1 teaspoon baking soda
⅛ teaspoon salt
2 cups low-fat buttermilk
¼ cup Egg Beaters
Butter-flavored spray

1. Combine oatmeal, flour, sugar, baking powder, baking soda, and salt in a bowl.

2. Whisk together buttermilk and Egg Beaters in a small bowl. Pour mixture over dry ingredients and stir together until just blended.

3. Pour ¼ cup pancake batter on a hot griddle prepared with butter-flavored spray. Cook until bubbles appear and edges are brown. Flip and cook until done.

PER SERVING Calories: 158 | Fat: 2 g | Protein: 7 g | Sodium: 183 mg | Carbohydrates: 29 g | Fiber: 1.1 g

Stuffed French Toast

For this recipe, be sure to cut thick slices of bread. This will make stuffing easier, and you'll get great big slices of stuffed French toast.

Vegetarian

INGREDIENTS	SERVES 4

Butter-flavored cooking spray

4 1"-thick slices French bread

4 teaspoons reduced-fat cream cheese

4 teaspoons favorite preserves

1 cup skim milk (divided into 4 servings)

1 teaspoon vanilla

1 teaspoon cinnamon or to taste

½ teaspoon nutmeg or to taste

A New Life for Stale Bread

Don't know what to do with that bread that's going stale? It's perfect for French toast! The fresher your bread, the more it will fall apart in the batter. Use bread that is nearing the end of its shelf life. It will be a little tougher and will hold together better when soaked in batter.

1. Prepare a skillet with the butter-flavored spray.

2. Cut a pocket through the top of each slice of bread, ¾ of the way through the bread.

3. Insert cream cheese and preserves.

4. Combine milk, vanilla, cinnamon, and nutmeg to make the batter.

5. Dip the bread in the batter and cook on the skillet.

PER SERVING Calories: 319 | Fat: 4 g | Protein: 11 g | Sodium: 258 mg | Carbohydrates: 58 g | Fiber: 1.4 g

Good-for-You Blueberry French Toast

Add ¼ cup of some fat-free ice cream to each serving to make it à la mode.

Vegetarian, Low-fat

INGREDIENTS | SERVES 6

14 slices bread
¾ cup blueberries
2 cups skim milk
1½ cups fat-free Egg Beaters
1 teaspoon ground cinnamon
2 teaspoons vanilla extract
2 tablespoons powdered sugar

Try Different Fruits

Peaches, pears, and cherries are good fruit fillings for this recipe. Whatever fruit you love best can be used. Buy fruit that's in season at your local market or use leftovers from fruitpicking expeditions.

1. Preheat oven to 400°F.

2. Arrange 7 slices of bread in the bottom of a baking dish.

3. Sprinkle the blueberries over the bread, spreading them out evenly.

4. Whisk the milk, Egg Beaters, ground cinnamon, and vanilla in a bowl.

5. Pour half of the milk mixture over the blueberries and bread, then top with the remaining bread slices and pour leftover milk mixture atop this.

6. Cover the dish with aluminum foil and bake for 20 minutes. Uncover the dish and bake until the top is a nice golden brown.

7. After baking, sprinkle with the powdered sugar and then slice into six servings.

PER SERVING Calories: 289 | Fat: 3 g | Protein: 17 g | Sodium: 529 mg | Carbohydrates: 50 g | Fiber: 2.1 g

Apple Yogurt Cinnamon Pancakes

You can substitute ½ cup berries for the apples in this recipe if you prefer.

Vegetarian

INGREDIENTS | SERVES 4

1 egg
1 cup plain fat-free yogurt
1 tablespoon canola oil
1 cup flour
1 tablespoon sugar
1 teaspoon baking powder
½ teaspoon baking soda
1 teaspoon cinnamon
Pinch of salt
Butter-flavored cooking spray
½ cup thinly sliced apple

Blender Pancakes

Think your blender is only good for making smoothies and a mess? Think again! These super-light pancakes are super easy to make in the blender. You can add the cinnamon to the ingredients or roll the apple slices in the cinnamon to coat them.

1. Combine the egg, yogurt, and oil in a blender until smooth.

2. Sift the flour, sugar, baking powder, baking soda, cinnamon, and salt together. Add to yogurt mixture and blend.

3. Prepare a hot griddle with the butter spray.

4. Ladle about ⅛ cup of the mixture onto the griddle.

5. Sprinkle each of the pancakes with apples and cook until bubbles form in the pancake. Flip over and cook until done.

PER SERVING Calories: 245 | Fat: 6 g | Protein: 8 g | Sodium: 218 mg | Carbohydrates: 35 g | Fiber: 1.5 g

Ginger Pear Wheat Pancakes

Add ¼ cup of chopped walnuts to the chopped pears to give these a little texture and kick.

Vegetarian, Lactose-free, High-fiber

INGREDIENTS | SERVES 3

1½ cups whole-wheat flour

2 tablespoons applesauce

1 tablespoon brown sugar

1 cup water

1½ teaspoons baking powder

1½ teaspoons ground ginger

1 teaspoon ground cinnamon

2 chopped pears

1. Combine the whole-wheat flour, applesauce, brown sugar, water, and baking powder in a medium bowl.

2. Add the ginger and ground cinnamon.

3. Fold in the chopped pears.

4. Pour the batter onto a hot griddle or skillet, ¼ cup for each pancake, and cook until golden.

PER SERVING Calories: 267 | Fat: 1 g | Protein: 9 g | Sodium: 11 mg | Carbohydrates: 60 g | Fiber: 6.4 g

What's the Deal with Ginger?

Ginger is a fibrous root that adds a warm, spicy flavor to dishes. It's also often used as a remedy for a cold or an upset stomach. (If you were ever given ginger ale for an upset stomach as a kid, that's why.) You'll find ginger in many different forms: fresh, ground, caramelized, or even pickled. Look out for more recipes in this book, such as Thai Chicken Sauté (page 101) that call for this wonderful ingredient.

Banana Chocolate-Chip Pancake Wrap

The chocolate chips sweeten this pancake recipe and are best when applied immediately after you take the pancakes off the griddle so they start to melt into the pancakes.

Vegetarian, High-fiber

INGREDIENTS | SERVES 2

½ cup dry oatmeal
½ cup nonfat cottage cheese
3 egg whites
2 tablespoons Splenda
1 teaspoon cinnamon
1 teaspoon vanilla
1 banana
¼ cup of semisweet chocolate chips

1. Combine oatmeal, cottage cheese, egg whites, Splenda, cinnamon, and vanilla in a blender until smooth.

2. Mash banana in a bowl and fold into pancake mix.

3. Pour four individual pancakes on griddle, thinly.

4. Remove from griddle and place a few chocolate chips on each pancake. Fold over like a wrap.

PER SERVING Calories: 318 | Fat: 8 g | Protein: 16 g | Sodium: 467 mg | Carbohydrates: 48 g | Fiber: 7.4 g

Fried Green Tomatoes

Invite a few friends over on a Saturday morning to watch the movie Fried Green Tomatoes *and enjoy your very own homemade version.*

Vegetarian

INGREDIENTS | SERVES 4

½ cup cornmeal
½ cup all-purpose flour
1 teaspoon baking powder
Salt and pepper to taste
1 egg
¼ cup 2% milk
2 very large green tomatoes
2 cups canola oil

1. Mix the dry ingredients together on a sheet of waxed paper. Whip the egg and milk in a small bowl.

2. Remove stem and core of the tomatoes and cut in ½" rounds. Place in the meal mixture; flip. Dip in the egg mixture and return to the meal mixture.

3. Heat the oil to 350°F in a deep frying pan. Fry tomatoes until brown and crisp. Drain on paper towels.

PER SERVING Calories: 596 | Fat: 57 g | Protein: 6 g | Sodium: 39 mg | Carbohydrates: 22 g | Fiber: 2.8 g

Blueberry Cornmeal Pancakes

You get a double dose of fiber from the blueberries and the cornmeal in these pancakes. These are dense and filling, great for a frosty morning before you head to class.

Vegetarian

INGREDIENTS | SERVES 4

1 cup flour

½ cup yellow cornmeal

3 tablespoons sugar

1½ teaspoons baking powder

½ teaspoon baking soda

½ teaspoon salt

2 eggs

3 tablespoons melted butter

1½ cups buttermilk

1 cup blueberries

1. Whisk together flour, cornmeal, sugar, baking powder, baking soda, and salt in a large bowl.

2. Whisk together eggs, melted butter, and buttermilk in another bowl.

3. Stir egg mixture into the flour mixture until combined. There will be lumps; be careful not to overmix.

4. Pour about ⅓ cup batter for each pancake onto hot oiled griddle or pan. Scatter several blueberries over batter. Flip pancakes when bubbles have formed and started to pop through the batter on top.

5. Cook on other side for about a minute. Serve hot with maple syrup.

PER SERVING Calories: 373 | Fat: 12 g | Protein: 10 g | Sodium: 514 mg | Carbohydrates: 55 g | Fiber: 3 g

Cornmeal Basics

Cornmeal isn't necessarily a staple like flour is, but it does show up in lots of great recipes. Just make sure you don't confuse cornmeal with cornstarch. Cornstarch, also called corn flour, is a fine chalky white powder that is useful for thickening sauces. Cornmeal is much coarser and is used to make polenta, muffins, and some breads, particularly corn bread.

Raspberry Almond Turnovers

Delicious for breakfast but also a good dessert or snack, these turnovers are a great source of fiber.

Vegetarian, High-fiber

INGREDIENTS | SERVES 4

1 cup sliced almonds
1 sheet puff pastry, thawed in the refrigerator
1 egg white
4 teaspoons almond paste
1 cup frozen raspberries
4 teaspoons sugar
2 teaspoons cornstarch
1 tablespoon wheat germ
2 tablespoons powdered sugar

Healthy Puff Pastry?

Unfortunately, you can't buy whole-grain puff pastry, but you can fill regular stuff pastry with fruit and nuts for wonderful turnovers. Wheat germ is also an excellent source of vitamins and fiber, and it can be added to everything from meatloaf to pancake batter.

1. Preheat the oven to 400°F. Grind half of the almonds in a food processor. Set aside.

2. Roll the puff pastry into an 11" × 11" square on a floured surface. Cut the square into four smaller squares. Paint the egg white on the pastry squares.

3. Put 1 teaspoon of almond paste in the middle of each square, layer ¼ cup raspberries on top, then sprinkle the ground almonds, sugar, cornstarch, and wheat germ over the berries.

4. Fold each square over to make a triangle to encase the filling. Press down on the outer edges with your fingers or a fork to seal.

5. Brush the egg white on the turnovers and sprinkle them with the remaining sliced almonds and powdered sugar. Bake for 10 minutes, turn the oven down to 350°F, and continue baking for about 10 to 15 minutes longer. Let cool before eating.

PER SERVING Calories: 562 | Fat: 37 g | Protein: 11 g | Sodium: 43 mg | Carbohydrates: 47 g | Fiber: 6 g

Oat Bran Griddlecakes

These oat bran cakes provide slow-release, long-term energy. Your stomach won't go to war to digest them, and you'll have loads of energy for the long haul.

Vegetarian, High-fiber

INGREDIENTS | SERVES 2

½ cup oat bran

1 cup low-fat buttermilk

½ cup dried cranberries

2 eggs, beaten until light in color

2 teaspoons honey

½ teaspoon salt

½ cup all-purpose flour

1 teaspoon baking powder

½ teaspoon baking soda

Options: Maple syrup, apple butter, any mono- or polyunsaturated spread

Nonstick butter-flavored spray

1. In a large bowl, mix together the oat bran, buttermilk, and cranberries. Let rest for 10 to 15 minutes.

2. In the blender, mix the eggs, honey, and salt. Slowly add the rest of the dry ingredients; then mix with the oat bran mixture.

3. Using nonstick butter-flavored spray, prepare a griddle and heat to medium. Drop cakes on griddle and cook until bubbles form on top, about 1 minute. Turn and cook until brown. Serve with choice of toppings.

PER SERVING Calories: 338 | Fat: 8 g | Protein: 11 g | Sodium: 1092 mg | Carbohydrates: 61 g | Fiber: 6.3 g

Oven-Roasted Tomatoes

This is an excellent side dish to accompany eggs. The tomatoes pick up the flavors of any herbs used with them, and you can add butter, cheese, and spices to add extra flavor.

Low-calorie, Gluten-free, Vegan, Lactose-free, Low-carb, High-fiber

INGREDIENTS | SERVES 1

1 large red, ripe, and juicy tomato

1 teaspoon olive oil or butter

1 teaspoon of your favorite herbs (rosemary, parsley, thyme, or basil)

Salt and pepper to taste

Impress Your Friends . . . with Tomatoes!

Roasted tomatoes are one of those amazingly simple foods that look and taste like a complicated gourmet specialty. The roasting brings out the sweetness in the tomatoes, making them a great accompaniment to many dishes. Try them alongside grilled steaks, mixed in with pasta, or in an omelet. You really can't go wrong with roasted tomatoes!

1. Preheat oven to 375°F. Cut the tomato in half, from top to bottom. Use a melon baller to remove seeds. Sprinkle with oil, herbs, salt, and pepper.

2. Individually nest the tomato halves in aluminum foil, leaving the top open. Place open-end up directly on the grill in the oven. Roast for 15 minutes.

PER SERVING Calories: 67 | Fat: 5 g | Protein: 1 g | Sodium: 23 mg | Carbohydrates: 6 g | Fiber: 5.5 g

Corn Cakes Topped with Fried Green Tomatoes

These corn cakes are a crispy and slightly sweet alternative to traditional pancakes. Paired with fried green tomatoes, these are a satisfying and unusual addition to the breakfast table!

Low-calorie, Low-fat, Vegetarian

INGREDIENTS | SERVES 4; MAKES 16 TO 18 CAKES

1 cup whole-wheat or all-purpose flour
2 teaspoons baking powder
1 tablespoon brown sugar
½ cup nonfat milk or low-fat buttermilk
2 eggs, well beaten
¾ cup corn (cooked, fresh, or canned)
¼ teaspoon nutmeg
Salt and freshly ground black pepper to taste
4 Fried Green Tomatoes (page 24)
Nonstick spray

Go Canned

Having certain canned foods on hand will make college cooking a lot quicker and easier—and it'll save you money. Canned tomatoes, beans, corn, and pumpkin are excellent for many purposes and save hours of time.

1. In a large bowl, whisk the flour, baking powder, and brown sugar into the milk. Stir in the eggs, corn, and spices.

2. Prepare a griddle with nonstick spray. Heat to medium.

3. Drop cakes on hot griddle and flatten with spoon before they rise. Cook about 4 minutes per side. Turn when bubbles start to form on uncooked side.

4. Serve topped with fried green tomatoes.

PER SERVING Calories: 187 | Fat: 3 g | Protein: 9 g | Sodium: 55 mg | Carbohydrates: 34 g | Fiber: 1.7 g

CHAPTER 3

High-Energy Breakfasts on the Go

Peach Yogurt Smoothie

You may use frozen peaches in this for a shortcut and a sherbet-like texture.
The combination of yogurt and fruit will give your day a delicious boost.

Low-fat, Gluten-free, Vegetarian

INGREDIENTS | SERVES 2

½ banana
1½ cups peaches, cubed
1 cup vanilla yogurt
¼ cup orange juice
1 teaspoon honey

1. Place all ingredients in a blender and blend until smooth.

2. Pour into two glasses and serve as a quick breakfast with a friend, or refrigerate one serving and take the other in a travel mug on the go.

PER SERVING Calories: 309 | Fat: 2 g | Protein: 8 g | Sodium: 82 mg | Carbohydrates: 68 g | Fiber: 4 g

Green Tea Smoothie

To kick this smoothie up a notch, add some fruit like a peach or banana.

Low-calorie, Low-fat, Vegetarian, Low-carb

INGREDIENTS | SERVES 2

1 cup brewed green tea, chilled
½ cup skim milk
½ cup fat-free vanilla ice cream

Combine all ingredients in a blender until smooth. Pour into a tall glass and enjoy at home or take with you on the go.

Green Means Good

This smoothie is packed with benefits. Green tea is chock full of antioxidants, which protect living cells from damage and deterioration. Researchers think antioxidants can help prevent cancer and some of the side effects of arthritis.

PER SERVING Calories: 67 | Fat: 0 g | Protein: 4 g | Sodium: 64 mg | Carbohydrates: 13 g | Fiber: 0.25 g

Creamy Carrot Smoothie

Yes, it sounds odd, but college is all about trying new things! The orange and lemon juices sweeten this smoothie, so you'll have all the benefits of carrot while still enjoying a tasty treat.

Low-calorie, Low-fat, Gluten-free, Vegetarian

INGREDIENTS | SERVES 1

5 large carrots
¼ cup carrot juice
1 tablespoon lemon juice
¼ cup orange juice
½ cup nonfat yogurt
½ cup skim milk

The Low-down on Carrots

Loaded with beta-carotene, which is essential for healthy eyes, skin, and cell respiration, carrots are a nutritious superfood that's cheap and available year-round. Always choose fresh carrots that are crisp and tight-skinned, not limp, marred, or covered in brown blemishes.

1. Grate 5 large carrots in a blender or food processor. Separate the grated carrot from the juice using a fine strainer. Reserve the juice.

2. Blend grated carrot, lemon juice, orange juice, yogurt and skim milk until smooth, then blend in the carrot juice. Pour into a tall glass.

PER SERVING Calories: 190 | Fat: 1 g | Protein: 13 g | Sodium: 188 mg | Carbohydrates: 34 g | Fiber: 1.8 g

Homemade Granola

Serve this granola with fruit and yogurt or just eat it by hand for an on-the-go breakfast. You can also turn this into trail mix by adding dried apples and/or raisins.

Vegetarian, Lactose-free, High-fiber

INGREDIENTS | SERVES 6

4 cups rolled oats
1 cup sliced almonds
½ teaspoon cinnamon
1 teaspoon vanilla
4 ounces orange blossom honey
2 ounces canola oil
½ cup wheat germ
¼ cup sesame seeds
¼ cup millet
¼ cup flaxseeds

1. Preheat oven to 350°F.

2. Toss oats, almonds, cinnamon, vanilla, honey, and canola oil together in a big bowl. Spread the mixture on a baking pan and bake for 10 minutes.

3. Stir and add wheat germ, sesame seeds, and millet. Bake for 15 minutes.

4. Stir and add flaxseeds. Bake for 10 minutes.

5. Remove from oven. Cool and break up large chunks.

PER SERVING Calories: 565 | Fat: 26 g | Protein: 16 g | Sodium: 161 mg | Carbohydrates: 69 g | Fiber: 11 g

What Are Flaxseeds?

Flaxseeds are slightly larger than sesame seeds and have a hard golden shell that is smooth and shiny. The warm, earthy, and subtly nutty flavor of flaxseeds combined with an abundance of omega-3 fatty acids makes them a great addition to anyone's diet. Whole and ground flaxseeds, as well as flaxseed oil, are available throughout the year.

Raspberry Almond Milk Frappé

You can substitute maple syrup for the honey in this recipe for a different flavor, or substitute other flavors of frozen yogurt to add variety.

Low-calorie, Low-fat, Gluten-free, Vegetarian

INGREDIENTS | SERVES 2

1 cup frozen raspberries
¾ cup vanilla frozen yogurt
½ cup almond milk
⅛ teaspoon almond extract
1 teaspoon honey

1. Place all ingredients in a blender and blend until smooth.

2. Pour into two glasses and serve as a quick breakfast.

PER SERVING Calories: 134 | Fat: 2 g | Protein: 4 g | Sodium: 74 mg | Carbohydrates: 26 g | Fiber: 4 g

Crunchy Creamy Yogurt Parfait

Yogurt parfaits are traditionally a healthy choice, and they're easy to make at home in no time at all. Mix and match different cereals, yogurt flavors, and fruits for more delicious combinations.

Low-fat, Gluten-free, Vegetarian, High-fiber

INGREDIENTS | SERVES 1

2 tablespoons bran flakes cereal
4 ounces sugar-free vanilla yogurt
¼ cup sliced strawberries

Layer the ingredients in a tall travel cup, starting with the bran flakes, then the yogurt, and finally the strawberries.

PER SERVING Calories: 210 | Fat: 1 g | Protein: 9 g | Sodium: 295 mg | Carbohydrates: 46 g | Fiber: 6 g

Basic Breakfast Sandwich

Light English muffins are almost always going to be your best choice when it comes to breads at breakfast. They're significantly lower in calories than bagels and regular white bread.

Low-calorie, Low-fat, Vegetarian, High-fiber

INGREDIENTS | SERVES 1

1 light-wheat English muffin
½ cup Egg Beaters
Dash of salt and pepper
1 slice fat-free American cheese

Step Away from the Fast Food

Why spend $5.00 at a greasy fast-food restaurant when you can make your own breakfast sandwich at home for half that? Try this easy recipe, and also try variations such as different cheeses and varieties of English muffins. You'll save time, money, and your waistline.

1. Toast English muffin halves.

2. Pour eggs, salt, and pepper into a microwave-safe bowl.

3. Microwave egg mixture for 1 minute on high or until egg is thoroughly cooked.

4. Place eggs on one side of the toasted muffin, add cheese, and top with the other half of the muffin. Wrap in foil and take to go.

PER SERVING Calories: 180 | Fat: 1 g | Protein: 22 g | Sodium: 680 mg | Carbohydrates: 27 g | Fiber: 8 g

Protein and Berry Pita

When deciding which berries to use in this recipe, test out a variety. In fact, it's always a good idea to give preferential treatment to in-season produce.

Low-calorie, Low-fat, Vegetarian

INGREDIENTS | SERVES 1

3 tablespoons fat-free ricotta cheese
½ teaspoon vanilla extract
½ teaspoon Splenda
3 tablespoons of your favorite berries
½ whole-wheat pita

1. In a small bowl mix ricotta, vanilla, and Splenda.

2. Add berries to ricotta mix.

3. Open pita and scoop ricotta mix into middle. Wrap pita in foil or put in a container and take with you.

PER SERVING Calories: 133 | Fat: 1 g | Protein: 10 g | Sodium: 261 mg | Carbohydrates: 23 g | Fiber: 3 g

Runner's Breakfast

Runners tend to eat lightly or not at all before a race. Nuts are a very high-fiber food with some good fat. Both the fiber and the fat take a while to digest without weighing you down.

Vegetarian, Lactose-free, High-fiber

INGREDIENTS | SERVES 1

½ cup 1-minute oats
Orange juice to cover oatmeal (about ¾ to 1 cup)
¼ cup of your favorite nuts (not peanuts)
10 raisins
½ banana
2 tablespoons honey or maple syrup

1. Boil the oatmeal in enough orange juice to cover the oats.

2. When the oatmeal has absorbed the orange juice, add the nuts, raisins, banana, and honey or maple syrup.

PER SERVING Calories: 672 | Fat: 37 g | Protein: 12 g | Sodium: 13 mg | Carbohydrates: 85 g | Fiber: 14 g

Peach Salad with Mint Dressing

The blueberries and raspberries in this recipe provide high levels of antioxidants, which are powerful cancer-fighting tools.

Low-calorie, Low-fat, Vegetarian, Gluten-free, Lactose-free

INGREDIENTS | SERVES 4

2 cups fresh peaches, sliced

1 cup cucumber, peeled, seeded, and thinly sliced

½ cup fresh raspberries

¼ cup fresh blueberries

½ teaspoon lemon rind, grated

1 tablespoon fresh lemon juice

2 teaspoons fresh mint, minced

2 teaspoons honey

½ teaspoon salt

¼ teaspoon black pepper

1. Thoroughly wash all fresh fruit and cucumber.

2. Once dry, combine in a large bowl.

3. Mix dressing ingredients in a separate bowl.

4. Gently toss dressing with fruit mixture and serve immediately.

PER SERVING Calories: 66 | Fat: 0 g | Protein: 1 g | Sodium: 268 mg | Carbohydrates: 17 g | Fiber: 3 g

Autumn Oatmeal

Oatmeal is the comfort food of the high-fiber diet—warm, nutritious, and delicious.

Low-calorie, Vegetarian

INGREDIENTS | SERVES 4

2 cups water

1 cup rolled oats

¼ teaspoon salt

½ cup dried currants

1 teaspoon ground cinnamon

4 teaspoons honey

2 tablespoons cream

1 cup almond milk, chilled

What Is Almond Milk?

Almond milk is a milky liquid made from ground almonds. Unlike animal milk, almond milk contains no cholesterol or lactose. It can be used as a substitute for animal milk in many recipes, and it is also completely vegan. Almond milk products you'll find in stores come in plain, vanilla, or chocolate flavors. They are often enriched with vitamins. You can also make your own almond milk at home by combining ground almonds with water and the flavorings of your choice in a blender.

1. Bring water to a boil. Add the oats and salt and stir. Turn the heat to low and simmer 5 minutes.

2. Stir in the currants and simmer for 10 minutes, stirring occasionally.

3. Remove from heat and spoon cooked oatmeal into four bowls.

4. Sprinkle ¼ teaspoon cinnamon and drizzle 1 teaspoon honey on each bowl.

5. Mix the cream with the cold almond milk and serve it on the side in a small pitcher.

PER SERVING Calories: 193 | Fat: 5 g | Protein: 4 g | Sodium: 217 mg | Carbohydrates: 35 g | Fiber: 4 g

Irish Oatmeal and Poached Fruit

This tasty breakfast has the perfect combination of slow-release starch and naturally sweet fruit. The nuts will help stave off hunger, too.

Vegetarian, High-fiber

INGREDIENTS | SERVES 4

1 fresh peach, chopped

½ cup raisins

1 tart apple, cored and chopped

½ cup water

3 tablespoons honey

½ teaspoon salt

2 cups Irish or Scottish oatmeal

1½ cups nonfat milk

1½ cups low-fat yogurt

1 cup toasted walnuts

1. In a saucepan, mix the peach, raisins, and apple with water, honey, and salt. Bring to a boil and remove from heat. Set aside.

2. Mix the oatmeal and skim milk with the low-fat yogurt. Cook according to package directions.

3. Mix the fruit into the oatmeal and cook for another 2 to 3 minutes. Serve hot, sprinkled with the walnuts.

PER SERVING Calories: 600 | Fat: 36 g | Protein: 32 g | Sodium: 457 mg | Carbohydrates: 61 g | Fiber: 6.5 g

Which Oatmeal Is Best?

You may have heard that instant oatmeal is not as nutritious as regular oatmeal. This is not really the case. The oats in instant oatmeal are cut thinner, so it cooks more quickly and produces a thinner consistency. Regular oatmeal contains larger pieces of rolled oat grains and produces a thicker, chewier texture.

Brown Rice and Spiced Peaches

Rice for breakfast? Don't knock it till you've tried it! This is an excellent cold-weather breakfast. You can prepare the rice and peaches in advance, mixing in milk and honey as desired, and heat in your microwave.

Low-fat, Gluten-free, Vegetarian, Lactose-free

INGREDIENTS | SERVES 4

1½ cups brown rice

3 cups water

1 teaspoon salt

2 cups fresh or frozen peaches, or canned peaches in water (no syrup) with ¾ cup natural juices

½ teaspoon cinnamon

¼ teaspoon nutmeg

Juice of ½ lemon

2 teaspoons honey

1. Add salt to water and boil. Cook rice in salted water until tender, following package directions.

2. In a separate saucepan, mix peaches, spices, lemon juice, and honey. Bring to a boil and set aside.

3. When ready to serve, mix the peaches and rice. Add warm milk and more honey if desired.

PER SERVING Calories: 260 | Fat: 1 g | Protein: 3 g | Sodium: 598 mg | Carbohydrates: 52 g | Fiber: 4.2 g

The Juice Solution

While it's always best to squeeze lemon or lime juice right out of the fruit, it's not always easy to keep fresh lemons and limes on hand. Luckily, you can buy bottles of lemon juice and lime juice that will stay good in the refrigerator for several weeks. These will come in handy in lots of recipes, from guacamole to fruit salad.

Brain Food Breakfast

Carbohydrates fuel the brain, so this recipe is perfect for the morning of an exam or presentation.

Vegetarian, High-fiber

INGREDIENTS | SERVES 1

½ cup cooked regular oatmeal (not instant)

½ banana

2 teaspoons honey

½ cup 2% milk

1 egg

1 slice whole-grain toast

½ ounce butter

1. When the oatmeal is cooked, slice the banana into it, drizzle with honey, and add milk.

2. To soft-boil the egg, place it on a teaspoon and lower it into simmering water for 2½ minutes. Run egg under cold water; peel off shell.

3. Serve egg on buttered whole-grain toast with oatmeal on the side.

PER SERVING Calories: 491 | Fat: 22 g | Protein: 17 g | Sodium: 490 mg | Carbohydrates: 63 g | Fiber: 7.6 g

California English Muffin

Food identified as "California-style" is traditionally fresh, uncomplicated cuisine that makes the most of locally grown ingredients.

Low-calorie, Low-fat, Vegetarian, High-fiber

INGREDIENTS | SERVES 2

1 light multigrain English muffin

2 tablespoons fat-free cream cheese

2 thick slices tomato

¼ cup sprouts

Salt and pepper to taste

Split and toast English muffin. Spread 1 tablespoon cream cheese on each English muffin half. Top each half with 1 slice of tomato and sprouts. Salt and pepper to taste.

PER SERVING Calories: 132 | Fat: 2 g | Protein: 8 g | Sodium: 318 mg | Carbohydrates: 24 g | Fiber: 5 g

Peanut Butter Banana Breakfast Wraps

Eating on the go? This wrap has all you need for a healthy breakfast, including whole grains, fresh fruit, and protein.

Vegan, High-fiber, Lactose-free

INGREDIENTS | SERVES 1

2 tablespoons peanut butter (or other nut butter)

1 whole-wheat flour tortilla

2 tablespoons granola (or any vegan breakfast cereal)

½ banana, sliced thin

¼ teaspoon cinnamon

1 tablespoon raisins

1 teaspoon agave nectar (optional)

1. Spread peanut butter down the center of the tortilla and layer granola and banana on top.

2. Sprinkle with cinnamon and raisins, and drizzle with agave nectar if desired.

3. Warm in the microwave for 10 to 15 seconds to slightly melt peanut butter.

PER SERVING Calories: 356 | Fat: 19 g | Protein: 13 g | Sodium: 210 mg | Carbohydrates: 54 g | Fiber: 7 g

Explore the World of Nut Butters

Peanut butter is delicious and a great source of protein, but you can also try other nut butters for variety. For example, cashew nut butter is a rich and creamy treat, and soy nut butter is similar to peanut butter but with an earthy taste.

Breakfast Fruit Salad

Mandarin oranges are a citrus fruit that really look more flat like a tangerine than round like an orange. They're high in vitamin C. When buying canned mandarins, always choose the ones without the heavy syrup.

Low-calorie, Gluten-free, Vegan, Lactose-free, High-fiber

INGREDIENTS | SERVES 4

2 cups Gala or Braeburn apples, cubed

1½ cups pears, cubed

1 cup mandarin orange slices

½ cup kiwi, sliced

¼ cup fresh blueberries

1 tablespoon dried cranberries

3 tablespoons sunflower seeds

Combine all ingredients in a large bowl. Put one serving in a container to take with you and refrigerate the leftovers.

Dried Fruits and Nuts

Dried fruits and nuts are the perfect foods for college students to have on hand. They make quick, healthy snacks and they can be thrown into all sorts of recipes, from trail mixes to salads. Also, if properly stored they can stay fresh for a long time, which means you'll always have some ready when you need them.

PER SERVING Calories: 148 | Fat: 4 g | Protein: 3 g | Sodium: 2 mg | Carbohydrates: 29 g | Fiber: 6 g

CHAPTER 4

Beyond Peanut Butter and Jelly: Sandwiches

Toasted Cheese and Turkey Sandwich

Traditional grilled cheese sandwiches made with white bread, butter, and full-fat cheeses are loaded with saturated fats and tons of unnecessary calories. This recipe is easier to make and far better for you!

Low-calorie, Low-fat, High-fiber

INGREDIENTS | SERVES 1

2 slices light-wheat bread
3 slices fat-free American cheese
2 slices roasted deli turkey

Freezing Sandwiches

Many sandwiches can be frozen. If they don't include mayonnaise, the end result will be better. Wrap sandwiches well in plastic wrap, label, and freeze for up to three months. You can let them thaw in a lunchbox until it's time for lunch, or wrap them in foil and bake in a 350°F oven for 15 to 25 minutes until warm, depending on the size of the sandwich.

1. Toast bread in toaster or toaster oven.

2. Place cheese and turkey between bread.

3. Microwave for 20 to 30 seconds.

4. Enjoy with a whole piece of fruit.

   PER SERVING Calories: 177 | Fat: 0 g | Protein: 23 g | Sodium: 1,057 mg | Carbohydrates: 26 g | Fiber: 6 g

Avocado Bagel Sandwich

This sandwich is on an untoasted bagel, so be sure to use a fresh, chewy bagel. You can also slice the bagel in thirds horizontally, adding another slice of onion and avocado.

Vegetarian, High-fiber

INGREDIENTS | SERVES 1

2 ounces whipped cream cheese

1 whole-wheat bagel, sliced

1 slice tomato

1 slice red onion

½ avocado, sliced

¼ cup alfalfa sprouts

1. Spread the cream cheese on both halves of the bagel.

2. Layer the tomato, red onion, avocado, and alfalfa sprouts on the bottom half of the bagel.

3. Top with the other half of the bagel and cut the sandwich in half.

PER SERVING Calories: 672 | Fat: 37 g | Protein: 19 g | Sodium: 461 mg | Carbohydrates: 75 g | Fiber: 16 g

Healthy Bagels

Bagels aren't typically thought of as a health food, but nowadays they come in so many different varieties—from whole wheat to honey oat—there are many kinds of bagels that are better for you than the standard plain. Also, try to stick with smaller bagels. They're very dense, which means that even a smaller one will still fill you up.

Mom's Egg Salad Sandwich

You may be in college, but that doesn't mean you can't make yourself a mean egg salad sandwich—just like Mom's.

Gluten-free, Vegetarian

INGREDIENTS | SERVES 4

6 hardboiled eggs

½ cup fat-free Miracle Whip salad dressing

¼ cup finely chopped celery

2 tablespoons finely chopped flatleaf parsley

Salt and pepper to taste

1. Separate the hardboiled egg whites from the yolks. Finely chop egg whites.

2. Press egg yolks through a sieve and add to chopped egg whites in small bowl.

3. Add salad dressing, celery, and parsley and blend well. Season with salt and pepper to taste.

4. Chill mixture for 1 hour. Spread on your favorite bread.

PER SERVING Calories: 283 | Fat: 11 g | Protein: 15 g | Sodium: 353 mg | Carbohydrates: 32 g | Fiber: 0.79 g

Turkey Walnut Wrap

The honey-roasted turkey slices create a sweet taste for this wrap, but feel free to try smoked turkey or any other sort of turkey breast that catches your eye.

INGREDIENTS | SERVES 1

1 small whole-wheat tortilla

2 deli slices of honey-roasted turkey breast

½ cup fresh spinach

1 teaspoon walnuts

1 tablespoon avocadoes, diced

2 tablespoons mushrooms, sliced

2 tablespoons sun-dried tomatoes, sliced

1 teaspoon crumbled bleu cheese

Place tortilla flat on a plate. Place turkey flat on tortilla. Cover turkey with the remaining ingredients. Roll tortilla into a wrap.

PER SERVING Calories: 280 | Fat: 10 g | Protein: 18 g | Sodium: 1,164 mg | Carbohydrates: 32 g | Fiber: 4 g

Teriyaki Chicken Power Pita

Teriyaki is the common Japanese term for grilled or broiled meat coated or glazed with a sweet soy sauce marinade.

Low-calorie, Low-fat, Lactose-free

INGREDIENTS | SERVES 2

1 large whole-wheat pita
1 Simple Grilled Chicken Breast (page 98)
½ cup chopped spring mix lettuce
4 tablespoons diced tomatoes
2 teaspoons white onions, diced
2 tablespoons sweet peppers
Dash of salt and pepper
2 tablespoons low-sodium teriyaki sauce

1. Slice pita in half to create 2 pita pockets.

2. Chop chicken breast and mix with other ingredients in a bowl.

3. Evenly divide chicken mixture and place into separate pita pockets.

PER SERVING Calories: 189 | Fat: 2 g | Protein: 21 g | Sodium: 440 mg | Carbohydrates: 23 g | Fiber: 3 g

Ultimate Veggie Wrap

Don't have alfalfa sprouts in your fridge? Substitute broccoli instead. Use what you have.

Vegetarian, High-fiber

INGREDIENTS | SERVES 1

1 (12") spinach tortilla
½ cup spinach leaves
1 tablespoon tomatoes, diced
1 tablespoon mushrooms, sliced
1 tablespoon roasted red peppers
1 tablespoon green pepper slices
¼ cup alfalfa sprouts
1 tablespoon shredded carrots
1 tablespoon fat-free crumbled feta cheese
1 tablespoon balsamic vinegar

Lay tortilla flat on a plate. Pile other ingredients on top of tortilla. Roll tortilla into a wrap.

PER SERVING Calories: 354 | Fat: 10 g | Protein: 11 g | Sodium: 961 mg | Carbohydrates: 57 g | Fiber: 5 g

Tuna Burgers

If you're having a luau or a pool party, these burgers are a perfect choice for your tropical theme. Your friends will think you're so clever. Aloha!

Low-calorie, Low-fat, Low-carb

INGREDIENTS | SERVES 6

1½ cups bread crumbs
10 ounces canned light tuna, in chunks
½ cup shredded fat-free cheddar cheese
½ cup fat-free peppercorn dressing
¼ cup Egg Beaters
¼ cup green onion, sliced

A New Take on Tuna

Tired of the same old traditional tuna salad? These burgers are the perfect way to mix things up. They're super quick and easy to make, they're good for you, and they make a great lunch or snack any time of year.

1. In a medium bowl, combine ¾ cup bread crumbs and all other ingredients. Blend well. Divide into six burgers and top with remaining bread crumbs.

2. Coat a large skillet with nonstick spray. Place burgers in skillet and cook each side on medium heat for 3 to 5 minutes or until golden brown.

PER SERVING Calories: 140 | Fat: 2 g | Protein: 16 g | Sodium: 507 mg | Carbohydrates: 13 g | Fiber: 0 g

Honey Mustard Tuna Melt

This twist on the classic tuna melt has a little extra flavor to spice things up when you're tired of the same old thing. Don't worry, though—it's still healthy!

Low-fat, High-fiber

INGREDIENTS | SERVES 1

1 (5-ounce) can light tuna in water

1 tablespoon fat-free honey mustard dressing

2 slices light-wheat bread, toasted

1 ounce shredded fat-free cheddar cheese

Mix tuna and honey mustard together in a bowl. Spread mixture on each slice of toast. Top each slice with cheese. Bake in oven at 400°F for 1 to 3 minutes, or until cheese has melted.

PER SERVING Calories: 308 | Fat: 3 g | Protein: 48 g | Sodium: 743 g | Carbohydrates: 23 g | Fiber: 6 g

The Scoop on Tuna

Canned tuna can be a good source of omega-3 fats, but the specific amounts depend on the product you choose. You'll find a variety of different terms used to describe tuna on canning labels. Nutritionally, these different types of tuna are quite similar except for their fat content, which can vary by as much as 10 grams per cup. Be sure to check the labels so you know exactly what you are getting.

Chicken Burrito, Hold the Rice

This lighter version of a traditional burrito makes a great lunch or light dinner.

High-fiber

INGREDIENTS | **SERVES 1**

1 small whole-wheat tortilla

½ Simple Grilled Chicken Breast (page 98)

2 tablespoons black beans

1 teaspoon white onions, diced

2 teaspoons salsa

1 tablespoon shredded fat-free cheddar cheese

¼ cup shredded romaine lettuce

Place tortilla flat on a plate. Slice chicken breast. Pile remaining ingredients in the center of the tortilla. Roll tortilla up burrito-style.

What's Wrong with Rice?

Traditional burritos are loaded with rice, which makes them feel hearty and filling. However, with little nutritional value and lots of calories, rice is not the best idea for those in search of a trim figure. Try to keep the rice content of your diet low, and whenever possible use more nutritious brown rice instead of white.

PER SERVING Calories: 317 | Fat: 4 g | Protein: 28 g | Sodium: 526 mg | Carbohydrates: 43 g | Fiber: 6 g

Naked Fajitas

Fajitas are fun! Although onions and peppers are the most traditional! sort of veggies used to make them, you can grill up any sort of produce to go with these.

Gluten-free, Low-carb

INGREDIENTS | **SERVES 1**

1 tablespoon yellow onions, sliced

1 tablespoon bell peppers, sliced

2 tablespoons frozen corn

1 Simple Grilled Chicken Breast (page 98)

2 tablespoons shredded fat-free Cheddar cheese

1 tablespoon fat-free sour cream

1 tablespoon salsa

1. Coat a skillet with nonstick spray. Cook onions, peppers, and corn on medium heat for 10 minutes. Slice chicken into thin strips.

2. Add precooked chicken to veggies and cook for 4 minutes. Place chicken and veggies on a plate and top with Cheddar. Serve with sour cream and salsa on the side.

PER SERVING Calories: 321 | Fat: 4 g | Protein: 60 g | Sodium: 322 mg | Carbohydrates: 8 g | Fiber: 1 g

Healthy Veggie Cuban

This take on a classic sandwich uses lots of veggies and healthy toppings to provide a yummy lunch.

Vegetarian, High-fiber

INGREDIENTS | SERVES 1

½ portobello mushroom, sliced

¼ zucchini, sliced lengthwise

¼ yellow squash, sliced lengthwise

¼ red bell pepper, sliced

Salt and pepper to taste

1 (4") portion Cuban bread

1 tablespoon Roasted Red Pepper Hummus (page 119)

1 teaspoon yellow mustard

1 slice fat-free Swiss cheese

1 slice sour pickle

What Is a Cuban Sandwich?

The Cuban sandwich was originally created by Cuban workers, either in Cuba or in the Cuban immigrant communities of Florida. Traditionally, the sandwich is made with ham, roasted pork, Swiss cheese, pickles, mustard, and sometimes salami on Cuban bread. Using vegetables in place of the meat, this variation is a lot better for you but still as delicious as the original.

1. Coat a nonstick pan with cooking spray and add mushroom, zucchini, squash, and red pepper on it. Season with salt and pepper to taste.

2. Bake veggies at 400°F for 8 minutes, flip veggies, then cook for about 6 to 8 minutes or until brown.

3. Remove veggies from pan and refrigerate for at least 1 hour.

4. Slice Cuban bread in half. Spread hummus on top and mustard on the bottom.

5. Top bottom slice of bread with vegetables, cheese, and pickle then cover with top slice.

6. Coat nonstick frying pan with cooking spray. Place sandwich in pan and cook each side for 3 minutes over medium heat.

PER SERVING Calories: 273 | Fat: 4 g | Protein: 16 g | Sodium: 1228 mg | Carbohydrates: 44 g | Fiber: 6 g

Turkey Parmesan Sandwich

Leftover turkey is great for whipping up quick lunches. This sandwich's melted Parmesan sets it apart from the usual post-Thanksgiving turkey sandwich.

INGREDIENTS | SERVES 2

4 slices whole-wheat bread
4 teaspoons low-fat mayonnaise
2 teaspoons Parmesan cheese
1 teaspoon thyme leaves, dried
Salt and pepper to taste
2 slices turkey breast
Shredded lettuce or Napa cabbage

1. Set your broiler on 400°F. Toast 4 slices of bread.

2. Mix the mayonnaise, cheese, thyme, salt, and pepper. Spread the mixture on one side of the bread.

3. Run under the broiler. Plate the toast and place turkey on two slices. Finally, add shredded lettuce or Napa cabbage for crunch and close sandwiches.

PER SERVING Calories: 251 | Fat: 8 g | Protein: 22 g | Sodium: 541 mg | Carbohydrates: 29 g | Fiber: 4 g

Ginger Peanut Chicken Salad Wrap

The chow mein vegetables in this recipe will taste better if they are chilled before use.

INGREDIENTS | SERVES 4

1 cup chopped chicken breast
¼ cup olive oil
1 (14-ounce) can oriental mixed vegetables, drained
⅔ cup Miracle Whip salad dressing
2 tablespoons reduced-sodium soy sauce
1 teaspoon ground ginger
4 (6") corn tortillas

1. Sauté chicken breast in olive oil in a large skillet over medium heat. Add vegetables and sauté until chicken is cooked. Transfer chicken and vegetables to a large bowl. Mix in the Miracle Whip, soy sauce, and ginger.

2. Heat the broiler, and warm the tortillas.

3. Spoon chicken mixture into tortillas. Roll up and serve.

PER SERVING Calories: 310 | Fat: 16 g | Protein: 16 g | Sodium: 1022 mg | Carbohydrates: 24 g | Fiber: 1 g

Smoked Salmon and Mascarpone Stuffed Pita Pockets

This recipe is a wonderful mixture of textures: melted and soft on the inside and slightly crisp on the outside.

High-fiber

INGREDIENTS | SERVES 2

2 whole-wheat pita pockets

2 thin slices of red onion

2 thin slices of lemon, seeded

⅛ pound smoked salmon

⅛ pound mascarpone cheese, sliced

1 teaspoon green peppercorns, packed in brine

Black pepper to taste

1. Preheat the oven to 350°F. Using half of each ingredient, stuff the pockets with onion, lemon, salmon, cheese, and peppercorns.

2. Bake for 15 to 20 minutes, until the pita is golden and the filling is hot.

PER SERVING Calories: 302 | Fat: 13 g | Protein: 13 g | Sodium: 856 mg | Carbohydrates: 36 g | Fiber: 6.8 g

Smoked Salmon

Smoked salmon is a preparation of salmon, typically a filet that has been cured and then hot or cold smoked. It can be expensive, but luckily you don't need much in most recipes. In the United States, smoked salmon is often sliced very thinly and served on bagels with cream cheese. This is called "bagels and lox," the lox being the smoked salmon.

Monte Cristo Sandwich

Bacon adds a salty crispness to these grilled sandwiches.
Serve them with more raspberry jam for dipping.

INGREDIENTS | SERVES 6

4 slices bacon

2 boneless, skinless chicken breasts

¼ cup raspberry jam

8 slices white bread

8 thin slices Gouda cheese

4 (1-ounce) slices ham

¼ cup butter, softened

1. In medium skillet, cook bacon until crisp. Remove from pan and drain on paper towels; crumble and set aside. Pour drippings from skillet and discard; do not wipe skillet. Add chicken; cook over medium heat, turning once, until browned and cooked, about 8 minutes. Remove chicken from pan and let stand.

2. Spread jam on one side of each slice of bread. Layer half of slices with cheese, then ham. Thinly slice chicken breasts and place over ham. Cover with remaining cheese slices, sprinkle with bacon, and top sandwiches with remaining bread slices.

3. Spread outsides of sandwiches with softened butter. Prepare and preheat griddle, indoor dual-contact grill, or panini maker. Grill sandwiches on medium for 4 to 6 minutes for dual-contact grill or panini maker, or 6 to 8 minutes, turning once, for griddle, until bread is golden brown and cheese is melted. Cut in half and serve immediately.

PER SERVING Calories: 373 | Fat: 19 g | Protein: 22 g | Sodium: 600 mg | Carbohydrates: 27 g | Fiber: 2 g

Classic Club Sandwich

*In restaurants, this sandwich is typically served with French fries or potato chips.
Choose a healthier alternative for your homemade club sandwiches, such
as a small portion of low-fat cottage cheese or some baked chips.*

Lactose-free

INGREDIENTS | SERVES 4

12 slices whole-wheat bread

3 tablespoons Miracle Whip salad dressing

1 head romaine lettuce

4 large tomatoes, thickly sliced

12 slices extra-lean bacon, broiled

½ pound thinly sliced smoked turkey

Salt and pepper to taste

12 toothpicks or cocktail sticks

1. Toast bread. Spread Miracle Whip thinly on 4 slices of bread. Cut romaine leaves to fit the bread. Place 2 tomato slices next on top of lettuce. Place bacon on top of the tomato. Top with turkey slices, salt, and pepper, and finish with another slice of bread.

2. Repeat for the second layer. Cover with a final bread slice spread with Miracle Whip.

3. Cut sandwich into 4 pieces, diagonally. Place toothpick or cocktail stick into center of each little sandwich to hold it together.

PER SERVING Calories: 513 | Fat: 21 g | Protein: 35 g | Sodium: 1500 mg | Carbohydrates: 50 g | Fiber: 4 g

What Is a Club Sandwich?

A club sandwich, also called a clubhouse or double-decker sandwich, includes two layers of fillings between three slices of bread. It is usually cut into quarters and held together with cocktail sticks. The traditional club ingredients are turkey on the bottom layer, and bacon, lettuce, and tomato on the top. Though it's a healthier version, this recipe is pretty darn close to the real thing.

Roast Beef Pitas

Fresh basil adds a lemony, peppery scent and taste to these simple sandwiches.

Low-fat

INGREDIENTS | SERVES 6

½ cup chopped fresh basil

2 tablespoons prepared horseradish

½ cup plain nonfat yogurt

⅛ teaspoon pepper

1 pound deli-sliced lean roast beef

1 head butter lettuce

3 whole-wheat pita breads, halved

2 tomatoes, sliced

1. In a large bowl, stir together the basil, horseradish, yogurt, and pepper. Spread the horseradish-yogurt mixture on the beef slices.

2. Separate lettuce into individual leaves and wrap each beef slice in a lettuce leaf. Put the lettuce-wrapped beef and 2 slices of tomato into each pita bread half. Serve immediately.

PER SERVING Calories: 201 | Fat: 3 g | Protein: 21 g | Sodium: 830 mg | Carbohydrates: 15 g | Fiber: 1 g

Horseradish Facts

The terms *horseradish* and *prepared horse-radish* refer to the grated root of the horseradish plant mixed with vinegar. Prepared horseradish is white to creamy-beige in color. It will keep for months in the refrigerator but eventually will start to darken, which means it should be replaced. Horseradish sauce, made from grated horseradish root, vinegar, and cream is also a popular condiment.

Peach Pita Sandwiches

Peaches and ham are a natural combination. The sweet peaches are a great contrast with the salty ham.

Low-fat

INGREDIENTS | SERVES 4

4 pita breads
8 curly lettuce leaves
2 cups 1%, low-sodium cottage cheese
8 tomato slices
6 extra-lean ham slices, chopped
1 (16-ounce) can sliced cling peaches, drained

Cut pita breads in half, forming 8 pockets. Line with the lettuce leaves. Add cottage cheese, tomato slices, ham, and drained peaches. Serve immediately.

Wonderful Pita Bread

You can find pita breads in most bakeries and large grocery stores. Cut the rounds in half to make two half-moons. You may need to slightly cut between the layers to form the pocket. These breads are baked at a very high temperature so the gas inside expands quickly, forming the pocket as the structure sets.

PER SERVING Calories: 450 | Fat: 6 g | Protein: 28 g | Sodium: 893 mg | Carbohydrates: 51 g | Fiber: 3 g

Peanut Butter Apple Wraps

This may sound like something you'd make for little kids, but it's healthy, delicious, and easy to make—which makes it perfect college food.

Vegetarian

INGREDIENTS | SERVES 4

½ cup natural crunchy peanut butter
1 apple, chopped
½ cup raisins
1 cup chopped celery
4 whole-wheat tortillas

In small bowl, combine peanut butter, apple, raisins, and celery. Arrange tortillas on work surface. Spread with peanut butter mixture and roll up. Cut into thirds and serve.

PER SERVING Calories: 279 | Fat: 13 g | Protein: 19 g | Sodium: 770 mg | Carbohydrates: 35 g | Fiber: 4 g

CHAPTER 5

Soups and Salads
You Can Make in Your Dorm

Leek and Potato Soup

There are many versions of this excellent soup, which tastes wonderful when served either hot or chilled. Some recipes have chunky potatoes, and others are smooth—you can prepare this one whichever way you like.

INGREDIENTS | SERVES 4

¼ cup olive oil
2 leeks, coarsely chopped
1 large sweet onion, chopped
2 large baking potatoes, peeled and chopped
2 cups chicken broth
1 teaspoon salt
1 cup 2% milk
1 cup whipping cream
¼ cup chopped chives
Salt and freshly ground pepper to taste
Garnish of ¼ cup chopped watercress

1. Heat the olive oil in a large soup kettle. Be sure to rinse the sand out of your leeks! Add the leeks and onion and sauté for 5 minutes over medium heat.

2. Add the potatoes, chicken broth, and salt. Simmer until the potatoes are tender. Set aside and cool.

3. Put the soup through a ricer or purée in the blender until smooth.

4. Pour the soup back into the pot, add the milk, whipping cream, and chives and reheat. Add salt and pepper to taste. Float the watercress on top for garnish.

PER SERVING Calories: 491 | Fat: 33 g | Protein: 8 g | Sodium: 469 mg | Carbohydrates: 40 g | Fiber: 4.4 g

Black Bean and Corn Soup

To add flavor and spice to any of your dishes, add chili powder, jalapeño peppers, chipotle peppers, cayenne pepper, red pepper, or serrano peppers.

Low-fat, High-fiber

INGREDIENTS | SERVES 6

4 cups black beans
1 teaspoon olive oil
1 clove fresh garlic, minced
½ teaspoon all-purpose seasoning
2 cups frozen corn
2 cups tomatoes, diced
2 cups crushed tomatoes
½ cup green onions, sliced
2 tablespoons chili powder
1 teaspoon cumin
½ cup bell peppers, diced
1 cup chicken broth
1 cup water

1. Combine all ingredients in a large saucepan.

2. Cook on medium heat for 15 minutes.

3. Reduce heat to low, simmer for another 10 minutes, then serve.

PER SERVING Calories: 267 | Fat: 3 g | Protein: 15 g | Sodium: 292 mg | Carbohydrates: 50 g | Fiber: 15 g

Green Onions

Green onions, also called scallions, are milder in flavor than most onions. They may be cooked or used raw, and they show up in lots of salads and Asian recipes. Diced scallions are used in soups as well as noodle and seafood dishes.

Veggies and Rice Soup

To make this an even lighter soup with fewer calories, reduce the amount of brown rice you use.

Vegan, High-fiber, Lactose-free

INGREDIENTS | SERVES 8

2 cups instant brown rice

4 cups California-blend vegetables, chopped

1 cup Brussels sprouts, cut in half

2 cups sweet potatoes, peeled and cubed

4 cups vegetable broth

½ teaspoon all-purpose seasoning

1 clove fresh garlic, minced

1 teaspoon Italian herbs

½ cup yellow onions, diced

1 tablespoon olive oil

1 teaspoon oregano

¼ cup fresh parsley

½ teaspoon black pepper

1 cup celery, chopped

2 cups water

1. Combine all ingredients in a large saucepan. Cook on medium-high heat for 15 minutes.

2. Reduce heat to low and simmer for another 10 minutes. Add additional water if soup dries out.

PER SERVING Calories: 352 | Fat: 5 g | Protein: 9 g | Sodium: 1,130 mg | Carbohydrates: 69 g | Fiber: 7 g

Chicken Soup Verde

It's very important to trim the bottom of the asparagus off or clean it very well, as this portion of the vegetable often contains sand.

Low-fat, Lactose-free, Low-carb

INGREDIENTS | SERVES 4

8 ounces fresh asparagus

4 cups low-sodium chicken broth

1 cup dry white wine

3 boneless, skinless chicken breasts, thinly sliced

½ teaspoon fresh garlic, minced

1 cup frozen green peas

¼ teaspoon parsley

¼ teaspoon dill

¼ teaspoon tarragon

½ teaspoon sesame oil

⅓ cup vermicelli rice noodles

1 tablespoon low-sodium soy sauce

½ cup green onions, sliced

Salt and pepper to taste

1. Wash and cut the woody end off asparagus, then cut into 1½" segments and set aside.

2. Add chicken broth and wine to a large saucepan and bring to a boil. Add chicken, asparagus, garlic, peas, and herbs to saucepan.

3. Simmer on low for 15 minutes and add sesame oil, noodles, soy sauce, and green onions to the saucepan. Simmer for an additional 10 minutes. Add salt and pepper to taste.

PER SERVING Calories: 272 | Fat: 2 g | Protein: 36 g | Sodium: 772 mg | Carbohydrates: 18 g | Fiber: 3 g

Spice It Up

A great but relatively inexpensive kitchen tool you might want to invest in is a pepper grinder. The flavor of freshly cracked pepper is much cleaner and more intense than store-bought ground pepper. Read the directions on the pepper grinder, as many models are adjustable for the size of the grind.

Tuscan Bean Soup

Tuscan cuisine combines a mixture of vegetables with the flavor of Mediterranean aromatic herbs.

Low-calorie, High-fiber, Lactose-free

INGREDIENTS | SERVES 6

1 clove fresh garlic, minced

2 cups zucchini, sliced

1 teaspoon oregano

½ cup bell peppers, diced

2 cups tomatoes, diced

1 teaspoon all-purpose seasoning

1 teaspoon cumin

½ cup carrots, sliced

1 cup red wine

3 cups white beans, cooked

4 cups chicken broth

½ teaspoon black pepper

1 tablespoon tomato paste

½ cup celery, sliced

1. Combine all ingredients in a large saucepan. Cook on medium-high heat for 15 minutes.

2. Reduce heat to low, simmer for another 10 minutes, then serve.

PER SERVING Calories: 242 | Fat: 4 g | Carbohydrates: 33 g | Protein: 14 g | Sodium: 595 mg | Fiber: 9 g

Cannellini Minestrone

Minestrone is an Italian soup that translates roughly to "the big soup." It is a thick soup made with vegetables, often with the addition of pasta or rice.

High-fiber, Low-fat, Vegan

INGREDIENTS | SERVES 6

1 clove fresh garlic, minced

½ teaspoon all-purpose seasoning

3 cups cannellini beans

1 cup white mushrooms, sliced

½ cup white onions, chopped

½ cup celery, chopped

1 teaspoon dried parsley

1 teaspoon dried basil

½ teaspoon red pepper flakes

2 cups diced tomatoes

1 cup frozen spinach

2 cups water

1. Combine all ingredients in a large saucepan. Cook on medium-high heat for 15 minutes.

2. Reduce heat to low, simmer for another 10 minutes, then serve.

PER SERVING Calories: 366 | Fat: 1 g | Protein: 25 g | Sodium: 53 mg | Carbohydrates: 67 g | Fiber: 17 g

What Are Cannellini Beans?

Cannellini beans are white Italian kidney beans, and they give this recipe a robust flavor. If you can't get a hold of cannellini beans, you can substitute great northern beans or navy beans. Always keep a few cans of different kinds of beans on hand for use in soups and salads.

Potato Garbanzo Stew

Potatoes and beans may sound like a strange combination, but it is heart-warming and delicious.

Low-fat, High-fiber, Lactose-free

INGREDIENTS | **SERVES 4**

1 tablespoon olive oil

1 onion, chopped

3 cloves garlic, minced

1 teaspoon paprika

3 tomatoes, chopped

1 teaspoon dried oregano leaves

2 potatoes, peeled and diced

4 cups fat-free, low-sodium chicken broth

1 (15-ounce) can garbanzo beans, rinsed and drained

½ cup chopped fresh basil leaves

¼ teaspoon salt

⅛ teaspoon pepper

½ cup chopped fresh parsley

1. In a large saucepan, heat olive oil over medium heat. Add onion and garlic; cook and stir until crisp-tender, about 5 minutes. Add paprika, tomatoes, and oregano. Reduce heat to low and cook, stirring frequently, for 5 minutes.

2. Add potatoes and broth, cover, and bring to a boil. Reduce heat to low and simmer for 5 minutes, stirring occasionally. Add garbanzo beans and cook until potatoes are tender, 5 to 8 minutes longer.

3. Add basil, salt, and pepper and simmer for 3 to 5 minutes longer to heat through. Sprinkle with parsley and serve.

PER SERVING Calories: 346 | Fat: 5 g | Protein: 9 g | Sodium: 361 mg | Carbohydrates: 45 g | Fiber: 8.5 g

Chickpea Soup

This fragrant, delicious soup is great any time of year, but especially once the weather has turned colder.

High-fiber, Low-calorie

INGREDIENTS | SERVES 6

1 clove fresh garlic, minced

1 cup bell peppers, diced

1 cup yellow onions, diced

3 teaspoons lemon juice

3 cups chicken broth

½ teaspoon red pepper

1 teaspoon ground ginger

½ teaspoon cumin

4 cups chickpeas, cooked

½ teaspoon all-purpose seasoning

2 cups carrots, sliced

3 tablespoons tomato paste

1 cup baking potatoes, cubed

1. Combine all ingredients in a large saucepan. Cook on medium-high heat for 15 minutes.

2. Simmer for another 10 minutes, then serve.

PER SERVING Calories: 250 | Fat: 4 g | Protein: 14 g | Sodium: 471 mg | Carbohydrates: 43 g | Fiber: 6 g

What Are Chickpeas?

Chickpeas, also known as garbanzo beans, are loaded with folate, zinc, protein, and dietary fiber—and they taste great! It's a great idea for vegetarians to toss these little guys in meals throughout the week.

Vegetable and Pasta Soup

To keep a quick and easy source of healthy veggies on hand, grab a bag of frozen mixed vegetables at a wholesale store and keep them in your freezer.

Low-fat, High-fiber, Lactose-free

INGREDIENTS | SERVES 6

1 clove fresh garlic, minced

1 cup bell peppers, diced

1 cup white onions, diced

1 cup celery, sliced

3 cups chicken broth

4 cups frozen mixed vegetables

½ teaspoon all-purpose seasoning

¼ cup fresh parsley

1 cup baking potatoes, diced

2 cups whole-wheat rotini pasta

2 cups water

1. Combine all ingredients in a large saucepan. Cook on medium-high heat for 15 minutes.

2. Reduce heat to low and simmer for another 10 minutes. Add additional water if soup dries out.

PER SERVING Calories: 259 | Fat: 2 g | Protein: 13 g | Sodium: 465 mg | Carbohydrates: 52 g | Fiber: 10 g

Salmon Spinach Salad

This salad makes perfect use of leftover salmon! Salmon will only remain good in the fridge for two days, so make sure you find a good use for it quickly!

Low-calorie, Low-carb, Gluten-free, Lactose-free

INGREDIENTS | SERVES 1

1 (5-ounce) salmon filet, cooked

1 cup spinach leaves

½ cup red grapes

¼ cup shredded carrots

½ tablespoon sliced almonds

1 tablespoon dried cranberries

Combine ingredients in a bowl and enjoy!

PER SERVING Calories: 211 | Fat: 7 g | Protein: 30 g | Sodium: 130 mg | Carbohydrates: 5 g | Fiber: 2 g

Moroccan Tagine of Chicken and Chickpeas

In Morocco, a traditional tagine is a stew cooked at very low temperatures so the meat has time to become very tender.

Low-fat, Lactose-free

INGREDIENTS | SERVES 6

1 clove fresh garlic, minced

½ teaspoon all-purpose seasoning

2 teaspoons paprika

1 teaspoon ground ginger

½ teaspoon turmeric

1 cup yellow onions, chopped

2 cups tomatoes, diced

2 cups chickpeas, cooked

¼ cup cilantro, chopped

2 cups low-sodium chicken broth

6 boneless, skinless chicken breasts, cut in chunks

Add all ingredients to a large saucepan. Cook on medium high for 10 to 12 minutes, stirring often. Simmer for 8 to 10 minutes.

PER SERVING Calories: 264 | Fat: 3 g | Protein: 37 g | Sodium: 260 mg | Carbohydrates: 22 g | Fiber: 3 g

Tortilla Tomato Soup

This soup is a fun alternative to tacos with the same great flavors. You might also add a dollop of fat-free sour cream for a cool, creamy taste.

High-fiber

INGREDIENTS | SERVES 8

½ cup red onions, diced

1 clove fresh garlic, minced

½ teaspoon all-purpose seasoning

4 cups tomatoes, diced

3 cups crushed tomatoes

¼ teaspoon black pepper

¼ cup fresh cilantro, chopped

3 cups chicken broth

3 cups whole-wheat tortilla strips

½ cup shredded fat-free Cheddar cheese

1. Combine all ingredients except tortillas and cheese in a large saucepan. Cook on medium-high heat for 15 minutes. Reduce heat to low and simmer for another 10 minutes.

2. Toast tortilla strips in toaster oven until crispy.

3. Serve soup and sprinkle with cheese and tortilla strips.

PER SERVING Calories: 426 | Fat: 8 g | Protein: 17 g | Sodium: 1,493 mg | Carbohydrates: 76 g | Fiber: 8 g

Slow Down!

Did you know that it takes your stomach about 20 minutes to let your brain know it's full? For this reason, it's important for you to slow down and give your body a chance to do its job. Chew each bite slowly, savor the taste of your food, and stop when your brain says "enough!"

Red Lentil and Sweet Potato Soup

For a creamier soup, add 1 cup of fat-free sour cream or plain yogurt after cooking. Swirl cream and soup together gently.

Low-calorie, Low-fat, High-fiber, Vegan, Lactose-free

INGREDIENTS | SERVES 4

1 white onion, chopped
1 celery stick, finely chopped
1 large carrot, sliced
1½ cups sweet potato, cubed
1 cup red lentils, cooked
1 bay leaf
½ teaspoon fresh garlic, minced
½ teaspoon all-purpose seasoning
5 cups vegetable or chicken broth
2 tablespoons fresh cilantro, chopped

Plentiful Lentils

Lentils come in many colors, from yellow to red-orange to green, brown, and black. Lentils can come whole or split, and many varieties come decorticated, or with their skins removed. All varieties are high in proteins, so they're a great choice all around!

1. Spray a large saucepan with nonstick cooking spray. Add onions and celery and cook on medium-high heat for 2 minutes, stirring often.

2. Add carrots, sweet potatoes, lentils, bay leaf, garlic, all-purpose seasoning, and broth to saucepan. Cover and cook on medium for 10 minutes.

3. Reduce heat to low and simmer for an additional 10 minutes. Remove bay leaf and blend soup in batches in a food processor.

4. Return soup to saucepan, add cilantro, and simmer for 5 minutes.

PER SERVING Calories: 184 | Fat: 2 g | Protein: 12 g | Sodium: 1,030 mg | Carbohydrates: 29 g | Fiber: 7 g

Pear and Watercress Salad

Chunky bleu cheese is the only type to serve with this salad.

Low-calorie, Low-carb, Vegan

INGREDIENTS | SERVES 4

2 pears

3 tablespoons canola oil

1½ tablespoons apple cider vinegar

Salt and pepper to taste

1 teaspoon whole-grain mustard

½ cup watercress, washed, dried, stems trimmed

1 cup arugula, washed, dried, stems trimmed

2 ounces bleu cheese, crumbled

1. Core the pears. Cut into ¾" slices. In 1 teaspoon of canola oil, sauté the pears until brown.

2. Mix the remaining oil with the vinegar, salt, and pepper. Add mustard, whisking until dressing is slightly thick.

3. Mix watercress and arugula in a plastic bag and pour into a salad bowl. Add bleu cheese, pears, and dressing. Toss and serve immediately.

PER SERVING Calories: 198 | Fat: 15 g | Protein: 4 g | Sodium: 202 mg | Carbohydrates: 14 g | Fiber: 3.2 g

Awesome Arugula

Arugula is a leafy green that is rich is vitamin C and potassium. It has a rich, peppery taste and is generally used in salads but also appears cooked as a vegetable with pasta sauces or meats in northern Italy. The strong flavor of the arugula is a great complement to the pears and bleu cheese in this salad.

Honey-Roasted Turkey Salad

Honey-roasted turkey offers a unique sweetness, but you can substitute regular roasted turkey if you prefer.

High-fiber

INGREDIENTS | SERVES 1

2 cups spinach

2 ounces honey-roasted turkey breast, sliced

4 tomato slices

1 tablespoon shredded low-fat mozzarella

4 red apple slices

1 tablespoon sweet vinaigrette dressing of choice

Combine all ingredients in a large bowl. Serve with a tablespoon of sweet dressing, such as fat-free raspberry vinaigrette, on the side if you'd like.

PER SERVING Calories: 379 | Fat: 4 g | Protein: 19 g | Sodium: 993 mg | Carbohydrates: 73 g | Fiber: 14 g

Cordon Bleu Salad

Traditional chicken cordon bleu is horribly high in fat and calories. This dish will allow you to enjoy some of those flavors without paying too high a caloric price.

High-fiber

INGREDIENTS | SERVES 1

2 cups romaine lettuce

2 ounces boneless, skinless chicken breast

1 ounce sliced deli ham

¼ cup plum tomatoes

¼ cup shiitake mushrooms

1 tablespoon low-fat shredded Swiss cheese

1 tablespoon fat-free honey Dijon dressing

Combine all ingredients in a bowl except for dressing. Serve with dressing on the side.

Shiitake Mushrooms

Fresh and dried shiitake mushrooms have many uses in East Asian cuisine. In Chinese dishes, they are often sautéed in vegetarian meals. In Japan, they are served in miso soup. In Korean cuisine, they are commonly used in dishes such as bulgogi (marinated grilled beef). Luckily, these tasty mushrooms have a place in American cuisine as well!

PER SERVING Calories: 381 | Fat: 5 g | Protein: 35 g | Sodium: 563 mg | Carbohydrates: 56 g | Flber: 9 g

Asian Chicken Salad

Use a prewashed, chopped, and ready-to-use bag of salad mix to save time.

Low-calorie, Low-fat, Low-carb, High-fiber, Lactose-free

INGREDIENTS | SERVES 1

2 cups green leaf lettuce

3 ounces grilled boneless, skinless chicken breast

¼ cup plum tomatoes

1 cup alfalfa sprouts

¼ cup shredded carrots

1 teaspoon sesame seeds

2 tablespoons mandarin oranges

1 tablespoon sesame ginger dressing, fat-free

Combine all ingredients except dressing in a bowl. Serve with dressing on the side.

PER SERVING Calories: 187 | Fat: 3 g | Protein: 23 g | Sodium: 204 mg | Carbohydrates: 16 g | Fiber: 5 g

Tropical Cobb Salad

The mango, feta, and pine nuts in this salad offer incredible textural differences yet perfectly complementary flavors.

Low-calorie, Low-carb, Gluten-free

INGREDIENTS | SERVES 1

2 cups romaine lettuce

3 ounces Simple Grilled Chicken Breasts (page 98)

¼ cup plum tomatoes

2 tablespoons chopped mangos

½ tablespoon toasted pine nuts

1 tablespoon feta cheese

Combine all ingredients in a large bowl. Choose a low-fat citrus dressing to serve on the side.

Fantastic Feta

Feta is a brined curd cheese traditionally made in Greece. It is an aged cheese, commonly produced in blocks, and has a slightly grainy texture. It is often used in salads (ever heard of Greek salad?—see the next page), pastries, and other baked dishes. You'll also find it in other recipes in this book, such as Hummus Tomato Pita Pizza (page 216).

PER SERVING Calories: 181 | Fat: 6 g | Protein: 24 g | Sodium: 174 mg | Carbohydrates: 9 g | Fiber: 3 g

Greek Salad

The Greek diet is associated with a decreased risk of cancer. To pursue Mediterranean-style eating habits, enjoy olives, fruit, beans, and fish on a regular basis.

Low-calorie, Low-carb, Vegetarian, Gluten-free

INGREDIENTS | SERVES 1

2 cups romaine lettuce

¼ cup tomatoes, diced

2 tablespoons cucumbers, diced ·

2 kalamata olives

2 pepperoncini

2 tablespoons red onions, diced

¼ cup bell pepper slices

1 tablespoon feta cheese

Combine all ingredients in a bowl. Serve with Greek dressing on the side.

PER SERVING Calories: 119 | Fat: 6 g | Protein: 6 g | Sodium: 344 mg | Carbohydrates: 12 g | Fiber: 4 g

Healthy Taco Salad

Use caution when ordering this at a restaurant. Taco salads are often comprised of fatty ground beef, full-fat cheese, sour cream, and a fried tortilla shell.

Low-calorie, Low-fat, High-fiber, Vegetarian, Gluten-free

INGREDIENTS | SERVES 1

2 cups romaine lettuce, chopped

3 ounces lean ground turkey or Boca Meatless Ground Burger, cooked

2 tablespoons tomatoes, diced

2 tablespoons black beans

2 tablespoons onions, caramelized

2 tablespoons corn

1 tablespoon shredded low-fat Cheddar cheese

1 jalapeño pepper, sliced

Layer all ingredients in a bowl. Serve with salsa.

PER SERVING Calories: 233 | Fat: 2 g | Protein: 29 g | Sodium: 462 mg | Carbohydrates: 34 g | Fiber: 12 g

Steak and Caesar Salad

Never heard of steak showing up in Caesar salad? Give it a try.
It's a great way to make a meal out of a side salad.

INGREDIENTS | SERVES 1

2 cups romaine lettuce
2 ounces grilled, lean steak
½ tablespoon reduced-fat grated
Parmesan cheese
2 tablespoons fat-free garlic Caesar
croutons

1. Wash lettuce and chop to desired size.

2. Slice steak into strips.

3. Combine all ingredients in a bowl and serve with 1 tablespoon fat-free Caesar dressing (optional).

PER SERVING Calories: 282 | Fat: 10 g | Protein: 14 g | Sodium: 529 mg | Carbohydrates: 24 g | Fiber: 2 g

Healthy Steak?

Steak isn't always considered health food, but that doesn't mean you can never have it. Just make sure the steak you choose is lean, and pair it with truly healthful fruits and vegetables. Beef provides much-needed iron and protein in a tasty package.

Macaroni Salad

Add a diced tomato for color if you like. It provides a touch of fiber with a negligible amount of calories.

Vegetarian, Lactose-free

INGREDIENTS | SERVES 4

2 cups elbow macaroni, cooked
according to package directions
⅓ cup diced celery
⅓ cup finely chopped Vidalia onion
⅔ cup Miracle Whip salad dressing
⅔ cup dry mustard
1 teaspoon Splenda
3 tablespoons fat-free sour cream
Salt and pepper to taste

Mix all ingredients together. Cover, refrigerate until cold, and serve.

Magnificent Macaroni

Cook the macaroni al dente so it's still chewy. *Al dente* is an Italian term meaning "to the tooth"—firm. A firmer pasta adds a great texture to salad. Pasta can also be cooked al dente for casseroles where the noodles will cook further in the oven.

PER SERVING Calories: 275 | Fat: 9 g | Protein: 11 g | Sodium: 376 mg | Carbohydrates: 36 g | Fiber: 1.8 g

Apple Gemelli Salad

You can use golden raisins or dark-colored raisins in this classic and easy salad. Substitute dried currants for a slightly sweeter taste.

Low-calorie, Low-fat, Vegetarian

INGREDIENTS | **SERVES 6**

1 (8-ounce) can crushed pineapple

2 Granny Smith apples, peeled and chopped

½ cup diced celery

⅓ cup raisins

½ (12-ounce) package gemelli pasta

½ cup plain low-fat yogurt

¼ cup plain nonfat mayonnaise

½ teaspoon cinnamon

⅛ teaspoon salt

1. Bring a large pot of salted water to a boil. Meanwhile, drain pineapple, reserving juice.

2. In a serving bowl, combine pineapple, apples, celery, and raisins and mix well. Cook pasta according to package directions until al dente; drain well.

3. Add pasta to apple mixture. In a small bowl, combine 3 tablespoons reserved pineapple liquid, yogurt, mayonnaise, cinnamon, and salt and mix well. Pour over salad and toss to coat. Cover and refrigerate for 3 to 4 hours before serving.

PER SERVING Calories: 180 | Fat: 2 g | Protein: 8 g | Sodium: 131 mg | Carbohydrates: 61 g | Fiber: 3.5 g

Crabmeat and Shrimp Salad

Make sure your seafood is thoroughly cooked before mixing this salad. Serve the salad by itself or on whole-wheat buns.

Low-calorie, Low-fat, Low-carb

INGREDIENTS | SERVES 4

¾ pound lump crabmeat, cooked

½ pound shrimp, cooked and diced

4 teaspoons dried chives

1 stalk celery, diced

¼ cup fat-free sour cream

1 teaspoon lemon juice

1 teaspoon Dijon mustard

Salt and pepper to taste

1 teaspoon Splenda

1 head iceberg lettuce

Combine all ingredients. Cover salad and refrigerate until chilled. Serve salad on iceberg lettuce leaves.

Expensive Seafood

Seafood can be expensive, but that doesn't mean it's off-limits to college students. Like most things, there's a cheaper way to do seafood; you just have to know what it is! Look in the freezer section of the grocery store for big bags of frozen shrimp, scallops, fish, and other types of seafood. These are much more affordable by the pound, and by keeping large bags of seafood in your freezer, you'll always have some on hand.

PER SERVING Calories: 170 | Fat: 2 g | Protein: 32 g | Sodium: 279 mg | Carbohydrates: 7 g | Fiber: 1 g

CHAPTER 6

Hearty, Easy-to-Prepare Pastas and Grains

Whole-Wheat Spaghetti with Jalapeño Tomato Sauce

Use Romano cheese instead of Parmesan cheese if you prefer.

Low-fat, Vegetarian

INGREDIENTS | **SERVES 6**

1 pound whole-wheat spaghetti

1 (28-ounce) can no-sodium diced tomatoes

¼ cup minced onions

½ teaspoon minced garlic

2 low-sodium vegetable bouillon cubes

3 jalapeño peppers, diced

⅓ cup grated Parmesan cheese

1. Cook spaghetti noodles as directed.

2. Combine tomatoes, onions, garlic, bouillon cubes, and jalapeño peppers in a food processor or blender until smooth.

3. Put blended mixture in a large saucepan and heat on medium for about 5 minutes.

PER SERVING Calories: 320 | Fat: 3 g | Protein: 14 g | Sodium: 340 mg | Carbohydrates: 65 g | Fiber: 3 g

Simple Vegetable Pasta

Warm your vegetables in a skillet or in the microwave. If you prefer to cook them for a softer texture, use a skillet and stir them until they are soft or slightly browned.

Low-fat, High-fiber, Vegetarian

INGREDIENTS | **SERVES 6**

1 pound whole-wheat spaghetti

10 ounces mixed frozen vegetables, thawed

1 teaspoon freshly grated rosemary

2 teaspoons minced onion

2 teaspoons minced garlic

Salt and pepper to taste

¼ cup Parmesan cheese

1. Cook spaghetti according to directions.

2. In a skillet over medium heat, toss the mixed vegetables to warm them.

3. Mix rosemary, onion, garlic, salt, and pepper with the vegetables.

4. Pour vegetables over spaghetti and serve, sprinkling with cheese.

PER SERVING Calories: 313 | Fat: 2 g | Protein: 14 g | Sodium: 345 mg | Carbohydrates: 64 g | Fiber: 6 g

Pasta Alfredo

If the pasta mixture has become thick and tight, thin it with some of the reserved cooking water.

Vegetarian

INGREDIENTS | SERVES 6

1 pound fettuccine noodles
½ cup margarine
2 cups skim milk
⅓ teaspoon nutmeg
1⅓ cups freshly grated Parmesan cheese

Counting Calories

A protein calorie is no different from a fat calorie, they are simply units of energy. However, fat packs more calories per gram than proteins or carbohydrates. The key to weight loss is to burn more calories than you take in.

1. Prepare the fettuccine according to package directions. When pasta is done, drain in a colander and reserve some of the cooking water.

2. Meanwhile, melt margarine in a saucepan over medium heat.

3. Whisk in the milk and nutmeg and bring the mixture to simmer.

4. Add the fettuccine to the cream mixture and top with the cheese.

PER SERVING Calories: 570 | Fat: 24 g | Protein: 24 g | Sodium: 327 mg | Carbohydrates: 61 g | Fiber: 3 g

Shells with Zucchini

Rosemary adds a rich depth of flavor to this simple summer pasta recipe, and the Parmesan cheese topping adds just the right texture and taste.

Vegetarian

INGREDIENTS | SERVES 4

1 tablespoon butter

2 cloves garlic, minced

3 zucchini, sliced

2 teaspoons fresh rosemary leaves, minced

¼ teaspoon salt

⅛ teaspoon white pepper

1 (12-ounce) package medium pasta shells

3 tablespoons chopped flat-leaf parsley

¼ cup grated Parmesan cheese

Cooking Pasta

Many chefs undercook pasta slightly and add it to the sauce in the pan. This way, the pasta absorbs flavors from the sauce. Remember that if you put pasta into a hot pan of sauce, it will continue to cook—be careful not to overcook and end up with mush!

1. Bring a large pot of water to a boil. In a large skillet, melt butter over medium heat. Add garlic and zucchini and cook until crisp-tender, about 5 to 6 minutes. Add rosemary and season with salt and pepper. Cook for 2 to 3 minutes to blend flavors. Remove from heat.

2. Meanwhile, cook pasta in boiling salted water until al dente. Drain and add to zucchini mixture. Return to the heat and toss until the shells are coated with sauce, 2 to 3 minutes. Add the parsley and cheese and toss again. Serve immediately.

PER SERVING Calories: 329 | Fat: 4 g | Protein: 14 g | Sodium: 420 mg | Carbohydrates: 68 g | Fiber: 4 g

Fresh Tomato with Angel Hair Pasta

This meal is simple but delicious. Throw in some leftover chicken or sausage if you want to add some protein and kick up the flavor a notch.

Vegetarian

INGREDIENTS | SERVES 4–6

½ cup pine nuts

4 ripe beefsteak tomatoes

¼ cup extra-virgin olive oil

1 tablespoon lemon juice

¼ cup packed fresh basil leaves

½ teaspoon salt

⅛ teaspoon white pepper

1 pound angel hair pasta

Fresh Basil

If you have a garden—or even just a sunny windowsill—by all means grow basil; it's easy to grow and requires very little maintenance. There are lots of kits available on the market or the Internet. Just be sure to use the basil before the plant starts to flower. You can also find fresh basil in the produce aisle of your supermarket.

1. Bring a large pot of water to a boil for the pasta. Place small skillet over medium heat for 3 minutes. Add pine nuts; cook and stir for 3 to 5 minutes or until nuts begin to brown and are fragrant. Remove from heat and pour nuts into a serving bowl.

2. Chop tomatoes into ½" pieces and add to pine nuts along with olive oil, lemon juice, basil, salt, and pepper. Add pasta to the boiling water; cook and stir until al dente, according to package directions. Drain and add to tomato mixture in bowl. Toss gently and serve immediately.

PER SERVING Calories: 277 | Fat: 18 g | Protein: 19 g | Sodium: 387 mg | Carbohydrates: 25 g | Fiber: 4 g

Fusilli with Ricotta

Ricotta is a soft cheese similar to cottage cheese, but it is made from whey instead of milk. It has a creamy texture and rich flavor.

Vegetarian

INGREDIENTS | SERVES 6

1 (15-ounce) container part-skim ricotta cheese

⅔ cup skim milk

¼ teaspoon salt

⅛ teaspoon white pepper

¼ cup grated Parmesan cheese

1 tablespoon olive oil

1 onion, chopped

4 cloves garlic, minced

½ cup chopped basil leaves

¼ cup chopped chives

¼ cup chopped flat-leaf parsley

1 (16-ounce) package fusilli pasta

1. In a food processor or blender, combine ricotta cheese, milk, salt, pepper, and Parmesan. Process or blend until smooth.

2. In a large skillet, heat oil over medium heat. Add onion and sauté until nearly browned, about 10 minutes. Add garlic and cook until softened.

3. Add ricotta mixture and stir in basil, chives, and parsley. Cook over low heat, stirring frequently, until hot and blended.

4. Meanwhile, cook pasta in boiling water until al dente. Drain and add to skillet. Toss well so pasta is coated with sauce. Transfer to a warm serving bowl and serve.

PER SERVING Calories: 429 | Fat: 9 g | Protein: 14 g | Sodium: 402 mg | Carbohydrates: 72 g | Fiber: 3 g

Classic Macaroni and Cheese

There are virtually hundreds of ways to make this macaroni and cheese your own. Using two different cheeses makes the flavor undeniable, but you can stick to one if you prefer.

Vegetarian

INGREDIENTS | **SERVES 4**

2 cups macaroni noodles
½ stalk celery, minced
¼ cup onion, minced
2 tablespoons canola oil
3 tablespoons fat-free milk
4 tablespoons flour
1 cup of low-fat grated Cheddar cheese
½ cup low-fat grated Swiss cheese
½ teaspoon grated nutmeg
Salt and pepper to taste

1. Cook macaroni according to package directions.

2. Sauté minced celery and onion in a skillet with the oil over medium heat.

3. Mix in the milk and flour, stirring until smooth.

4. Mix in the cheese, stirring constantly until thick.

5. Remove immediately from heat.

6. Stir in the nutmeg and season with salt and pepper.

7. Pour mixture over the macaroni. Toss and serve.

PER SERVING Calories: 368 | Fat: 11 g | Protein: 19 g | Sodium: 430 mg | Carbohydrates: 48 g | Fiber: 3 g

Nutmeg Is Nice

Nutmeg always adds a slight hint of spice and helps bring out the flavor in cheese sauces. You can use a pinch of pre-ground nutmeg, but fresh nutmeg has much more flavor and aroma. Grate a bit of fresh nutmeg over everything from cheese sauce to potatoes.

Pad Thai

This simple and quick dish uses the flavors and textures of Southeast Asia in a recipe perfect for a late-night dinner.

Lactose-free

INGREDIENTS | SERVES 4

¼ pound dried rice noodles

3 tablespoons rice vinegar

1 tablespoon fish sauce

2 tablespoons sugar

1 teaspoon Chinese chili paste with garlic

1 tablespoon peanut oil

3 cloves garlic, minced

1 egg, beaten

½ pound medium shrimp, peeled

2 cups mung bean sprouts

½ cup sliced green onions

¼ cup chopped peanuts

Bean Sprouts, Baby

You can grow your own bean sprouts; there are books and lots of information online on the subject. You can also find them in the grocery store, either fresh in the produce aisle or canned. They are very perishable. If you buy them fresh, use them within 2 days or they may start to spoil.

1. Place noodles in a large bowl and cover with warm water. Let soak until noodles are soft, about 20 minutes. Drain noodles well and set aside.

2. In a small bowl, combine rice vinegar, fish sauce, sugar, and chili paste and mix well; set aside. Have all ingredients ready.

3. In wok or large skillet, heat peanut oil over medium-high heat. Add garlic; cook until golden, about 15 seconds. Add egg; stir-fry until set, about 30 seconds. Add shrimp and stir-fry until pink, about 2 minutes.

4. Add noodles to the wok, tossing with tongs until they soften and curl, about 1 minute. Add bean sprouts and green onions; stir-fry for 1 minute. Stir vinegar mixture and add to wok; stir-fry until mixture is hot, about 1 to 2 minutes longer. Sprinkle with peanuts and serve immediately.

PER SERVING Calories: 321 | Fat: 10 g | Protein: 18 g | Sodium: 721 mg | Carbohydrates: 66 g | Fiber: 4 g

Basic Polenta with Butter and Cheese

You can enjoy this basic polenta recipe by itself, with different kinds of cheese, or with added meat or veggies.

Low-calorie, Low-carb, Vegetarian, Gluten-free

INGREDIENTS | SERVES 4

3½ cups water

1 teaspoon salt

1 cup yellow cornmeal, coarsely ground

1 tablespoon butter or heart-healthy margarine

2 tablespoons Parmesan or fontina cheese, grated

Pepper to taste

Parsley for garnish

1. Bring the water to a boil. Add salt. Stir in the cornmeal in a thin stream, stirring constantly. Reduce heat to low; continue to stir for 20 minutes or until the polenta comes away from the pot.

2. Stir in the butter, cheese, pepper, and parsley.

PER SERVING Calories: 68 | Fat: 4 g | Protein: 2 g | Sodium: 147 mg | Carbohydrates: 6 g | Fiber: 0 g

What Is Polenta?

In some parts of Italy, polenta is used more than pasta! It is simply cornmeal cooked in boiling water until soft and fluffy like mashed potatoes. When polenta is cooled, it stiffens up, making it useful for frying or grilling. This classic can be used instead of pasta or potatoes. Serve as a base for stews, veggies, or pasta sauces.

Polenta with Broccoli Rabe

Broccoli rabe is a leafy vegetable whose florets resemble those of broccoli. It packs a wonderful and slightly bitter, acidic punch that contrasts with the mildness of the polenta.

Low-calorie, Low-carb, Vegetarian, Gluten-free

INGREDIENTS | SERVES 4

Basic Polenta with Butter and Cheese (page 89)

1 pound broccoli rabe

1 quart boiling, salted water

2 tablespoons olive oil

2 cloves garlic, minced

Juice of ½ lemon

Red pepper flakes to taste

1. Rinse the broccoli rabe and cut in 1½" pieces, trimming off very bottoms of stems. Drop the broccoli rabe into the boiling water and cook for 5 minutes. Shock in cold water. Drain thoroughly.

2. Heat the olive oil and sauté garlic over medium heat. Add the lemon juice, pepper flakes, and drained broccoli rabe. Cook and stir until well coated.

3. Serve over hot polenta.

PER SERVING Calories: 74 | Fat: 7 g | Protein: 1 g | Sodium: 176 mg | Carbohydrates: 3 g | Fiber: 3 g

Herbed Rice Pilaf

The tiny thyme leaves will drop off the stem as the pilaf cooks, adding a lemony-mint flavor to this easy recipe.

Low-calorie, Lactose-free, Vegan, Gluten-free

INGREDIENTS | SERVES 4

1 tablespoon olive oil

1 onion, chopped

2 stalks celery, chopped

2 cloves garlic, minced

1 fresh thyme sprig

½ teaspoon salt

⅛ teaspoon pepper

1 bay leaf

2½ cups water

1 cup long-grain brown rice

1. In a large saucepan, heat oil over medium heat. Add onion, celery, garlic, and thyme and sauté until onion is translucent, about 5 minutes. Add salt, pepper, bay leaf, and water, and bring to a boil.

2. Add rice, bring to a simmer, then cover, reduce heat to low, and simmer until all the water is absorbed and rice is tender, about 20 minutes. Remove and discard the bay leaf and the thyme stem; stir gently. Serve immediately.

PER SERVING Calories: 230 | Fat: 4 g | Protein: 6 g | Sodium: 211 mg | Carbohydrates: 29 g | Fiber: 2 g

Basic Bulgur Wheat

You can stuff the cooked bulgur into red or yellow tomatoes for baking. It's also an excellent stuffing for red, yellow, or green peppers, adding flavor and fiber.

Low-calorie, High-fiber, Lactose-free

INGREDIENTS | SERVES 4

2 tablespoons olive oil

1 cup medium bulgur wheat

3 chopped green onions

2 cups chicken broth

¼ teaspoon oregano

1 teaspoon salt

½ teaspoon pepper

1. Heat the olive oil in a skillet over medium-high heat and cook the bulgur in it for 1 minute; then add the green onions.

2. Sauté for another minute and add the chicken broth.

3. Add the seasonings and stir. Cover with a lid and turn the heat to low.

4. Simmer for 20 minutes.

PER SERVING Calories: 194 | Fat: 8 g | Protein: 5 g | Sodium: 198 mg | Carbohydrates: 29 g | Fiber: 7 g

Bulgur Wheat

Bulgur is usually sold parboiled, dried, and de-branned. Don't confuse bulgur with cracked wheat, which is crushed wheat grain that has not been parboiled. Although traditionally de-branned, whole-grain, high-fiber bulgur and cracked wheat can be found in natural food stores. Bulgur is a common ingredient in Turkish, Middle Eastern, Indian, and Mediterranean dishes. It has a light, nutty flavor.

Citrus Rice Salad

A flavorful creamy dressing coats a blend of rice, fruit, and vegetables in this satisfying salad. Serve it with a grilled steak for a complete meal.

Vegetarian

INGREDIENTS | SERVES 4

2 stalks celery, sliced

4 green onions, sliced

1 (8-ounce) can mandarin oranges, drained

½ cup sliced cucumber

¼ cup golden raisins

2 cups cooked rice

¾ cup plain low-fat yogurt

2 tablespoons orange juice

1 tablespoon lemon juice

1 teaspoon orange zest

2 tablespoons honey

½ teaspoon ground ginger

¼ teaspoon salt

⅛ teaspoon white pepper

1. In a large bowl, combine the celery, green onions, oranges, cucumber, and raisins. Gently stir in the rice to combine.

2. In a small bowl, stir together the yogurt, orange juice, lemon juice, orange zest, honey, ginger, salt, and pepper, mixing well. Pour over the salad and toss gently to coat. Cover and chill for 2 to 3 hours before serving.

PER SERVING Calories: 275 | Fat: 6 g | Protein: 6 g | Sodium: 294 mg | Carbohydrates: 38 g | Fiber: 4 g

Go for Citrus

Citrus is a great flavor profile to use in many different kinds of dishes, from salads to fish. You can use both the juices of citrus fruits, such as oranges and lemons, as well as the fruits themselves. This is a great way to get your daily dose of vitamins without taking a vitamin!

Chinese Fried Rice with Tofu and Cashews

On busy weeknights, pick up some plain white rice from a Chinese take-out restaurant and turn it into a home-cooked meal in no time. Garnish with fresh lime wedges and a sprinkle of sea salt and fresh black pepper on top.

Macrobiotic, Vegan, High-fiber

INGREDIENTS | **SERVES 3**

2 cloves garlic, minced

1 container silken tofu, mashed with a fork

3 tablespoons olive oil

3 cups leftover rice

½ cup frozen mixed diced veggies

3 tablespoons soy sauce

1 tablespoon sesame oil

2 tablespoons lime juice

3 scallions (greens and whites), sliced

⅓ cup chopped cashews (optional)

1. In a large skillet or wok, sauté the garlic and tofu in 2 tablespoons of olive oil over medium-high heat, stirring frequently, until tofu is lightly browned, about 6 to 8 minutes.

2. Add remaining 1 tablespoon of olive oil, rice, and veggies, stirring well to combine.

3. Add soy sauce and sesame oil and combine well.

4. Allow to cook, stirring constantly, for 3 to 4 minutes.

5. Remove from heat and stir in remaining ingredients.

PER SERVING Calories: 498 | Fat: 22 g | Protein: 13 g | Sodium: 57 mg | Carbohydrates: 50 g | Fiber: 5 g

Quick and Easy Vegetable Fried Rice

Oyster sauce is literally made of oysters, reduced down to a thick brown sauce. It's very savory, with lots of umami.

Low-calorie, High-fiber, Vegetarian, Lactose-free

INGREDIENTS | SERVES 6

1 tablespoon peanut oil

1 onion, chopped

2 cloves garlic, minced

2 red bell peppers, diced

2 cups sliced zucchini

1 cup celery, sliced

4 cups cooked cold rice

2 eggs, beaten

1 cup bean sprouts

¼ cup oyster sauce

1. In a large skillet, heat oil over medium heat. Add onion and garlic; stir-fry for 3 minutes. Add bell pepper, zucchini, and celery; stir-fry for 3 minutes more. Add rice; stir-fry for 1 minute longer.

2. Stir in the eggs and stir-fry for 2 to 3 minutes until cooked. Add bean sprouts; stir-fry for 1 minute until hot. Add oyster sauce and mix gently, then serve immediately.

PER SERVING Calories: 231 | Fat: 5 g | Protein: 7 g | Sodium: 549 mg | Carbohydrates: 49 g | Fiber: 5 g

Quick Healthy Meals

Like stir-fries and an easy pasta recipe, fried rice is a quick and easy meal you can turn to again and again. The formula is always the same—rice, oil and seasonings—but the variations are endless. Besides tofu, try adding tempeh, seitan, or store-bought mock meats to fried rice. Make it Hawaiian-style with diced pineapple, add kimchi for a Korean spice, or season with a mixture of cumin, curry, ginger, and turmeric for an Indian-inspired dish.

Vegetable Risotto

Arborio rice is a short-grain rice. It has more starch than long-grain, which is why it's used in creamy risotto.

Vegetarian

INGREDIENTS | SERVES 4

4 cups fat-free vegetable broth
2 tablespoons butter
1 onion, chopped
3 cloves garlic, minced
1 cup Arborio rice
¼ teaspoon salt
⅛ teaspoon white pepper
1 cup chopped zucchini
1 cup chopped green beans
⅓ cup minced flat-leaf parsley
¼ cup grated Parmesan cheese

1. In a medium saucepan, place broth and heat over low heat. Melt 1 tablespoon butter in large skillet over medium heat. Add onion and garlic and sauté until softened, about 6 minutes. Add rice, salt, and pepper and stir to coat.

2. Reduce heat to low and add ½ cup broth at a time, stirring frequently, until absorbed. Continue adding broth, ½ cup at a time, cooking and stirring until absorbed.

3. When last ½ cup of broth is added, stir in zucchini and green beans; cook and stir for 6 minutes. Risotto is done when rice is still slightly firm in the center and mixture is creamy. Add the parsley, Parmesan, and remaining 1 tablespoon butter and stir gently; serve immediately.

PER SERVING Calories: 277 | Fat: 8 g | Protein: 4 g | Sodium: 540 mg | Carbohydrates: 38 g | Fiber: 4 g

Asian Orange Rice Pilaf

Orange and raisins add flavor and wonderful aroma to this simple pilaf. It makes a great lunch or snack by itself, or a delicious side dish alongside grilled salmon.

Vegan

INGREDIENTS | SERVES 4

⅓ cup slivered almonds

⅓ cup orange juice

1 teaspoon grated orange zest

1 teaspoon Asian sesame oil

1 tablespoon olive oil

1 cup long-grain brown rice

1 onion, chopped

¼ teaspoon salt

½ teaspoon dried tarragon leaves

⅛ teaspoon white pepper

½ cup raisins

2 cups water

1. Combine almonds, orange juice, zest, and sesame oil in a blender or food processor. Blend or process until smooth, about 10 to 15 seconds.

2. In a large saucepan, heat olive oil over medium heat. Add rice and onion and sauté for 3 minutes. Add salt, tarragon, pepper, and raisins and stir.

3. Add orange mixture and water. Bring to a simmer, then reduce heat to low, cover, and cook until rice is tender, about 18 to 23 minutes. Fluff with a fork before serving.

PER SERVING Calories: 288 | Fat: 9 g | Protein: 4 g | Sodium: 239 mg | Carbohydrates: 40 g | Fiber: 4 g

All about Almonds

You can buy almonds in all shapes and sizes: halved, slivered, sliced, blanched, with their shells off, and with their shells on. Whatever variety you go with, it's a good choice. Almonds are both delicious and good for you. They're a rich source of vitamin E, which is great for your skin, as well as monounsaturated fat, one of the two "good" fats responsible for lowering LDL cholesterol.

Minimal-Effort Main Dishes

Simple Grilled Chicken Breasts

Grill more chicken than you can eat when you make this recipe. Seal the leftovers in plastic containers; they're perfect to use in salads and soups throughout your week.

Low-calorie, Low-fat, Low-carb, Lactose-free

INGREDIENTS | SERVES 6

6 boneless, skinless chicken breasts
½ teaspoon all-purpose seasoning

1. Trim visible fat from chicken breasts.

2. Sprinkle chicken with all-purpose seasoning.

3. Coat skillet with nonstick spray.

4. Place chicken in skillet and cook on medium heat for 12 to 15 minutes or until internal temperature of chicken is 165°F or juices run clear when pricked.

PER SERVING Calories: 130 | Fat: 1 g | Protein: 27 g | Sodium: 97 mg | Carbohydrates: 0 g | Fiber: 0 g

Turkey with Couscous

This easy recipe can be doubled to serve six. You could also add a chopped apple or some sliced mushrooms.

High-fiber

INGREDIENTS | SERVES 3

1 (8-ounce) box instant couscous
½ teaspoon cinnamon
1 cup diced cooked turkey
1 (15-ounce) can garbanzo beans, drained
⅓ cup raisins
½ cup low-fat plain yogurt
⅛ teaspoon pepper

1. In a medium saucepan, cook the couscous according to package directions, adding the cinnamon at the start of cooking.

2. When the couscous is done, stir in the turkey, garbanzos, raisins, yogurt, and pepper. Cook over low heat, stirring constantly, until hot, about 4 to 5 minutes. Serve immediately.

PER SERVING Calories: 494 | Fat: 5 g | Protein: 24 g | Sodium: 292 mg | Carbohydrates: 47 g | Fiber: 9 g

Chicken Breasts with Rosemary

These simple chicken breasts are great on their own or included in a main dish.

Low-calorie, Low-fat, Low-carb, Lactose-free

INGREDIENTS | SERVES 6

6 boneless, skinless chicken breasts
½ tablespoon olive oil
1 clove fresh garlic, minced
½ teaspoon all-purpose seasoning
2 teaspoons balsamic vinegar
2 tablespoons lemon juice
1 cup red cooking wine
1 teaspoon rosemary
1 cup tomatoes, diced
¼ teaspoon black pepper

1. Coat a large skillet with nonstick spray. Place chicken on skillet, being careful not to crowd the meat.

2. In a separate bowl, mix remaining ingredients. Pour mixture over chicken.

3. Cook on medium high for 10 to 12 minutes, turn chicken, and simmer for 8 minutes.

PER SERVING Calories: 177 | Fat: 3 g | Protein: 28 g | Sodium: 125 mg | Carbohydrates: 3 g | Fiber: 0 g

Rosemary: Ancient Brain Food

According to the ancient Greeks, rosemary was believed to enhance intelligence and memory. It wasn't uncommon to see Greek students wearing this spice in their hair to help them excel in school. Keep this in mind as you study for your next exam!

Spicy Honey-Brushed Chicken Breast

This chicken breast is delicious accompanied by rice or vegetables, on a sandwich, or even chopped up in a salad.

Low-calorie, Low-fat, Lactose-free

INGREDIENTS | SERVES 6

½ tablespoon olive oil
1 clove fresh garlic, minced
½ teaspoon all-purpose seasoning
3 teaspoons chili powder
1 teaspoon cumin
1 teaspoon paprika
½ teaspoon red pepper
½ cup honey
1 tablespoon cider vinegar
6 boneless, skinless chicken breasts

1. Mix all ingredients except chicken in a large bowl. Add chicken to mixture and coat each breast well on each side.

2. Spray a skillet with nonstick spray. Add chicken to skillet and cook over medium heat for 6 to 8 minutes on each side.

PER SERVING Calories: 233 | Fat: 3 g | Protein: 28 g | Sodium: 112 mg | Carbohydrates: 25 g | Fiber: 1 g

Sweet Crusted Chicken Nuggets

This recipe may surprise you and everyone you serve it to. Sweet chicken sounds strange, but it is guaranteed to please.

Low-fat, Lactose-free

INGREDIENTS | SERVES 4

4 boneless, skinless chicken breasts, trimmed of fat and cut into chunks
1 cup Egg Beaters
2 cups frosted flakes cereal, crumbled
1 tablespoon Splenda

Not Just Kid Food

Chicken nuggets may sound like kid food, but they're a great snack or light meal for folks of any age. Try this easy recipe and see for yourself!

1. Preheat oven to 400°F.

2. Coat chicken chunks in Egg Beaters.

3. Roll coated chicken in frosted flakes until covered.

4. Place chicken on 2 large cookie sheets and sprinkle with Splenda.

5. Bake for 20 minutes or until internal temperature reaches 165°F.

PER SERVING Calories: 360 | Fat: 2 g | Protein: 32 g | Sodium: 392 mg | Carbohydrates: 55 g | Fiber: 1 g

Thai Chicken Sauté

Thai food traditionally combines a variety of sweet and fiery flavors. This particular dish combines the sweetness of coconut milk with the spice of hot sauce.

Low-calorie, Low-carb, Lactose-free

INGREDIENTS | SERVES 6

½ tablespoon olive oil

1 clove fresh garlic, minced

6 boneless, skinless chicken breasts, cut in chunks

½ teaspoon all-purpose seasoning

2 tablespoons cornstarch

1 teaspoon ground ginger

2 tablespoons hoisin sauce

½ cup coconut milk

1 tablespoon hot sauce

1 tablespoon sugar or Splenda

1 tablespoon lemon juice

1 cup onions, sliced

3 tablespoons cilantro

1. Heat olive oil in a large skillet over medium heat. Sauté garlic for 1 to 2 minutes until garlic is fragrant but not brown.

2. Add chicken to skillet and sauté for 5 minutes.

3. In a separate bowl, mix all-purpose seasoning, cornstarch, ginger, hoisin sauce, coconut milk, hot sauce, sugar, and lemon juice. Blend well.

4. Add mixture to chicken. Cook for 10 minutes.

5. Add onions and cilantro and simmer for 8 to 10 minutes or until sauce thickens.

PER SERVING Calories: 224 | Fat: 8 g | Protein: 28 g | Sodium: 255 mg | Carbohydrates: 10 g | Fiber: 1 g

Hungarian Chicken Paprikas

This is a great, hearty meal for an evening with friends. They'll be impressed with your knowledge of international cuisine!

Low-calorie, Low-fat, Low-carb

INGREDIENTS | SERVES 6

½ tablespoon olive oil

1 clove fresh garlic, minced

6 boneless, skinless chicken breasts, cut in chunks

½ teaspoon all-purpose seasoning

1 cup bell peppers, diced

1 cup white onions, diced

1 cup chicken broth

1 tablespoon paprika

½ teaspoon chili powder

¼ cup tomato paste

1 cup fat-free sour cream

1. Spray skillet with nonstick spray. Add olive oil, garlic, and chicken chunks to skillet. Sauté on medium high for 5 minutes, stirring often.

2. Add remaining ingredients except sour cream to skillet. Cook for 5 minutes.

3. Add sour cream, stirring well, and simmer for 5 to 8 minutes.

PER SERVING Calories: 202 | Fat: 3 g | Protein: 32 g | Sodium: 343 mg | Carbohydrates: 11 g | Fiber: 2 g

What Is Paprikas?

Paprikas is a Hungarian dish made with diced meat and covered with a sauce made with paprika. Paprika is a spice made from the grinding of dried peppers (for example, bell peppers or chili peppers). The seasoning is used in many cuisines to add color and flavor to dishes.

Lime Turkey Tenderloin

Turkey tenderloins are quite low in fat and are also tender when properly cooked. Serve this dish with couscous or rice to soak up the sauce.

Low-fat, Lactose-free

INGREDIENTS | SERVES 4

1 tablespoon olive oil

2 shallots, minced

1 turkey tenderloin, cubed

½ teaspoon salt

⅛ teaspoon white pepper

2 tablespoons flour

½ teaspoon dried thyme leaves

3 tablespoons lime juice

1 cup apple juice

2 tablespoons cornstarch

½ cup fat-free chicken broth

1. Heat olive oil in large skillet over medium heat. Cook shallots for 2 to 3 minutes, stirring frequently. Sprinkle turkey with salt, pepper, and flour. Add turkey to skillet and cook, turning to brown evenly, until tender and juices run clear when a piece is pierced, about 8 to 10 minutes.

2. In a small bowl combine thyme, lime juice, apple juice, cornstarch, and broth. Add to skillet; cook and stir over medium heat until thickened and bubbly, about 3 to 4 minutes. Serve immediately.

PER SERVING Calories: 202 | Fat: 2 g | Protein: 22 g | Sodium: 398 mg | Carbohydrates: 18 g | Fiber: 1 g

Lime with Turkey?

It may sound like a strange pairing, but lime with turkey is a great flavor combination. With only 3 tablespoons of lime juice, the lime flavor in this recipe is subtle. Give it a try. You may be pleasantly surprised!

Sweet-and-Sour Turkey Burgers

Sweet and sour is an excellent flavor combination to use in low-fat cooking because the main ingredients are fat-free. These tender and juicy burgers are really delicious.

Lactose-free

INGREDIENTS | SERVES 4

1 tablespoon soy sauce

1 tablespoon honey

1 tablespoon apple cider vinegar

¼ cup dried bread crumbs

1 pound ground turkey breast

¼ cup chopped green onions

¼ cup chili sauce

6 hamburger buns, split

6 slices canned pineapple, drained

6 butter lettuce leaves

Great Ground Turkey

When you buy ground turkey, look for an evenly colored product that has very little liquid in the package. If there is a lot of liquid, the meat will be dry when cooked. Ground turkey freezes very well, so purchase a lot when there's a sale. You can also grind your own turkey in a food processor using the pulse function.

1. In a medium bowl, combine soy sauce, honey, vinegar, and bread crumbs until blended. Add ground turkey and green onions and mix well. Shape into 4 patties.

2. In a nonstick skillet over medium heat, fry patties, turning once, until done, about 8 to 10 minutes. To serve, spread chili sauce on hamburger buns and top with a patty, pineapple ring, and lettuce. Top with half of the bun and serve immediately.

PER SERVING Calories: 358 | Fat: 9 g | Protein: 25 g | Sodium: 404 mg | Carbohydrates: 45 g | Fiber: 3 g

Raspberry Pork Chops

This is a great variation on the basic pork chops you might've eaten as a kid.

Low-carb, Lactose-free

INGREDIENTS | SERVES 4

4 boneless pork chops
¼ teaspoon salt
⅛ teaspoon pepper
1 tablespoon olive oil
¼ cup fat-free chicken broth
3 tablespoons raspberry vinegar
1 tablespoon low-sodium soy sauce
⅓ cup seedless raspberry jam
1 cup fresh raspberries

Raspberries and Pork?

Don't balk! Raspberries have a wonderful sweet and tart flavor that complements the meaty tenderness of the pork chops in this recipe. In fact, lots of fruit flavors go well with pork, such as cranberry and currant. Try different variations to see which one you like best.

1. Sprinkle chops with salt and pepper. Heat olive oil in medium skillet over medium heat. Add chops; brown well on both sides, turning once, about 6 to 7 minutes total.

2. Add chicken broth, vinegar, and soy sauce to pan. Bring to a boil, then cover pan, reduce heat to low, and simmer for 10 minutes.

3. Uncover pan and remove pork. Add jam to sauce in pan and stir to blend. Return pork to pan and simmer for 2 to 4 minutes longer or until pork is just cooked and still slightly pink in center. Sprinkle with raspberries and serve immediately.

PER SERVING Calories: 284 | Fat: 9 g | Protein: 29 g | Sodium: 435 mg | Carbohydrates: 9 g | Fiber: 1 g

Sweet-and-Sour Pork

This is a healthy take on the classic combination of sweet-and-sour flavors found in Asian cuisine.

Lactose-free

INGREDIENTS | SERVES 8

2 pounds boneless pork loin chops
½ teaspoon salt
⅛ teaspoon pepper
1 (20-ounce) can pineapple tidbits
¼ cup brown sugar
½ cup apple cider vinegar
2 tablespoons reduced-sodium soy sauce
3 tablespoons ketchup
¼ teaspoon ground ginger
2 tablespoons cornstarch
1 tablespoon olive oil
1 cup sliced celery
1 red bell pepper, chopped
1 onion, chopped

1. Sprinkle pork with salt and pepper and cut into 1" cubes. Drain pineapple, reserving liquid. In a small bowl, combine 1 cup pineapple liquid with brown sugar, vinegar, soy sauce, ketchup, ginger, and cornstarch; mix well and set aside.

2. In a large skillet or wok, heat oil over medium heat and add pork; stir-fry until pork is browned, about 5 minutes; remove from skillet. Add celery, bell pepper, and onion; stir-fry until crisp-tender, about 5 minutes.

3. Return pork to skillet and stir-fry for 1 minute. Stir pineapple liquid mixture and add to skillet along with pineapple tidbits. Cook and stir until bubbly, then continue cooking, stirring frequently, until pork and vegetables are tender. Serve immediately with hot cooked brown rice.

PER SERVING Calories: 338 | Fat: 6 g | Protein: 25 g | Sodium: 500 mg | Carbohydrates: 26 g | Fiber: 1 g

Steak Stroganoff

This comforting meal is quick to prepare and satisfying after a long day of classes. It'll even taste great the next day as leftovers.

INGREDIENTS | SERVES 6

1 pound boneless round steak
2 tablespoons olive oil
1 onion, chopped
1 (8-ounce) package sliced mushrooms
3 tablespoons tomato paste
3 tablespoons water
½ teaspoon basil leaves
1 tablespoon cornstarch
1 cup plain low-fat yogurt
¼ cup fat-free beef broth
3 cups hot cooked noodles

1. Trim off excess fat from the steak and slice against the grain into ¼" strips. In a large skillet, heat olive oil over medium heat. Add onion and mushrooms; cook and stir until tender, about 5 minutes.

2. Add beef and cook, stirring frequently, until browned, about 4 minutes longer.

3. Meanwhile, in small bowl combine tomato paste, water, basil, cornstarch, yogurt, and broth and mix with wire whisk until blended. Add to skillet and bring to a simmer. Simmer for 3 to 4 minutes or until sauce thickens. Serve immediately over hot cooked noodles.

PER SERVING Calories: 359 | Fat: 11 g | Protein: 19 g | Sodium: 92 mg | Carbohydrates: 30 g | Fiber: 3 g

Terrific Tomato Paste

Tomato paste is an excellent ingredient to add lots of flavor to a dish without extra fat. If you can find tomato paste in a tube, just store it in the refrigerator and use it as you need it. If you can only find it in a can, remove the paste from the can and freeze it in a small freezer bag. Cut off what you need when you need it.

Spicy Beef and Cabbage

Cabbage is delicious when lightly cooked. It adds color, crunch, and fiber to this simple dish.

High-fiber, Lactose-free

INGREDIENTS | SERVES 4

¾ pound top round beef steak

½ cup orange juice

2 tablespoons hoisin sauce

2 tablespoons rice vinegar

1 tablespoon cornstarch

⅛ teaspoon cayenne pepper

1 tablespoon vegetable oil

1 tablespoon minced ginger root

1 onion, chopped

1 (10-ounce) package shredded cabbage

1½ cups shredded carrots

3 green onions, julienned

1. Trim excess fat from steak and cut into ⅛" × 3" strips against the grain. In a small bowl, combine orange juice, hoisin sauce, rice vinegar, cornstarch, and pepper and mix well; set aside.

2. In a large skillet, heat vegetable oil over medium-high heat. Add ginger root and onion; cook and stir for 3 to 4 minutes until onion is crisp-tender. Add beef and cook for 2 to 3 minutes or until browned. Remove beef and onion from skillet with slotted spoon and set aside.

3. Add cabbage, carrots, and green onion to skillet; stir-fry for 3 minutes. Stir orange juice mixture and add to skillet along with beef. Stir-fry until sauce thickens slightly and beef and vegetables are tender. Serve immediately over hot cooked rice.

PER SERVING Calories: 324 | Fat: 9 g | Protein: 22 g | Sodium: 236 mg | Carbohydrates: 32 g | Fiber: 5 g

Chinese Beef Stir-Fry

You can use any quick-cooking vegetable in this super-fast recipe.
Mushrooms, eggplant, or summer squash are delicious.

Lactose-free

INGREDIENTS | SERVES 8

¼ cup oyster sauce

2 teaspoons chili paste

½ cup low-fat beef broth

1 tablespoon peanut oil

2 onions, chopped

4 cloves garlic, minced

1 tablespoon minced fresh ginger root

1 pound lean round steak, thinly sliced

2 tomatoes, cubed

2 green bell peppers, sliced

2 cups chopped Chinese cabbage

4 cups cold cooked brown rice

¼ cup chopped peanuts

¼ cup chopped green onions

1. In a small bowl, combine oyster sauce, chili paste, and beef broth; mix well. Prepare all ingredients.

2. In wok or large skillet, heat oil over high heat. Add onion, garlic, and ginger; stir-fry for 3 minutes. Add beef; stir-fry for 2 minutes until beef is browned.

3. Add tomatoes, bell peppers, and cabbage; stir-fry for 3 minutes longer. Stir oyster sauce mixture and add to skillet along with rice; stir-fry for 3 to 5 minutes or until hot.

4. Scoop onto serving plate, sprinkle with peanuts and green onions, and serve immediately.

PER SERVING Calories: 308 | Fat: 9 g | Protein: 23 g | Sodium: 334 mg | Carbohydrates: 42 g | Fiber: 3 g

Stir-Fry It Up!

It may take some time to prepare ingredients for stir-frying, but once the actual cooking starts, everything goes together quickly. It's easiest to have all of the ingredients prepared and ready before you start cooking. It's also important to use high heat and keep the food moving while it cooks.

Surf and Turf Pasta

The combination of seafood and beef is classic; who knew you could have it in a low-fat recipe?

Lactose-free

INGREDIENTS | SERVES 5

½ pound sirloin steak

2 tablespoons flour

¼ teaspoon salt

Dash pepper

¼ pound medium shrimp, peeled

¼ pound scallops

1 tablespoon olive oil

4 cloves garlic, minced

1 cup fat-free chicken broth

1 (12-ounce) package radiatore pasta

1 cup chopped spinach leaves

6 dry-packed, sun-dried tomatoes, chopped

1 teaspoon dried basil leaves

1. Bring a large pot of water to a boil. Trim excess fat from meat; cut into ¼" slices across the grain. Combine flour, salt, and pepper on plate; toss with shrimp and scallops.

2. Heat olive oil in large skillet over medium heat. Add beef; stir-fry for 2 to 3 minutes until browned; remove to bowl.

3. Add shrimp and scallops to skillet; stir-fry until cooked, about 4 to 5 minutes; remove to bowl with beef. Add garlic and chicken broth to skillet; bring to a simmer; simmer until thickened, about 5 minutes. Cook pasta according to package directions until al dente.

4. Return beef, shrimp, and scallops to skillet along with spinach, tomatoes, and basil leaves; bring to a simmer. Drain pasta and add to skillet; cook and stir until mixed. Serve immediately.

PER SERVING Calories: 434 | Fat: 8 g | Protein: 26 g | Sodium: 337 mg | Carbohydrates: 45 g | Fiber: 3 g

Louisiana Seafood

This combination of seafood is reminiscent of a clam bake but is much easier to make.

Gluten-free, Low-fat

INGREDIENTS | SERVES 4

2 shallots, chopped

3 cloves garlic, minced

¼ cup dry white wine

½ teaspoon dried basil leaves

¼ teaspoon dried thyme leaves

12 raw sea scallops

8 large raw shrimp

8 clams, scrubbed

8 mussels, debearded

2 (6-ounce) frozen lobster tails, thawed, chopped

2 tomatoes, chopped

3 cups hot cooked brown rice

1. In a large stock pot, combine shallots, garlic, and wine; bring to a simmer. Simmer until vegetables soften, about 5 minutes. Add basil and thyme.

2. Add seafood except lobster; cover and cook for 6 to 8 minutes, shaking pot frequently, until shrimp curl, scallops are opaque, and clams and mussels open. Discard any clams and mussels that do not open.

3. Remove cover and add lobster and tomato; cook and stir until lobster is hot, about 2 to 3 minutes longer. Serve over hot cooked rice.

PER SERVING Calories: 360 | Fat: 4 g | Protein: 26 g | Sodium: 429 mg | Carbohydrates: 30 g | Fiber: 2 g

Why Louisiana?

The combination of rice and seafood is commonly found in Louisiana Creole cuisine, which is a melting pot that blends French, Spanish, Caribbean, Mediterranean, Indian, and African influences. For a taste of the real thing, take a trip to New Orleans for your next vacation!

Scallop and Pepper Stir-Fry

For a stir-fry, make sure that you have all of the ingredients prepared before you start cooking since the cooking time is so short.

Gluten-free, Low-fat

INGREDIENTS | SERVES 4

1 pound bay scallops
1 tablespoon cornstarch
¼ teaspoon salt
⅛ teaspoon cayenne pepper
1 tablespoon olive oil
1 red onion, chopped
2 cloves garlic, minced
1 green bell pepper, chopped
1 red bell pepper, chopped
2 cups cold cooked white rice
3 tablespoons apple juice
1 tablespoon lemon juice

1. In a medium bowl, combine scallops with cornstarch, salt, and pepper; toss to coat. In a large skillet or wok, heat olive oil over medium-high heat.

2. Add onion and garlic; stir-fry for 2 minutes. Add scallop mixture and bell peppers; stir-fry until scallops are just cooked, about 4 to 5 minutes.

3. Add rice, then sprinkle with apple juice and lemon juice. Stir-fry until rice is heated through, about 2 to 4 minutes. Serve immediately.

PER SERVING Calories: 273 | Fat: 5 g | Protein: 26 g | Sodium: 334 mg | Carbohydrates: 36 g | Fiber: 2 g

Curried Shrimp and Vegetables

Adding lots of vegetables to seafood not only enhances the flavor, it increases the nutrition of a dish and lowers the fat and cholesterol content.

Gluten-free, Low-fat, High-fiber, Lactose-free

INGREDIENTS | SERVES 6

1 tablespoon olive oil

1 onion, chopped

3 cloves garlic, minced

1 tablespoon curry powder

½ teaspoon cinnamon

1½ cups water

2 carrots, sliced

2 russet potatoes, peeled and cubed

1 zucchini, sliced

1 (14.5-ounce) can diced tomatoes

1 pound raw shrimp

4 cups hot cooked brown rice

Cooking with Curry

The flavors in curry powder are enhanced when they are heated, which is why the powder is often cooked in the first step of many Indian recipes. It's still good when uncooked. You can buy curry powder in many blends, from hot to mild. Curry powder is a blend of spices, and each blend is usually unique to a particular area of India.

1. In a large skillet, heat oil over medium heat. Add onion and garlic; cook and stir until crisp-tender, about 4 minutes. Add curry powder and cinnamon; cook and stir for 1 minute longer.

2. Add water, carrots, and potatoes; bring to a simmer. Then reduce the heat to low, cover, and cook for 8 to 10 minutes or until carrots are crisp-tender. Add zucchini, tomatoes, and shrimp, cover again, and simmer for 5 to 8 minutes longer or until shrimp are pink.

3. Spoon rice onto individual plates and top with shrimp and vegetables; serve immediately.

PER SERVING Calories: 372 | Fat: 5 g | Protein: 23 g | Sodium: 164 mg | Carbohydrates: 45 g | Fiber: 5 g

Baked Sole Amandine

Almonds contain lots of healthy monounsaturated fat. Just a few add great flavor and crunch to this classic recipe.

Low-carb

INGREDIENTS | SERVES 4

1 egg
¼ cup skim milk
½ cup dried bread crumbs
¼ cup ground almonds
1 teaspoon dried basil leaves
¼ teaspoon salt
½ teaspoon dried thyme leaves
1 pound sole filets
2 tablespoons lemon juice
1 tablespoon water
1 tablespoon butter, melted
¼ cup sliced almonds
3 green onions, chopped

Almonds of All Kinds

Almonds come in several types. Plain whole almonds come with the skin attached. Blanched almonds have had their skins removed. Sliced almonds are thinly sliced unblanched whole almonds. Slivered almonds are blanched almonds cut into little sticks. If a recipe calls for ground almonds, slivered almonds are the best choice; grind them in a food processor.

1. Preheat oven to 425°F. Line a baking sheet with parchment paper and set aside.

2. In shallow dish, combine egg and milk; beat until combined. On plate, combine bread crumbs, ground almonds, basil, salt, and thyme and mix well.

3. Dip the fish into the egg mixture, then in the crumb mixture to coat. Place on prepared baking sheet.

4. In a small bowl, combine lemon juice, water, and melted butter. Sprinkle over the fish. Sprinkle with sliced almonds. Bake for 8 to 10 minutes or until fish flakes easily when tested with fork. Sprinkle with green onions and serve immediately.

PER SERVING Calories: 300 | Fat: 12 g | Protein: 27 g | Sodium: 404 mg | Carbohydrates: 13 g | Fiber: 2 g

Pork Tenderloin with Caraway Sauerkraut

Caraway is a popular flavor in Scandinavian and Eastern European cooking. It is excellent with veal and pork. Tenderloin of pork is lean, moist, and delicious. It is very low in calories and a real treat with the sauerkraut.

Low-carb, Lactose-free

INGREDIENTS | SERVES 2

1 teaspoon olive oil

8 ounces pork tenderloin

Salt and pepper to taste

1 teaspoon Wondra flour

2 medium red onions, chopped

¼ cup low-salt chicken broth

8 ounces sauerkraut, drained

1 teaspoon caraway seeds

1. Heat the oil in a frying pan over medium heat. Sprinkle the pork tenderloin with salt, pepper, and flour. Sauté the pork over medium heat for 4 minutes; turn the pork and add onions.

2. Continue to sauté until the pork is lightly browned on both sides and the onions have softened slightly.

3. Add the chicken broth, sauerkraut, and caraway seeds. Cover and simmer for 25 minutes. Pork should be pink.

PER SERVING Calories: 309 | Fat: 15 g | Protein: 36 g | Sodium: 98 mg | Carbohydrates: 4 g | Fiber: 1 g |

CHAPTER 8

Vegetarian and Vegan Delights

Green and Black Olive Tapenade

Mediterranean olive tapenade can be used as a spread or dip for baguettes or crackers. If you don't have a food processor, you could also mash the ingredients together with a mortar and pestle or a large fork.

Vegan

INGREDIENTS | YIELDS 1 CUP

½ cup green olives
¾ cup black olives
2 cloves garlic
1 tablespoon capers (optional)
2 tablespoons lemon juice
2 tablespoons olive oil
¼ teaspoon oregano
¼ teaspoon black pepper

Process all ingredients in a food processor until almost smooth.

PER TABLESPOON Calories: 29 | Protein: 0 g | Fat: 3 g | Sodium: 116 mg | Carbohydrates: 15 g | Fiber: 0 g

Easy Asian Dipping Sauce

Tangy, salty, spicy, and a bit sour—this easy dipping sauce has it all! Use it for dipping Fresh Mint Spring Rolls (pg 122). It would also make an excellent marinade for a baked tofu dish.

Vegan, Low-fat, Low-carb

INGREDIENTS | YIELDS ⅓ CUP

¼ cup soy sauce
2 tablespoons rice vinegar
2 teaspoons sesame oil
1 teaspoon sugar
1 teaspoon fresh ginger, minced
2 cloves garlic, minced and crushed
¼ teaspoon crushed red pepper flakes, or to taste

Whisk together all ingredients.

PER TABLESPOON Calories: 29 | Fat: 2 g | Protein: 1 g | Sodium: 719 mg | Carbohydrates: 10 g | Fiber: 0 g

Roasted Red Pepper Hummus

As a veggie dip or sandwich spread, hummus is always a favorite. Up the garlic in this recipe, if that's your thing, and don't be ashamed to lick the spoons or spatula.

Vegan, Low-fat, Low-carb

INGREDIENTS | MAKES 1½ CUPS

1 (15-ounce) can chickpeas, drained

⅓ cup tahini

⅔ cup chopped roasted red peppers

3 tablespoons lemon juice

2 tablespoons olive oil

2 cloves garlic

½ teaspoon cumin

⅓ teaspoon salt

¼ teaspoon cayenne pepper (optional)

Process all ingredients together in a blender or food processor until smooth, scraping the sides down as needed.

PER TABLESPOON Calories: 53 | Fat: 3 g | Protein: 1 g | Sodium: 110 mg | Carbohydrates: 10 g | Fiber: 1 g

Do-It-Yourself Roasted Red Peppers

Sure, you can buy them in a jar, but it's easy to roast your own. Here's how: Fire up your oven to 450°F (or use the broiler setting) and drizzle a few whole peppers with olive oil. Bake for 30 minutes, turning over once. Direct heat will also work, if you have a gas stove. Hold the peppers with tongs over the flame until lightly charred. Let your peppers cool, then remove the skin before making hummus.

Fresh Basil Bruschetta with Balsamic Reduction

Your friends will go so crazy for the rich flavor of the balsamic reduction sauce that they won't even notice that the cheese is missing from this vegan bruschetta. Use a fresh artisan bread, if you can.

Vegan

INGREDIENTS | SERVES 4

¾ cup balsamic vinegar

1 tablespoon sugar

2 large tomatoes, diced small

3 cloves garlic, minced

¼ cup chopped fresh basil

2 tablespoons olive oil

Salt and pepper to taste

8–10 slices French bread

A Tuscan Tradition

A true Italian chef will prepare the bread for bruschetta by toasting homemade bread over hot coals, then quickly rubbing a sliced clove of garlic over both sides of the bread before drizzling with just a touch of the finest olive oil. In lieu of hot coals, a toaster or five minutes in the oven at 350°F will work just fine.

1. Whisk together the balsamic vinegar and sugar in a small saucepan. Bring to a boil then reduce to a slow simmer. Allow to cook for 6 to 8 minutes, until almost thickened. Remove from heat.

2. Combine the tomatoes, garlic, olive oil, basil, salt, and pepper in a large bowl. Gently toss with balsamic sauce.

3. Spoon tomato mixture over bread slices and serve immediately.

PER SERVING Calories: 321 | Fat: 8 g | Protein: 9 g | Sodium: 434 mg | Carbohydrates: 30 g | Fiber: 3 g

Hot Artichoke Spinach Dip

Serve this creamy dip hot with some baguette slices, crackers, pita bread, or sliced bell peppers and jicama. If you want to get fancy, you can carve out a bread bowl for an edible serving dish.

Vegan

INGREDIENTS | SERVES 6–8

1 (12-ounce) package frozen spinach, thawed

1 (14-ounce) can artichoke hearts, drained

¼ cup vegan margarine

2 cups soy milk

¼ cup flour

½ cup nutritional yeast

1 teaspoon garlic powder

1½ teaspoons onion powder

¼ teaspoon salt

1. Preheat oven to 350°F.

2. Purée spinach and artichokes together until almost smooth and set aside.

3. In a small saucepan, melt the vegan margarine over low heat. Slowly whisk in flour, 1 tablespoon at a time, stirring constantly to avoid lumps, until thick.

4. Remove from heat and add spinach and artichoke mixture, stirring to combine. Add remaining ingredients.

5. Transfer to an ovenproof casserole dish or bowl and bake for 20 minutes. Serve hot.

PER SERVING Calories: 134 | Fat: 7 g | Protein: 6 g | Sodium: 378 mg | Carbohydrates: 10 g | Fiber: 4 g

Fresh Mint Spring Rolls

Wrapping spring rolls is a balance between getting them tight enough to hold together, but not so tight the thin wrappers break! It's like riding a bike: Once you've got it, you've got it, and then spring rolls can be very quick and fun to make.

Vegan, Low-fat

INGREDIENTS | SERVES 3–4

1 (3-ounce) package clear bean thread noodles

1 cup hot water

1 tablespoon soy sauce

½ teaspoon powdered ginger

1 teaspoon sesame oil

¼ cup shiitake mushrooms, diced

1 carrot, grated

10–12 spring roll wrappers

Warm water

½ head green leaf lettuce, chopped

1 cucumber, sliced thin

1 bunch fresh mint

To Dip, or Not to Dip?

Store-bought sweet chili sauce, spicy sriracha sauce, or a Japanese salad dressing or marinade will work in a pinch, but a simple homemade dip is best for these spring rolls. Try the Easy Asian Dipping Sauce (page 118).

1. Break noodles in half to make smaller pieces, then submerge in 1 cup hot water until soft, about 6 to 7 minutes. Drain.

2. In a large bowl, toss together the hot noodles with the soy sauce, ginger, sesame oil, mushrooms, and carrots, tossing well to combine.

3. In a large shallow pan, carefully submerge spring roll wrappers, one at a time, in warm water until just barely soft. Remove from water and place a bit of lettuce in the center of the wrapper. Add about 2 tablespoons of noodles mixture and a few slices of cucumber and place 2 to 3 mint leaves on top.

4. Fold the bottom of the wrapper over the filling, fold in each side, then roll.

PER SERVING Calories: 216 | Fat: 1 g | Protein: 4 g | Sodium: 262 mg | Carbohydrates: 18 g | Fiber: 2 g

Mango Citrus Salsa

Salsa has a variety of uses, and this recipe adds color and variety to your usual chips and dip or Mexican dishes.

Vegan, Low-fat, Low-calorie

INGREDIENTS | YIELDS 2 CUPS

1 mango, chopped
2 tangerines, chopped
½ red bell pepper, chopped
½ red onion, minced
3 cloves garlic, minced
½ jalapeño pepper, minced
2 tablespoons lime juice
½ teaspoon salt
¼ teaspoon black pepper
3 tablespoons chopped fresh cilantro

1. Gently toss together all ingredients.

2. Allow to sit for at least 15 minutes before serving, to allow flavors to mingle.

Hello, Mango!

A ripe mango is sweet, with a unique taste that varies from variety to variety. The texture of the flesh varies as well, some having a soft, pulpy texture similar to an overripe plum, while others have firmer flesh like a cantaloupe or avocado. Mango lassi, or a mango smoothie, is a very popular choice in many Indian restaurants.

PER ¼ CUP Calories: 37 | Fat: 0 g | Protein: 1 g | Sodium: 147 mg | Carbohydrates: 37 g | Fiber: 1 g

Ten-Minute Cheater's Chili

No time? No problem! This is a quick and easy way to get some veggies and protein on the table with no hassle. Instead of veggie burgers, you could toss in a handful of any other mock meat.

Vegan, Lactose-free, Low-fat, High-fiber

INGREDIENTS | SERVES 4–5

1 (12-ounce) jar salsa
1 (14-ounce) can diced tomatoes
2 (14-ounce) cans kidney beans or black beans, drained
1½ cups frozen veggies
4 veggie burgers, crumbled (optional)
2 tablespoons chili powder
1 teaspoon cumin
½ cup water

In a large pot, combine all ingredients. Simmer for 10 minutes, stirring frequently.

The Many Lives of Veggie Burgers

Don't believe the hype: Veggie burgers don't have to always sit on buns! They're also great when crumbled up in soups and stews, like this one, or when used as an ingredient in omelets and lots of other recipes. Don't be afraid to get creative!

PER SERVING Calories: 271 | Fat: 3 g | Protein: 15 g | Sodium: 1154 mg | Carbohydrates: 19 g | Fiber: 17 g

Chili Masala Tofu Scramble

Tofu scramble is an easy and versatile vegan breakfast. This version adds chili and curry for subcontinental flavor. Toss in whatever veggies you have on hand— tomatoes, spinach, or diced broccoli would work well.

Vegan, High-fiber, Lactose-free

INGREDIENTS | SERVES 2

1 container firm or extra-firm tofu, pressed
1 small onion, diced
2 cloves garlic, minced
2 tablespoons olive oil
1 small red chili pepper, minced
1 green bell pepper, chopped
¾ cup sliced mushrooms
1 tablespoon soy sauce
1 teaspoon curry powder
½ teaspoon cumin
¼ teaspoon turmeric
1 teaspoon nutritional yeast (optional)

1. Cut or crumble pressed tofu into 1" cubes.

2. Sauté onions and garlic in olive oil for 1 to 2 minutes, until onions are soft.

3. Add tofu, chili pepper, bell pepper, and mushrooms, stirring well to combine.

4. Add remaining ingredients, except nutritional yeast, and combine well. Allow to cook until tofu is lightly browned, about 6 to 8 minutes.

5. Remove from heat and stir in nutritional yeast if desired.

PER SERVING Calories: 410 | Fat: 28 g | Protein: 29 g | Sodium: 482 mg | Carbohydrates: 31 g | Fiber: 6 g

The Next Day

Leftover tofu scramble makes an excellent lunch. Or, you can wrap leftovers in a warmed flour tortilla to make breakfast-style burritos, perhaps with some salsa or beans. Whatever you do, don't let these leftovers go to waste!

Vegan Pancakes

A touch of sugar and hint of sweet banana flavor more than makes up for the lack of eggs and butter in this pancake recipe.

Vegan, Low-calorie, Low-fat, Lactose-free

INGREDIENTS | YIELDS 8–10 PANCAKES

1 cup flour
1 tablespoon sugar
1¾ teaspoons baking powder
¼ teaspoon salt
½ banana
1 teaspoon vanilla
1 cup soy milk

Don't Overmix!

When it comes to mixing pancake batter, less is more! Pancakes should be light and fluffy, but overmixing the batter will make them tough and rubbery. Gently combine the wet ingredients with the dry ones and don't be afraid of a few lumps; they'll sort themselves out when heated. If you let the batter sit for about five minutes, you'll need to stir even less.

1. Mix together flour, sugar, baking powder, and salt in a large bowl.

2. In a separate small bowl, mash banana with a fork. Add vanilla and whisk until smooth and fluffy. Add soy milk and stir to combine well.

3. Add soy milk mixture to the flour and dry ingredients, stirring just until combined.

4. Heat a lightly greased griddle or large frying pan over medium heat. Drop batter about 3 tablespoons at a time and heat until bubbles appear on surface, about 2 to 3 minutes. Flip and cook other side until lightly golden brown, another 1 to 2 minutes.

PER 1 PANCAKE Calories: 56 | Fat: 0 g | Protein: 2 g | Sodium: 128 mg | Carbohydrates: 32 g | Fiber: 0 g

Quick Breakfast Burrito with Avocado and Soy Cheese

Toss in a fresh diced chili if you need something to really wake you up in the morning. There's no reason you can't enjoy these burritos for lunch, either!

Vegan, Lactose-free, High-fiber

INGREDIENTS | **SERVES 2**

1 block firm or extra-firm tofu, well pressed
2 tablespoons olive oil
½ cup salsa
½ teaspoon chili powder
Salt and pepper to taste
2 flour tortillas, warmed
Ketchup or hot sauce, to taste
2 slices vegan cheese
½ avocado, sliced

1. Cube or crumble the tofu into 1" chunks. Sauté in olive oil over medium heat for 2 to 3 minutes.

2. Add salsa and chili powder, and cook for 2 to 3 more minutes, stirring frequently. Season generously with salt and pepper.

3. Layer each warmed flour tortilla with half of the tofu and salsa mix and drizzle with ketchup or hot sauce.

4. Add vegan cheese and avocado slices and wrap like a burrito.

PER SERVING Calories: 728 | Fat: 45 g | Protein: 34 g | Sodium: 986 mg | Carbohydrates: 68 g | Fiber: 12 g

Soy Cheese

Soy cheese is a variety of cheese analogue, which is a dairy cheese substitute most commonly made from soy but also from rice, almonds, or other nondairy foods. Many soy cheeses have calcium added, so that you still get the benefits of dairy cheese.

Veggie Burger Chili

For vegetarians and carnivores alike, ground veggie burger is an excellent food to keep in your freezer. It is low in calories and fat, offers a decent amount of protein, and can be cooked in 60 seconds!

Vegan, Lactose-free, Low-calorie, High-fiber

INGREDIENTS | SERVES 6

1 tablespoon vegetable oil

1 cup yellow onions, diced

1 cup bell peppers, diced

½ cup celery stalk, stemmed and diced

1 tablespoon roasted garlic

3 (8-ounce) packets Boca Meatless Ground Burger

1 (1.25-ounce) packet chili seasoning mix

4 cups canned chili beans, undrained

1 (10-ounce) can milder diced tomatoes and green chilies, undrained

1 cup tomato sauce

½ teaspoon all-purpose seasoning

1. Spray a large saucepan with nonstick cooking spray. Add oil, onion, pepper, celery, and garlic. Cook on medium-high heat for 6 to 8 minutes or until veggies have browned, stirring often.

2. Reduce heat to medium and add Boca Meatless Ground Burger to saucepan. Cook for an additional 5 to 7 minutes.

3. Add remaining ingredients to saucepan and bring to a boil, stirring often. Simmer for an additional 10 to 12 minutes or until thoroughly cooked.

PER SERVING Calories: 215 | Fat: 4 g | Protein: 29 g | Sodium: 1,129 mg | Carbohydrates: 29 g | Fiber: 10 g

Cashew Cream of Asparagus Soup

A dairy-free and soy-free asparagus soup with a rich cashew base brings out the natural flavors of the asparagus without relying on other enhancers.

Vegan, Lactose-free, Low-carb, High-fiber

INGREDIENTS | SERVES 4

1 onion, chopped

4 cloves garlic, minced

2 tablespoons olive oil

2 pounds asparagus, trimmed and chopped

4 cups vegetable broth

¾ cup raw cashews

¾ cup water

¼ teaspoon sage

½ teaspoon salt

¼ teaspoon black pepper

2 teaspoons lemon juice

2 tablespoons nutritional yeast (optional)

1. In a large soup or stock pot, sauté onion and garlic in olive oil for 2 to 3 minutes, until onion is soft. Reduce heat and carefully add asparagus and vegetable broth.

2. Bring to a simmer, cover, and cook for 20 minutes. Cool slightly, then purée in a blender, working in batches as needed, until almost smooth. Return to pot over low heat.

3. Purée together cashews and water until smooth and add to soup. Add sage, salt, and pepper, and heat for a few more minutes, stirring to combine.

4. Stir in lemon juice and nutritional yeast just before serving, and adjust seasonings to taste.

PER SERVING Calories: 271 | Fat: 18 g | Protein: 10 g | Sodium: 1241 mg | Carbohydrates: 11 g | Fiber: 6 g

Varieties of Veggie Broths

A basic vegetable broth is made by simmering vegetables, potatoes, and a bay leaf or two in water for at least 30 minutes. While you may be familiar with the canned and boxed stocks available at the grocery store, vegan chefs have a few other tricks up their sleeves to impart extra flavor to recipes calling for vegetable broth. Check your natural grocer for specialty flavored bouillon cubes such as vegetarian "chicken" or "beef" flavor, or shop the bulk bins for powdered vegetable broth mix.

Indian Curried Lentil Soup

Similar to a traditional Indian lentil dal recipe but with added vegetables to make it into an entrée, this lentil soup is perfect as is or perhaps paired with rice or some warmed Indian flatbread.

Vegan, Lactose-free, High-fiber, Gluten-free

INGREDIENTS | SERVES 4

1 onion, diced

1 carrot, sliced

3 whole cloves

2 tablespoons vegan margarine

1 teaspoon cumin

1 teaspoon turmeric

1 cup yellow or green lentils

2¾ cups vegetable broth

2 large tomatoes, chopped

1 teaspoon salt

¼ teaspoon black pepper

1 teaspoon lemon juice

1. In a large soup or stock pot, sauté the onion, carrot, and cloves in margarine until onions are just turning soft, about 3 minutes. Add cumin and turmeric and toast for 1 minute, stirring constantly to avoid burning.

2. Reduce heat to medium low and add lentils, vegetable broth, tomatoes, and salt. Bring to a simmer, cover, and cook for 35 to 40 minutes, until lentils are done.

3. Season with black pepper and lemon juice just before serving.

PER SERVING Calories: 265 | Fat: 6 g | Protein: 14 g | Sodium: 1328 mg | Carbohydrates: 30 g | Fiber: 17 g

Cream of Carrot Soup with Coconut

This carrot soup will have you begging for more. The addition of coconut milk transforms an ordinary carrot and ginger soup into an unexpected treat.

Vegan, Lactose-free, Gluten-free, Low-calorie

INGREDIENTS | SERVES 6

3 medium carrots, chopped
1 sweet potato, chopped
1 yellow onion, chopped
3½ cups vegetable broth
3 cloves garlic, minced
2 teaspoons fresh ginger, minced
1 (14-ounce) can coconut milk
1 teaspoon salt
¾ teaspoon cinnamon (optional)

Eat Carrots for Your Eyes

In addition to being crunchy and tasty, carrots are also really good for you. They're rich in dietary fiber, antioxidants, and minerals, as well as vitamin A, which helps maintain your vision. An urban legend says that eating large amounts of carrots will allow you to see in the dark! While this isn't exactly true, it is a good indicator that you should work more carrots into your diet.

1. In a large soup or stock pot, bring the carrots, sweet potato, and onion to a simmer in the vegetable broth. Add garlic and ginger, cover, and heat for 20 to 25 minutes, until carrots and potatoes are soft.

2. Allow to cool slightly, then transfer to a blender and purée until smooth.

3. Return soup to pot. Over very low heat, stir in the coconut milk and salt, stirring well to combine. Heat just until heated through, another 3 to 4 minutes.

4. Garnish with cinnamon just before serving.

PER SERVING Calories: 177 | Fat: 14 g | Protein: 2 g | Sodium: 978 mg | Carbohydrates: 36 g | Fiber: 2 g

Barley Vegetable Soup

Barley and vegetable soup is an excellent "kitchen sink" recipe, meaning that you can toss in just about any fresh or frozen vegetables or spices you happen to have on hand.

Vegan, Lactose-free, High-fiber, Low-calorie

INGREDIENTS | **SERVES 6**

1 onion, chopped

2 carrots, sliced

2 ribs celery, chopped

2 tablespoons olive oil

8 cups vegetable broth

1 cup barley

1½ cups frozen mixed vegetables

1 (14-ounce) can crushed or diced tomatoes

½ teaspoon parsley

½ teaspoon thyme

2 bay leaves

Salt and pepper to taste

1. In a large soup or stock pot, sauté the onion, carrot, and celery in olive oil for 3 to 5 minutes, just until onions are almost soft.

2. Reduce heat to medium-low, and add remaining ingredients, except salt and pepper.

3. Bring to a simmer, cover, and allow to cook for at least 45 minutes, stirring occasionally.

4. Remove cover and allow to cook for 10 more minutes.

5. Remove bay leaves, season with salt and pepper to taste.

PER SERVING Calories: 228 | Fat: 5 g | Protein: 6 g | Sodium: 1380 mg | Carbohydrates: 30 g | Fiber: 9 g

Sesame and Soy Coleslaw Salad

Good news: You don't need mayonnaise to make a crispy, delicious coleslaw!

Vegan, Low-calorie, High-fiber, Lactose-free

INGREDIENTS | SERVES 4

1 head Napa cabbage, shredded

1 carrot, grated

2 green onions, chopped

1 red bell pepper, sliced thin

2 tablespoons olive oil

2 tablespoons apple cider vinegar

2 teaspoons soy sauce

½ teaspoon sesame oil

2 tablespoons maple syrup

2 tablespoons sesame seeds (optional)

1. Toss together the cabbage, carrot, green onions, and bell pepper in a large bowl.

2. In a separate small bowl, whisk together the olive oil, vinegar, soy sauce, sesame oil, and maple syrup until well combined.

3. Drizzle dressing over cabbage and veggies, add sesame seeds, and toss well to combine.

PER SERVING Calories: 168 | Fat: 8 g | Protein: 4 g | Sodium: 203 mg | Carbohydrates: 42 g | Fiber: 7 g

Eat Your Cabbage

While cabbage may not be your favorite vegetable, it's a good one to work into your diet here and there. Because it's mild in flavor, it serves as a great base for soups, salads, and other dishes. It's also an excellent source of vitamin C.

Spicy Southwestern Two-Bean Salad

This cold bean salad with Tex-Mex flavors is even better the next day—if it lasts that long!

Vegan, Lactose-free, High-fiber, Gluten-free

INGREDIENTS | SERVES 6–8

1 (15-ounce) can black beans, drained and rinsed

1 (15-ounce) can kidney beans, drained and rinsed

1 red or yellow bell pepper, chopped

1 large tomato, diced

⅔ cup corn (fresh, canned, or frozen)

⅓ cup olive oil

¼ cup lime juice

½ teaspoon chili powder

½ teaspoon garlic powder

¼ teaspoon cayenne pepper

½ teaspoon salt

¼ cup chopped fresh cilantro

1 avocado, diced

1. In a large bowl, combine the black beans, kidney beans, bell pepper, tomato, and corn.

2. In a separate small bowl, whisk together the olive oil, lime juice, chili powder, garlic powder, cayenne, and salt.

3. Pour over bean mixture, tossing to coat. Stir in fresh cilantro.

4. Chill for at least 1 hour before serving, to allow flavors to mingle.

5. Add avocado and gently toss again just before serving.

PER SERVING Calories: 320 | Fat: 18 g | Protein: 11 g | Sodium: 573 mg | Carbohydrates: 38 g | Fiber: 13 g

Make It a Pasta Salad

Guess what? This recipe can also double as another kind of salad. Just omit the avocado and add some cooked pasta and extra dressing to turn it into a high-protein Tex-Mex pasta salad! Have this salad for lunch or a light dinner, and take the rest for leftovers the next day.

Tempeh "Chicken" Salad

Turn this great dish into a sandwich, or slice up some tomatoes and serve on a bed of lettuce.

Vegan, Lactose-free, Low-calorie

INGREDIENTS | SERVES 3–4

1 package tempeh, diced small

3 tablespoons vegan mayonnaise

2 teaspoons lemon juice

½ teaspoon garlic powder

1 teaspoon Dijon mustard

2 tablespoons sweet pickle relish

½ cup green peas

2 stalks celery, diced small

1 tablespoon chopped fresh dill (optional)

1. Cover tempeh with water and simmer for 10 minutes, until tempeh is soft. Drain and allow to cool completely.

2. Whisk together mayonnaise, lemon juice, garlic powder, mustard, and relish.

3. Combine tempeh, mayonnaise mixture, peas, celery, and dill and gently toss to combine.

4. Chill for at least 1 hour before serving to allow flavors to combine.

PER SERVING Calories: 237 | Fat: 14 g | Protein: 16 g | Sodium: 233 mg | Carbohydrates: 21 g | Fiber: 2 g

Try Curried Chicken Tempeh

For curried chicken salad, omit the dill and add half a teaspoon curry powder and a dash cayenne and black pepper. If you don't feel up to dicing and simmering tempeh, try combining the dressing with store-bought mock chicken, or even veggie turkey or deli slices.

Sweet Potato Apple Latkes

Use your food processor to quickly process the potatoes, apples, and onion to a fine grate and cut the preparation time in half for this recipe. Serve topped with applesauce or nondairy sour cream.

Vegan, Low-calorie

INGREDIENTS | YIELDS 12 LATKES

3 large sweet potatoes, grated
1 apple, grated
1 small yellow onion, grated
Egg replacer for 2 eggs
3 tablespoons flour
1 teaspoon baking powder
½ teaspoon cinnamon
½ teaspoon nutmeg
½ teaspoon salt
Oil for frying

1. Using a cloth or paper towel, gently squeeze out excess moisture from potatoes and apples, and combine with onions in a large bowl.

2. Combine remaining ingredients, except for oil and mix well.

3. Heat a few tablespoons of oil in a frying pan. Drop potato mixture in the hot oil a ¼ cup at a time, and use a spatula to flatten, forming a pancake. Cook for 3 to 4 minutes on each side, until lightly crisped.

PER 1 LATKE Calories: 89 | Fat: 4 g | Protein: 1 g | Sodium: 162 mg | Carbohydrates: 31 g | Fiber: 2 g

Cuban Black Beans and Sweet Potatoes

Stir some plain steamed rice right into the pot, or serve it alongside these well-seasoned beans.

Vegan, Lactose-free, High-fiber

INGREDIENTS | SERVES 4

3 cloves garlic, minced
2 large sweet potatoes, chopped small
2 tablespoons olive oil
2 (15-ounce) cans black beans, drained
¾ cup vegetable broth
1 tablespoon chili powder
1 teaspoon paprika
1 teaspoon cumin
1 tablespoon lime juice
Hot sauce, to taste
2 cups cooked rice

1. In a large skillet or soup pot, sauté garlic and sweet potatoes in olive oil for 2 to 3 minutes.

2. Reduce heat to medium-low and add beans, vegetable broth, chili powder, paprika, and cumin. Bring to a simmer, cover, and allow to cook for 25 to 30 minutes, until sweet potatoes are soft.

3. Stir in lime juice and hot sauce, to taste. Serve hot over rice.

PER SERVING Calories: 387 | Fat: 8 g | Protein: 13 g | Sodium: 491 mg | Carbohydrates: 42 g | Fiber: 13 g

Sun-Dried Tomato Risotto with Spinach and Pine Nuts

The tomatoes carry the flavor in this easy risotto—no butter, cheese, or wine is needed.

Vegan

INGREDIENTS | SERVES 4

1 yellow onion, diced

4 cloves garlic, minced

2 tablespoons olive oil

1½ cups Arborio rice

5–6 cups vegetable broth

⅔ cup rehydrated sun-dried tomatoes, sliced

½ cup fresh spinach

1 tablespoon chopped fresh basil (optional)

2 tablespoons vegan margarine (optional)

2 tablespoons nutritional yeast

Salt and pepper to taste

¼ cup pine nuts

Sun-Dried Tomatoes

If you're using dehydrated tomatoes, rehydrate them first by covering in water for at least 10 minutes, and add the soaking water to the broth. If you're using tomatoes packed in oil, add 2 tablespoons of the oil to risotto at the end of cooking, instead of the vegan margarine.

1. Heat onion and garlic in olive oil until just soft, about 2 to 3 minutes. Add rice and toast for 1 minute, stirring constantly.

2. Add ¾ cup vegetable broth and stir to combine. When most of the liquid has been absorbed, add another ½ cup, stirring constantly. Continue adding liquid ½ cup at a time until rice is cooked, about 20 minutes.

3. Add another ½ cup broth, tomatoes, and spinach and reduce heat to low. Stir to combine well. Heat for 3 to 4 minutes, until tomatoes are soft and spinach is wilted.

4. Stir in basil, margarine, and nutritional yeast. Taste, then season lightly with a bit of salt and pepper.

5. Allow to cool slightly, then top with pine nuts. Risotto will thicken a bit as it cools.

PER SERVING Calories: 441 | Fat: 13 g | Protein: 8 g | Sodium: 1322 mg | Carbohydrates: 47 g | Fiber: 4 g

Spanish Artichoke and Zucchini Paella

Traditional Spanish paellas are always cooked with saffron, but this version with zucchini, artichokes, and bell peppers uses turmeric instead for the same golden hue.

Vegan, Lactose-free, High-fiber, Low-fat

INGREDIENTS | SERVES 4

3 cloves garlic, minced

1 yellow onion, diced

2 tablespoons olive oil

1 cup white rice

1 (15-ounce) can diced or crushed tomatoes

1 green bell pepper, chopped

1 red or yellow bell pepper, chopped

½ cup artichoke hearts, chopped

2 zucchinis, sliced

2 cups vegetable broth

1 tablespoon paprika

½ teaspoon turmeric

¾ teaspoon parsley

½ teaspoon salt

1. In the largest skillet you can find, heat garlic and onions in olive oil for 3 to 4 minutes, until onions are almost soft. Add rice, stirring well to coat, and heat for another minute, stirring to prevent burning.

2. Add tomatoes, bell peppers, artichokes, and zucchini, stirring to combine. Add vegetable broth and remaining ingredients, cover, and simmer for 15 to 20 minutes, or until rice is done.

PER SERVING Calories: 260 | Fat: 1 g | Protein: 7 g | Sodium: 1016 mg | Carbohydrates: 44 g | Fiber: 6 g

Orange Ginger Mixed Veggie Stir-Fry

Rice vinegar can be substituted for the apple cider vinegar, if you prefer. As with most stir-fry recipes, the vegetables are merely a suggestion; use your favorites or whatever looks like it's been sitting too long in your crisper.

Vegan, Lactose-free, Low-calorie, Low-fat, High-fiber

INGREDIENTS | SERVES 4

3 tablespoons orange juice

1 tablespoon apple cider vinegar

2 tablespoons soy sauce

2 tablespoons water

1 tablespoon maple syrup

1 teaspoon powdered ginger

2 cloves garlic, minced

2 tablespoons oil

1 bunch broccoli, chopped

½ cup sliced mushrooms

½ cup snap peas, chopped

1 carrot, sliced

1 cup chopped cabbage or bok choy

1. Whisk together the orange juice, vinegar, soy sauce, water, maple syrup, and ginger.

2. Heat garlic in oil and add veggies. Allow to cook, stirring frequently, over high heat for 2 to 3 minutes, until just starting to get tender.

3. Add sauce and reduce heat. Simmer, stirring frequently, for another 3 to 4 minutes, or until veggies are cooked.

PER SERVING Calories: 117 | Fat: 3 g | Protein: 6 g | Sodium: 518 mg | Carbohydrates: 46 g | Fiber: 6 g

Oodles of Noodles

When stir-frying a saucy veggie dish, you can add quick-cooking Asian-style noodles right into the pan. Add some extra sauce ingredients and a fourth to a third cup of water. Add the noodles, stir up the sauce, reduce the heat so the veggies don't scald, and keep covered for just a few minutes.

Gingered Tofu and Bok Choy Stir-Fry

Dark leafy bok choy is a highly nutritious vegetable that can be found in well-stocked groceries. Keep an eye out for light green baby boy choy, which are a bit more tender but carry a similar flavor.

Vegan, Lactose-free, Low-calorie, Low-carb

INGREDIENTS | SERVES 3

3 tablespoons soy sauce

2 tablespoons lemon or lime juice

1 tablespoon fresh ginger, minced

1 block firm or extra-firm tofu, well pressed

2 tablespoons olive oil

1 head bok choy or 3–4 small baby bok choys

½ teaspoon sugar

½ teaspoon sesame oil

1. Whisk together soy sauce, lemon or lime juice, and ginger in a shallow pan. Cut tofu into cubes, and marinate for at least 1 hour. Drain, reserving marinade.

2. In a large skillet or wok, sauté tofu in olive oil for 3 to 4 minutes.

3. Carefully add reserved marinade, bok choy, and sugar, stirring well to combine.

4. Cook, stirring, for 3 to 4 more minutes, or until bok choy is done.

5. Drizzle with sesame oil and serve over rice.

PER SERVING Calories: 243 | Fat: 18 g | Protein: 19 g | Sodium: 732 mg | Carbohydrates: 8 g | Fiber: 4 g

It's Easy Being Green

Learn to love your leafy greens! Pound for pound and calorie for calorie, dark, leafy green vegetables are the most nutritious food on the planet. Try a variety of greens: bok choy, collard greens, spinach, kale, mustard greens, Swiss chard, or watercress. When you find one or two that you like, sneak it in as many meals as you can!

Potatoes "Au Gratin" Casserole

You'll never miss the boxed version after trying these easy potatoes!

Vegan, Lactose-free, High-fiber

INGREDIENTS | SERVES 4

4 potatoes

1 onion, chopped

1 tablespoon vegan margarine

2 tablespoons flour

1½ cups unsweetened soy milk

2 teaspoons onion powder

1 teaspoon garlic powder

2 tablespoons nutritional yeast

1 teaspoon lemon juice

½ teaspoon salt

½ teaspoon paprika

Pepper, to taste

¾ cup bread crumbs or French fried onions (optional)

1. Preheat oven to 375°F.

2. Slice potatoes into thin coins and arrange half the slices in a casserole or baking dish. Layer half of the onions on top of the potatoes.

3. Melt the margarine over low heat and add flour, stirring to make a paste. Add soy milk, onion powder, garlic powder, nutritional yeast, lemon juice, and salt, stirring to combine. Stir over low heat until sauce has thickened.

4. Pour half of sauce over potatoes and onions, then layer the remaining potatoes and onions on top of the sauce. Pour the remaining sauce on top.

5. Sprinkle with paprika and black pepper, and top with bread crumbs or French fried onions.

6. Cover and bake for 45 minutes; then bake uncovered for an additional 10 minutes. Allow to cool for at least 10 minutes before serving, as sauce will thicken as it cools.

PER SERVING Calories: 264 | Fat: 5 g | Protein: 9 g | Sodium: 406 mg | Carbohydrates: 28 g | Fiber: 7 g

Roasted Brussels Sprouts with Apples

Brussels sprouts are surprisingly delicious when prepared properly, so if you have bad memories of being force fed soggy, limp baby cabbages as a child, don't let it stop you from trying this recipe!

Vegan, Lactose-free, Low-calorie

INGREDIENTS | SERVES 4

2 cups Brussels sprouts, chopped into quarters

8 whole cloves garlic, peeled

2 tablespoons olive oil

2 tablespoons balsamic vinegar

¾ teaspoon salt

½ teaspoon black pepper

2 apples, chopped

Reuse and Recycle

Recycle this basic recipe by adding an extra garnish or two each time you make it: a touch of fresh rosemary, a couple shakes of a vegan Parmesan cheese, some chopped toasted nuts, or vegetarian bacon bits for crunch. For a Thanksgiving side dish, toss in some rehydrated dried cranberries.

1. Preheat oven to 425°F.

2. Arrange Brussels sprouts and garlic on a single layer on a baking sheet. Drizzle with olive oil and balsamic vinegar and season with salt and pepper. Roast for 10 to 12 minutes, tossing once.

3. Remove tray from oven and add apples, tossing gently to combine. Roast for 10 more minutes, or until apples are soft, tossing once again.

PER SERVING Calories: 143 | Fat: 7 g | Protein: 2 g | Sodium: 451 mg | Carbohydrates: 19 g | Fiber: 4 g

Gnocchi and Purple Potatoes with Broccolini

This colorful dish is as delicious and nutritious as it is pretty!

Vegetarian, High-fiber

INGREDIENTS | SERVES 4

1 (17.6-ounce) package fresh gnocchi

1 bunch broccolini, chopped and cooked

10 baby purple potatoes, cooked and cubed

1 (13.75-ounce) can artichoke hearts, drained and quartered

3 tablespoons capers

½ cup olive oil

3 tablespoons red wine vinegar

2 tablespoons pesto

Salt and freshly ground black pepper to taste

1. Cook the gnocchi according to package directions, drain, and put into a serving bowl. Add the broccolini, potatoes, artichoke hearts, and capers.

2. Whisk together the oil, vinegar, pesto, salt, and pepper. Pour over the vegetables and toss to combine. Serve.

PER SERVING Calories: 750 | Fat: 40 g | Protein: 15 g | Sodium: 970 mg | Carbohydrates: 85 g | Fiber: 9 g

What Are Gnocchi?

A knot-shaped pasta most commonly made with mashed potatoes and flour, gnocchi, when freshly made and right from the boiling water, are so delicate they seem to whisper. Another less common version is made with semolina flour, milk, and cheese. You can make potato gnocchi yourself, but fresh ones are sold at Italian markets and some supermarkets.

Mexi Mac 'n' Cheese

This grownup version of mac 'n' cheese will rouse you with its fiery bite. You can kick this up a notch or two by adding both jalapeño and habanero chilies as a garnish . . . but you may need a fire extinguisher.

Vegetarian

INGREDIENTS | SERVES 6

3 cups crushed taco chips

1 (8-ounce) package elbow macaroni

3 tablespoons butter

3 tablespoons flour

2 cups milk

1 cup hot or mild salsa

2 cups shredded Cheddar cheese

Salt and freshly ground black pepper to taste

4 ounces habanero cheese, cubed

Jalapeño slices to taste

Flour tortillas for serving

1. Preheat the oven to 350°F. Layer 2 cups taco chips on the bottom of a 2-quart heatproof dish.

2. Cook the macaroni in lightly salted water until al dente. Drain and set aside.

3. Meanwhile, melt the butter and whisk in the flour and milk, stirring for a few minutes until the mixture begins to thicken and is lump-free. Stir in the salsa, Cheddar cheese, salt, and pepper. Combine the pasta with the cheese sauce and spoon into the prepared dish. Top with the remaining chips, the habanero cheese, and jalapeño slices.

4. Bake for about 30 minutes or until the cheese is melted throughout. Serve with softened flour tortillas.

PER SERVING Calories: 640 | Fat: 32 g | Protein: 25 g | Sodium: 960 mg | Carbohydrates: 62 g | Fiber: 3 g

Apple, Quince, and Barley Tart

For convenience's sake, use a readymade piecrust just out of the freezer. This meal comes together quickly. Despite its sweetness, the dish makes a pleasant supper or brunch main course because the barley provides an earthy flavor counterpoint to the apple and jelly.

Vegetarian, High-fiber

INGREDIENTS | SERVES 4–6

2 large eggs, lightly beaten

1 cup shredded Swiss cheese

2 cups cooked and cooled barley

1 firm cooking apple, cored and sliced

1 quince, peeled, cored, and sliced

½ cup chopped dates

1 (9") deep-dish piecrust

3 tablespoons apple jelly

1. Preheat the oven to 350°F.

2. Combine the eggs and cheese in a large mixing bowl and stir in the barley, apple, quince, and dates. Mix together well and spoon the mixture into the piecrust. Spoon the apple jelly over top.

3. Bake for about 30 minutes or until the crust browns. Cool slightly before serving.

PER SERVING Calories: 523 | Fat: 16 g | Protein: 17 g | Sodium: 211 mg | Carbohydrates: 81 g | Fiber: 13 g

What Is Quince?

A favorite Mediterranean, Asian, and Hispanic fruit, the quince resembles a green-yellow apple, but its flesh is very firm and its flavor is tart. Quince is high in pectin and adds a thickening power to jams and jellies. Some folktales attribute healing powers to quince: it purportedly cures upset stomachs, among other ills.

CHAPTER 9

Mom Was Right: Eat Your Fruits and Veggies

Banana Berry Smoothie

You can replace the yogurt with soy yogurt and the milk with soy or rice milk in this recipe if you have a milk allergy.

Low-fat, High-fiber, Vegetarian, Gluten-free

INGREDIENTS | SERVES 1

1 banana
1 cup raspberries
1 cup nonfat yogurt
½ cup skim milk

Combine all ingredients in a blender until smooth. Pour into a tall glass.

Pack in Some Protein

Give your smoothie an instant protein boost by adding a tablespoon of peanut butter to the smoothie mixture. Let's be honest: Peanut butter tastes great in pretty much everything! You can also add protein powder to the smoothie to really pack a punch.

PER SERVING Calories: 365 | Fat: 2 g | Protein: 21 g | Sodium: 154 mg | Carbohydrates: 71 g | Fiber: 9.4 g

Blackberry Apple Smoothie

When berries are not in season, frozen berries will work just as well. Frozen berries can also add a nice texture to a berry smoothie. Test the texture as you blend to get the perfect fruity, crunchy blend.

Vegetarian, Low-fat, High-fiber, Gluten-free

INGREDIENTS | SERVES 1

1 cup blackberries
1 apple, sliced
1 cup nonfat yogurt
½ cup skim milk

Combine all ingredients in a blender until smooth. Pour into a tall glass.

PER SERVING Calories: 380 | Fat: 2 g | Protein: 20 g | Sodium: 164 mg | Carbohydrates: 75 g | Fiber: 8 g

Sinless Strawberry Smoothie

This smoothie is thick and creamy, but won't thicken the thighs!

Vegetarian, Low-fat

INGREDIENTS | SERVES 1

½ cup fat-free vanilla ice cream
1 cup fresh strawberries
½ cup nonfat yogurt
½ cup skim milk

Combine all ingredients in a blender until smooth. Pour into a tall glass.

Strawberries and Cream

You probably see lots of items in the grocery store with the flavor of strawberries and cream, from popsicles to ice cream to hard candies. That's because it's one of the oldest and best combos in the cookbook! Don't fight what works. Enjoy this smoothie in good health.

PER SERVING Calories: 251 | Fat: 1 g | Protein: 15 g | Sodium: 198 mg | Carbohydrates: 46 g | Fiber: 3 g

Apple with Yogurt and Cinnamon

You can use any other kind of apples, but Granny Smith apples have a tart taste that goes well with the yogurt. Use vanilla-flavored nonfat yogurt for an additional full-tasting treat.

Vegetarian, Gluten-free, Low-calorie, Low-fat

INGREDIENTS | SERVES 1

1 apple
½ cup plain nonfat yogurt
2 teaspoons Splenda
½ teaspoon cinnamon

1. Wash, peel, and cut up apple in small pieces.

2. Mix the yogurt, Splenda, and cinnamon in a small bowl. Mix in apple slices.

3. Chill for 20 minutes and serve.

PER SERVING Calories: 170 | Fat: 0 g | Protein: 6 g | Sodium: 53 mg | Carbohydrates: 41 g | Fiber: 2 g

Homemade Fruit Popsicles

If you do not have an ice crusher, place the ice in a plastic bag and smash it with a hammer or other hard object to crush it before adding it to a blender. The ice is important for bulking up the mixture.

Vegan, Gluten-free, Low-calorie, Low-fat, Lactose-free

INGREDIENTS | SERVES 6

1 (12-ounce) bag frozen strawberries
3 cups 100% fruit strawberry juice
1 cup crushed ice

Popsicle Tools

If you don't have a popsicle mold, don't fret. Just use paper cups! Allow the popsicles to freeze about 1 hour, then insert popsicle sticks just as you would in the original recipe. If you don't have popsicle sticks, try plastic spoons. Anything that stays in the center of the popsicle and makes a decent handle will work.

1. Place fruit, juice, and ice in a blender, in that order. Blend on high.

2. Pour mixture into popsicle molds.

3. Freeze for 1 hour. Remove popsicles from the freezer and insert a popsicle stick into the center of each treat. Return to the freezer and let solidify for another 7 to 9 hours before eating.

PER SERVING Calories: 55 | Fat: <1 g | Protein: 1 g | Sodium: 19 mg | Carbohydrates: 14 g | Fiber: 3 g

Pineapple Chunks in Cream Cheese

You can use fresh strawberries instead of pineapple chunks for a sweeter, less tangy treat.

Vegetarian, Low-calorie, Low-fat, Gluten-free

INGREDIENTS | SERVES 4

1 cup canned pineapple chunks in water, drained
½ cup fat-free cream cheese, softened
⅓ cup finely chopped mint

Fat-Free Cream Cheese

If you're used to full-fat cream cheese, the low-fat or fat-free variety will probably take some getting used to. However, once you've grown accustomed to the lighter flavor, you'll really enjoy the classic creamy texture without all the fat!

1. Dry pineapple chunks lightly with paper towel.

2. Carefully spread cream cheese over each pineapple chunk.

3. Roll each chunk in the chopped mint.

4. Refrigerate for 20 minutes and serve.

PER SERVING Calories: 58 | Fat: <1 g | Protein: 5 g | Sodium: 176 mg | Carbohydrates: 18 g | Fiber: 1 g

Fruity Coleslaw

Coleslaw is usually made with cabbage and root vegetables like carrots and broccoli. This fruity version is a fun alternative that's super easy to make.

Vegetarian, Low-fat, Low-calorie

INGREDIENTS | SERVES 6

2 cups shredded green cabbage
2 cups shredded red cabbage
3 pears, diced
1 Granny Smith apple, diced
3 tablespoons lemon juice
½ cup dried currants
1 cup vanilla low-fat yogurt
1 teaspoon grated lemon zest
2 tablespoons honey
⅛ teaspoon salt

1. Place cabbages in large bowl. Toss pears and apple with lemon juice and add to cabbage mixture along with currants.

2. In a small bowl, combine yogurt, lemon zest, honey, and salt and mix well. Pour over cabbage mixture, toss to coat, and cover. Refrigerate for 1 to 2 hours before serving to blend flavors.

PER SERVING Calories: 148 | Fat: 1 g | Protein: 4 g | Sodium: 183 mg | Carbohydrates: 46 g | Fiber: 3 g

Avocado Citrus Salad

This unusual salad features a tangy combination of textures, colors, and flavors that will make it one of your new favorites.

Vegetarian, Low-calorie

INGREDIENTS | SERVES 6

3 (6") corn tortillas
1 tablespoon chili powder
¼ teaspoon fine salt
4 oranges
4 grapefruits
3 tablespoons honey
2 tablespoons raspberry vinegar
2 tablespoons extra-virgin olive oil
1 avocado, peeled and diced
6 mint sprigs

Making Salad ahead of Time

Most fruit and vegetable salads can be made ahead of time. Omit any vegetables that may wilt and fruits that will turn brown. Add them just before serving time. Do not make salads using lettuce or spinach ahead of time because the dressing will wilt the greens.

1. Preheat oven to 275°F. Slice tortillas into very thin strips, about ¼" wide and arrange in single layer on cookie sheet. Bake until golden brown, about 15 minutes, turning with spatula halfway through cooking time. Toss with chili powder and salt while still warm. Remove to cool on wire rack.

2. Grate 2 teaspoons orange zest and set aside. Remove peel from oranges and grapefruits, and cut fruit into wedges between the sections. Squeeze the membrane to retrieve 3 tablespoons juice; reserve. Place fruit in serving bowl.

3. In a small bowl, combine reserved juice, honey, raspberry vinegar, olive oil, and orange zest and whisk to blend. Drizzle over fruit.

4. Top with avocado, tortilla strips, and mint and serve immediately.

PER SERVING Calories: 209 | Fat: 6 g | Protein: 3 g | Sodium: 130 mg | Carbohydrates: 45 g | Fiber: 4 g

Peach Spinach Salad

This fresh, colorful, and tender salad is full of sweet and tangy flavor. It's perfect for a side salad with an entrée or all by itself on a warm day.

Vegetarian, Low-calorie, Low-fat

INGREDIENTS | SERVES 6

3 cups baby spinach

1 cup peeled, sliced cucumber

1 peach, peeled and sliced

2 plums, pitted and sliced

¼ cup sliced green onion

⅔ cup low-fat lemon yogurt

2 tablespoons sugar

¼ teaspoon dried dill weed

1. In serving bowl, combine spinach, cucumber, peaches, plums, and green onion and toss to coat.

2. In a small bowl, combine yogurt, sugar, and dill weed; stir to combine. Let stand for 10 minutes, then drizzle over salad; toss to coat and serve immediately.

PER SERVING Calories: 69 | Fat: 1 g | Protein: 2 g | Sodium: 41 mg | Carbohydrates: 35 g | Fiber: 4 g

Give Baby Spinach a Try

If you think you don't like spinach, try fresh baby spinach. It's tender and nutty, with a sweet aftertaste. To prepare, rinse in cold water. You may want to pull off the stems, but they are usually tender enough to eat. Arrange spinach in a kitchen towel, roll up, and refrigerate for 1 to 2 hours. Then use in salads and recipes.

Simple Sweet and Fruity Salad

Always rinse fresh produce under cool water. This will help remove things you don't want to eat such as pesticides, fertilizers, and bacteria.

Vegan, Low-calorie, Low-fat, High-fiber, Gluten-free, Lactose-free

INGREDIENTS | SERVES 1

2 cups shredded romaine lettuce

4 cherry tomatoes

½ cup Gala apple, sliced

2 tablespoons golden raisins

2 tablespoons mandarin oranges

Combine all ingredients in a bowl and enjoy!

PER SERVING Calories: 135 | Fat: 1 g | Protein: 3 g | Sodium: 18 mg | Carbohydrates: 33 g | Fiber: 5 g

Cucumber Cilantro Salad

Cooling cucumbers and cold creamy yogurt are coupled with a dash of cayenne pepper for a salad that keeps you guessing.

Vegan, Low-calorie, Low-fat

INGREDIENTS | SERVES 2–3

4 cucumbers, diced

2 tomatoes, chopped

½ red onion, diced small

1 cup soy yogurt, plain or lemon flavored

1 tablespoon lemon juice

2 tablespoons chopped fresh cilantro

Salt and pepper to taste

¼ teaspoon cayenne (optional)

1. Toss together all ingredients, stirring well to combine.

2. Chill for at least 2 hours before serving, to allow flavors to marinate. Toss again just before serving.

PER SERVING Calories: 134 | Protein: 6 g | Fat: 2 g | Sodium: 23 mg | Carbohydrates: 36 g | Fiber: 4 g

Broccoli Salad

This tantalizing salad makes a healthy, hearty side and helps spice up your entrée.

Vegetarian, Low-calorie, Low-fat

INGREDIENTS | SERVES 6

5 cups fresh broccoli florets
⅓ cup raisins
¼ cup sunflower seeds
¼ cup red onion, chopped
1 cup frozen peas, thawed
1 cup fat-free mayonnaise
2 tablespoons vinegar
½ cup Splenda

1. In a large bowl, combine first five ingredients and toss.

2. In a separate bowl, combine mayonnaise, vinegar, and Splenda.

3. Pour dressing over broccoli mixture and toss to mix.

4. Chill for at least 2 hours before serving.

PER SERVING Calories: 130 | Fat: 3 g | Protein: 5 g | Sodium: 551 mg | Carbohydrates: 27 g | Fiber: 4 g

Broccoli Is Your Friend

Broccoli is one of those great veggies. It's crunchy when raw, soft and tasty when cooked, and it has a great texture. To top it all off, it's absolutely packed with vitamins. Broccoli is high in vitamins C, K, and A, as well as dietary fiber.

Tangerine and Mint Salad

Fennel and mint are a wonderful combination, but the sweet tangerines will carry the salad if you can't find fennel.

Vegan, Lactose-free, High-fiber

INGREDIENTS | **SERVES 2**

1 head green lettuce, chopped

2 tablespoons chopped fresh mint

2 tangerines, clementines, or satsuma oranges, sectioned

⅓ cup chopped walnuts

1 bulb fennel, sliced thin (optional)

2 tablespoons olive oil

Salt and pepper to taste

1. Gently toss together the lettuce, mint, tangerines, walnuts, and sliced fennel.

2. Drizzle with olive oil, salt, and pepper.

PER SERVING Calories: 322 | Fat: 27 g | Protein: 6 g | Sodium: 55 mg | Carbohydrates: 17 g | Fiber: 6 g

Get to Know Fresh Mint

If you haven't yet become acquainted with fresh mint, now's the time. It comes in multiple varieties (spearmint, peppermint, even chocolate mint!), and it has dozens of great uses. Fresh mint tastes great in salads, meat dishes, and desserts, and of course, it's wonderful all by itself in hot or iced tea.

Carrot and Date Salad

If you're used to carrot and raisin salads with pineapples that are drowning in mayonnaise, this lighter version with tahini, dates, and mandarin oranges will be a welcome change.

Vegan, High-fiber, Lactose-free

INGREDIENTS | SERVES 4–6

⅓ cup tahini

1 tablespoon olive oil

2 tablespoons agave nectar (or 2 teaspoons sugar)

3 tablespoons lemon juice

¼ teaspoon salt

4 large carrots, grated

½ cup chopped dates

3 satsuma or mandarin oranges, sectioned

⅓ cup coconut flakes (optional)

1. In a small bowl, whisk together the tahini, olive oil, agave nectar, lemon juice, and salt.

2. Place grated carrots in a large bowl and toss well with tahini mixture. Add dates, oranges, and coconut flakes and combine well.

3. Allow to sit for at least 1 hour before serving, to soften carrots and raisins. Toss again before serving.

PER SERVING Calories: 307 | Fat: 15 g | Protein: 5 g | Sodium: 220 mg | Carbohydrates: 57 g | Fiber: 7 g

Edamame Salad

If you can't find shelled edamame, try this recipe with lima beans instead.

Vegan, High-fiber, Lactose-free

INGREDIENTS | SERVES 4

2 cups frozen shelled edamame, thawed and drained

1 red or yellow bell pepper, diced

¾ cup corn kernels

3 tablespoons chopped fresh cilantro (optional)

3 tablespoons olive oil

2 tablespoons red wine vinegar

1 teaspoon soy sauce

1 teaspoon chili powder

2 teaspoons lemon or lime juice

Salt and pepper to taste

1. Combine edamame, bell pepper, corn, and cilantro in a large bowl.

2. Whisk together the olive oil, vinegar, soy sauce, chili powder, and lemon or lime juice and combine with the edamame. Add salt and pepper to taste.

3. Chill for at least 1 hour before serving.

PER SERVING Calories: 246 | Fat: 16 g | Protein: 10 g | Sodium: 133 mg | Carbohydrates: 42 g | Fiber: 9 g

Eda-what?

You're probably familiar with the lightly steamed and salted edamame served as an appetizer at Japanese restaurants, but many grocers sell shelled edamame in the frozen foods section. Edamame, or baby green soybeans, are a great source of unprocessed soy protein.

Sweet Red Salad with Strawberries and Beets

Colorful and nutritious, this vibrant red salad can be made with roasted or canned beets, or even raw grated beets, if you prefer.

Vegan, Lactose-free, High-fiber

INGREDIENTS | SERVES 4

3–4 small beets, chopped
Spinach or other green lettuce
1 cup sliced strawberries
½ cup chopped pecans
¼ cup olive oil
2 tablespoons red wine vinegar
2 tablespoons agave nectar
2 tablespoons orange juice
Salt and pepper to taste

1. Boil beets until soft, about 20 minutes. Allow to cool completely.

2. In a large bowl, combine spinach, strawberries, pecans, and cooled beets.

3. In a separate small bowl, whisk together the olive oil, vinegar, agave nectar, and orange juice, and pour over salad, tossing well to coat.

4. Season generously with salt and pepper, to taste.

PER SERVING Calories: 295 | Fat: 24 g | Protein: 3 g | Sodium: 73 mg | Carbohydrates: 57 g | Fiber: 5 g

Vegetable Chowder

This is what you make when it's cold outside and you don't want to run to the store. It's easy, filling, and delicious.

Vegetarian, Low-calorie

INGREDIENTS | SERVES 8

3 tablespoons margarine

1 onion, chopped

1 cup chopped celery

2 cups sliced carrots

½ cup water

3 cups low-sodium chicken or vegetable broth

3 potatoes, peeled and diced

3 cups skim milk

¼ cup flour

1. Melt margarine in a large, deep skillet over medium heat. Add the vegetables until tender, tossing occasionally. Add the water, broth, and potatoes; boil for 15 minutes or until potatoes are tender.

2. Add the milk, stirring to combine, and turn heat down to medium high. Add the flour to thicken. If you need to thicken further, add more flour. Serve hot.

PER SERVING Calories: 158 | Fat: 5 g | Protein: 8 g | Sodium: 37 mg | Carbohydrates: 24 g | Fiber: 3.5 g

Chowder for Everyone

Who says chowder has to have clams in it? Chowder is basically just a cream- or milk-based soup that you can enjoy a thousand different ways. Corn chowder is a popular variation, as is seafood chowder. This veggie-packed recipe is a favorite of vegetarians and meat-eaters alike!

Heirloom Tomato Sandwich

Select a rustic-peasanty round loaf, such as a sourdough, and cut thick slices from the center for a full-sized sandwich. To kick this up a notch, use fresh mozzarella, which you should find in a specialty cheese shop or in the imported cheeses section of well-stocked supermarkets.

Vegetarian, High-fiber

INGREDIENTS | SERVES 1

1 teaspoon extra-virgin olive oil, or more as desired

2 thick slices bread, preferably sourdough

1 teaspoon minced garlic

2 teaspoons mayonnaise, or more as desired

Fresh basil leaves

1 large heirloom tomato, thinly sliced

2 thin slices fresh mozzarella cheese

Salt and freshly ground black pepper to taste

1. Drizzle the olive oil on 1 slice of bread.

2. Mix together the garlic and mayonnaise and spread the mixture on the other slice.

3. Cover this slice with basil leaves. Top the leaves with the tomato and the mozzarella slices, layering the slices if necessary. Sprinkle the slices with salt and pepper and close the sandwich.

PER SERVING Calories: 680 | Fat: 29 g | Protein: 25 g | Sodium: 1,190 mg | Carbohydrates: 76 g | Fiber: 6 g

Veggie-Stuffed Peppers

When you place the peppers on the baking pan, add a little water to the pan so that the peppers don't burn.

Vegetarian, High-fiber, Gluten-free

INGREDIENTS | **SERVES 4**

4 green bell peppers

6 cups water

1 (15-ounce) can pinto beans, rinsed and drained

2 cups whole kernel corn

¾ cup low-fat shredded cheddar cheese

½ tablespoon vegetable oil

1 clove garlic, crushed

½ onion, chopped

1 teaspoon black pepper

No Meat?

Stuffed peppers is another meal that is traditionally made with meat but doesn't have to be. In fact, there are lots of varieties, some including rice, others including bread, and so on. If you're vegetarian or simply looking for a lighter meal, try this meatless version. You'll find it's just as satisfying as any other variation.

1. Preheat oven to 375°F.

2. Cut off the tops of the green peppers. Remove the seeds.

3. Boil 6 cups of water; add peppers and cook for 5 minutes. Remove peppers, place upside down on a paper towel to drain.

4. Mix all remaining ingredients in a medium bowl. Divide ingredients evenly among peppers and stuff them. Place peppers on a baking dish, filled side up; bake about 20 minutes. Serve hot.

PER SERVING Calories: 278 | Fat: 6 g | Protein: 14 g | Sodium: 105 mg | Carbohydrates: 41 g | Fiber: 8 g

Veggie-Stuffed Zucchini

Stuff the zucchini with any vegetables you like. The vegetables in this recipe can easily be substituted with your favorites.

Vegan, High-fiber, Low-calorie

INGREDIENTS | SERVES 4

4 medium zucchini
1 teaspoon salt
2 teaspoons vegan margarine
2 teaspoons vegetable oil
1 onion, chopped
1 clove garlic, crushed
½ cup chickpeas
2 tablespoons flour
1 teaspoon ground coriander
1 potato, peeled, cooked, and diced
1 cup green peas
2 tablespoons chopped cilantro

1. Preheat oven to 375°F.

2. Cut each zucchini in half lengthwise and scoop out the pulp. Place each half with the open side up on a shallow roasting pan and sprinkle with salt.

3. Heat margarine and oil in a skillet over medium heat. Add onion and garlic; sauté for 4 minutes, then stir in chickpeas, flour, coriander, potato, peas, and cilantro.

4. Spoon ¼ of potato mixture into each zucchini half and cover with foil.

5. Bake for 15 minutes or until zucchini is tender.

PER SERVING Calories: 205 | Fat: 5 g | Protein: 8 g | Sodium: 68 mg | Carbohydrates: 35 g | Fiber: 5 g

Fresh Fruit Pizza Bites

Fresh fruit is the best fiber-rich diet dessert to have every day, and this pizza dresses it up for a party.

Vegetarian

INGREDIENTS | SERVES 6

1 pound sugar cookie dough

1 (8-ounce) package cream cheese, softened

½ cup powdered sugar

6 sliced strawberries

½ mango, cut in slices

1 sliced banana

¼ cup blueberries

¼ cup apple jelly

Mix It Up!

You can use other fruits as they come into season, including nectarines, peaches, pears, and melons. Toss a few roasted nuts on top for an extra crunch and more fiber.

1. Preheat oven to 350°F. Press the sugar cookie dough out onto a 12" pizza pan.

2. Bake the cookie dough for 20 minutes, then let cool on a rack.

3. Whip the cream cheese. Add the powdered sugar and mix well.

4. Spread the cookie dough with the cream cheese mixture.

5. Arrange the fruit on top of the cream cheese, glaze the fruit with warm apple jelly, and chill for 10 minutes. Cut into wedges to serve.

PER 1 WEDGE Calories: 517 | Fat: 25 g | Protein: 6 g | Sodium: 204 mg | Carbohydrates: 68 g | Fiber: 2 g

CHAPTER 10

Appease Your Sweet Tooth: Healthy Desserts

Coffee Almond Float

Floats are fun desserts. You could use this cold coffee mixture over any flavor of frozen yogurt or sorbet.

Low-calorie, Low-fat, Vegetarian

INGREDIENTS | SERVES 2

1 tablespoon brown sugar
½ cup cold brewed coffee
1 teaspoon orgeat (almond) syrup or vanilla
¼ cup ice cubes
1 cup 1% milk
½ cup chocolate low-fat frozen yogurt

1. In a small bowl, combine sugar and coffee; stir until dissolved. Add orgeat, stirring to mix well. Add ice cubes and milk and stir well; let stand for 5 minutes. Remove ice cubes.

2. Divide milk mixture between two parfait glasses and top with the frozen yogurt. Serve immediately.

PER SERVING Calories: 174 | Fat: 3 g | Protein: 7 g | Sodium: 128 mg | Carbohydrates: 58 g | Fiber: 0 g

Simple, Sweet Ricotta Dessert

Ricotta cheese is a grainy, slightly sweet fresh cheese that is delicious in both savory and sweet dishes.

Vegetarian, Low-calorie, Low-fat, Low-carb

INGREDIENTS | SERVES 1

¼ cup fat-free ricotta cheese
½ teaspoon vanilla extract
1 teaspoon Splenda

Combine ingredients in a bowl, stir well, and enjoy!

PER SERVING Calories: 51 | Fat: 0 g | Protein: 9 g | Sodium: 120 mg | Carbohydrates: 4 g | Fiber: 0 g

Forget the Ice Cream!

Instead of crawling into bed with a big bowl of ice cream, try this. It's sweet and creamy like ice cream, but it's far lower in calories and the high protein content will actually fill you up! Add some fresh fruit if you'd like some variety.

Fruit and Yogurt Parfait

This simple recipe is very flexible. Cream cheese, ricotta cheese, or even ice cream can all be used in place of the yogurt. Feel free to substitute seasonal fresh fruit for the blueberries.

Vegetarian, Low-calorie, Low-fat

INGREDIENTS | **SERVES 6–8**

1 cup sliced banana
1 cup fresh blueberries
1 cup plain or vanilla-flavored yogurt
1 tablespoon lime juice
¼ cup sweetened coconut flakes

Divide the sliced banana among 4 wine or parfait glasses, then the blueberries, and finally the yogurt. Drizzle with the lime juice and sprinkle the coconut flakes over the top. Chill in the refrigerator, and serve.

PER SERVING Calories: 121 | Fat: 2 g | Protein: 2 g | Sodium: 24 g | Carbohydrates: 16 g | Fiber: 1.5 g

Homemade Graham Cracker Crust

Egg white helps hold together the crumbs and reduces the fat in this crisp and crunchy pie crust.

Low-calorie

INGREDIENTS | **SERVES 8**

9 double low-fat graham crackers
2 tablespoons finely chopped walnuts
2 tablespoons brown sugar
2 tablespoons butter, melted
1 egg white, slightly beaten

1. Preheat oven to 375°F. Crush graham crackers until very fine crumbs form. In a medium bowl, combine with walnuts and brown sugar; toss to mix well.

2. Add melted butter and egg white; mix well with a fork until well blended. Press mixture onto bottom and up sides of 9" pie plate.

3. Bake pie crust for 8 to 10 minutes or until set. Cool completely on wire rack before filling.

PER SERVING Calories: 119 | Fat: 4 g | Protein: 2 g | Sodium: 125 mg | Carbohydrates: 48 g | Fiber: 1 g

Buttermilk Fruit Sherbet

This almost-instant dessert can be served as is or topped with a dessert sauce.

Vegetarian, Low-calorie, Low-fat

INGREDIENTS | SERVES 4

2 cups frozen blueberries

1 cup frozen raspberries

¾ cup low-fat buttermilk, divided

2 tablespoons honey

Pinch salt

1 teaspoon vanilla

Sweeten the Pot with Honey

Even if you're used to desserts and drinks made with refined sugar, don't be afraid to give honey-sweetened options a try. Honey is a natural sweetener, so it isn't typically processed and refined the way white and brown sugars are. Look for all-natural, organic varieties of honey in your local natural foods store.

1. In a food processor, combine frozen berries with ½ cup buttermilk; process until berries are chopped.

2. Continue processing, adding remaining ¼ cup buttermilk, honey, salt, and vanilla. Uncover and stir, then process again until mixture is smooth and has the texture of frozen custard. Don't overprocess. Serve immediately.

PER SERVING Calories: 66 | Fat: 1 g | Protein: 2 g | Sodium: 33 mg | Carbohydrates: 20 g | Fiber: 2.3 g

Frozen Yogurt with Berry Sauce

This beautiful dessert can be made any time of year. It's nice to serve in the winter, when fresh fruits are more expensive and of lesser quality.

Vegetarian, Low-calorie, Low-fat

INGREDIENTS | SERVES 4

1 (10-ounce) package frozen strawberries, thawed

1 teaspoon vanilla

½ cup raspberries

1 tablespoon lemon juice

1 pint low-fat frozen vanilla yogurt

1. In a blender or food processor, combine strawberries, vanilla, raspberries, and lemon juice; blend or process until smooth.

2. Spoon yogurt into 4 dessert dishes and top with strawberry sauce. Sauce can be stored, covered, in refrigerator up to 4 days. Use for other things, like topping cake or other fruits.

PER SERVING Calories: 187 | Fat: 2 g | Protein: 7 g | Sodium: 69 mg | Carbohydrates: 34 g | Fiber: 3 g

Berry Combinations

Use your imagination when making sauces with fresh or frozen berries. Blackberries and raspberries are delicious together, as are boysenberries and blueberries. Use this basic formula to make the sauce. The sauce can be frozen after it is made; freeze in pint containers for up to 3 months. To thaw, let stand in refrigerator overnight.

Baked Pears

This recipe may not sound like much, but it can be the perfect finish after a hearty meal when all you want is something small and sweet.

Vegetarian, Low-calorie, Low-fat

INGREDIENTS | SERVES 6

2 tablespoons lemon juice

6 pears, peeled

4 tablespoons sugar

3 cups nonfat frozen yogurt

Baked Fruit

Baked fruit is a simple and nutritious low-fat dessert. You can make this dessert using other fruits like peaches or apples. The peaches would bake for about 15 minutes, and apples for about 40 to 50 minutes. Also think about adding some spices to the sugar glaze; cinnamon, cardamom, and nutmeg are delicious.

1. Preheat oven to 375°F. Place lemon juice in a 2-quart baking dish and add just enough water to cover the bottom. Cut pears in half, remove cores, and place pears in baking dish, cut-side down. Cover and bake until pears are tender when pierced with a knife, 20 to 25 minutes.

2. Remove from oven and sprinkle each pear with 2 teaspoons sugar. Bake, uncovered, for 10 minutes longer to glaze. Serve warm or chilled with frozen yogurt.

PER SERVING Calories: 143 | Fat: 0 g | Protein: 5 g | Sodium: 1 mg | Carbohydrates: 27 g | Fiber: 3 g

Banana Nut Cake

You can drizzle honey over each slice of cake to add some scrumptious sweetness.

Low-fat, Low-calorie

INGREDIENTS | SERVES 16

1 (18-ounce) box yellow cake mix
½ cup chopped walnuts
1 cup fat-free milk
1 cup mashed bananas
1 cup Egg Beaters
1 tablespoon olive oil

Don't Throw Away Brown Bananas!

Overripe bananas work best for this recipe because they are easier to mash. If you have way too many overripe bananas, refrigerate them to keep the flesh firm and use them in banana baking recipes. They also make fantastic additions to any shake or smoothie.

1. Preheat oven to 350°F.

2. Lightly spray a 9" × 13" cooking pan and set aside.

3. In a large mixing bowl, combine the cake mix and walnuts.

4. Add the milk, bananas, Egg Beaters, and oil, and mix well.

5. Spread batter into baking pan.

6. Bake for 30 minutes or until browned on top.

PER SERVING Calories: 199 | Fat: 4 g | Protein: 4 g | Sodium: 120 mg | Carbohydrates: 30 g | Fiber: 3 g

Chocolate Chip Banana Cake

The only thing missing from unsweetened applesauce is several scoops of sugar. The flavors are almost identical, so save the calories and always choose the unsweetened variety.

Low-calorie

INGREDIENTS | SERVES 9

¾ cup whole-wheat flour

¾ cup all-purpose flour

1 teaspoon baking powder

¼ teaspoon baking soda

¾ cup Splenda

⅛ teaspoon salt

⅔ cup dark chocolate chips

⅔ cup mashed ripe bananas

⅓ cup unsweetened applesauce

⅓ cup fat-free plain yogurt

½ cup Egg Beaters

1 teaspoon banana extract

1. Preheat oven to 350°F.

2. Combine flour, baking powder, baking soda, Splenda, salt, and chocolate chips in a large bowl and stir well. Add remaining ingredients; stir until smooth.

3. Pour batter into an 8" square pan. Bake for 30 minutes. Cool and cut into 9 squares.

PER SERVING Calories: 163 | Fat: 4 g | Protein: 5 g | Sodium: 146 mg | Carbohydrates: 33 g | Fiber: 3 g

Caramel Sour Cream Cake

Drizzle this cake with some purchased caramel ice cream topping for a decadent dessert with a minimal amount of calories!

Low-calorie

INGREDIENTS | SERVES 16

1 cup sour cream
½ cup sugar
½ cup brown sugar
2 eggs
2 teaspoons vanilla
1¾ cups flour
1 teaspoon baking powder
1 teaspoon baking soda
¼ teaspoon salt
¼ teaspoon ground nutmeg

Mmm . . . Caramel

Caramel is created when sugar is melted. When sugar is melted and reaches 338°F, the molecules in the sugar begin to break down and recombine to form other compounds. These new compounds create the color and complex, rich flavor of caramel. Brown sugar does not break down into caramel; it's regular granulated sugar combined with molasses.

1. Preheat oven to 350°F. Grease 9" × 13" pan with unsalted butter and set aside.

2. In a large bowl, combine sour cream and sugar; beat well. Add brown sugar and beat. Add eggs, one at a time, beating well after each addition. Stir in vanilla.

3. Sift flour with baking powder, baking soda, salt, and nutmeg. Stir into sour cream mixture and beat at medium speed for 1 minute. Pour into prepared pan.

4. Bake for 25 to 35 minutes or until cake pulls away from sides of pan and top springs back when lightly touched in center. Cool completely on wire rack; store covered at room temperature.

PER SERVING Calories: 140 | Fat: 4 g | Protein: 3 g | Sodium: 125 mg | Carbohydrates: 24 g | Fiber: 2 g

Light and Sweet Strawberry Pie

This light and airy dessert is delicious when strawberries are in season. Garnish with a few whole berries.

Low-calorie

INGREDIENTS | SERVES 8

1 Homemade Graham Cracker Crust
(page 165)
2 pasteurized egg whites
⅛ teaspoon cream of tartar
¼ teaspoon lemon juice
⅓ cup sugar
1½ cups sliced strawberries

1. Bake and cool the pie crust; set aside. In a large bowl, combine egg white with cream of tartar and lemon juice. Beat until foamy, then add the sugar and strawberries. Continue to beat until the mixture holds soft peaks, about 10 to 12 minutes.

2. Spoon into pie crust and chill thoroughly before serving. Pie can also be frozen; let stand at room temperature for 15 minutes before slicing.

PER SERVING Calories: 250 | Fat: 5 g | Protein: 2 g | Sodium: 156 mg | Carbohydrates: 48 g | Fiber: 3 g

Egg White Foams

Egg white foams are created when air is beaten into egg whites. You'll have a higher foam if you let the egg white stand at room temperature for about 20 minutes before you start beating. Cream of tartar and lemon juice help stabilize the foam by adding acid to the protein web of the foam.

Easy, Low-Fat Key Lime Pie

Premade graham cracker crusts are sold at most grocery stores and make piemaking much more doable.

INGREDIENTS | SERVES 8

½ cup Egg Beaters
½ cup Key lime juice
1 (14-ounce) can fat-free condensed milk
4 egg whites
½ teaspoon cream of tartar
½ cup Splenda
1 prepared graham cracker crust

What's a Key Lime?

Key limes are a unique breed of limes often as small as a ping-pong ball or as large as a golf ball. They are also incredibly aromatic, which makes them a delight in the kitchen. Key limes are not indigenous to the Florida Keys, but they've earned their resident status.

1. Preheat oven to 350°F.

2. In a medium mixing bowl, mix Egg Beaters, Key lime juice, and fat-free condensed milk for filling.

3. In a small mixing bowl, beat egg whites and cream of tartar until peaks form. Slowly beat in Splenda until stiff but not dry to form the meringue.

4. Fold ¼ of the meringue into pie filling. Pour into pie shell. Spread remaining meringue on top of pie, extending to the edge of the shell.

5. Bake for 12 to 15 minutes or until golden brown. Cool and chill well before serving.

PER SERVING Calories: 307 | Fat: 7 g | Protein: 8 g | Sodium: 270 mg | Carbohydrates: 55 g | Fiber: 1 g

Peanut Butter Chocolate Bars

This crunchy and creamy bar cookie is really delicious, and only ⅓ of its calories come from fat!

Low-calorie

INGREDIENTS | **MAKES 36 SQUARES**

5 tablespoons butter, softened

⅓ cup reduced-fat peanut butter

1 egg

1 egg white

1 cup brown sugar

1 cup flour

¾ cup crisp peanut butter–flavored cereal squares, finely crushed

1 cup quick-cooking oatmeal

¼ teaspoon salt

½ teaspoon baking soda

1 (13-ounce) can nonfat sweetened condensed milk

2 cups semisweet chocolate chips

1. Preheat oven to 350°F. Spray a 9" × 13"- baking pan with nonstick cooking spray containing flour; set aside.

2. In a large bowl combine butter, peanut butter, egg, and egg white; beat until combined. Add brown sugar and beat until smooth. Stir in flour, finely crushed cereal, oatmeal, salt, and baking soda and mix until crumbly. Press half into prepared pan.

3. In a medium microwave-safe bowl, combine sweetened condensed milk and 1½ cups chocolate chips; microwave on 50 percent power for 2 minutes, then remove and stir until smooth. Spoon evenly over the crumbs in pan.

4. Top with remaining ½ cup chocolate chips, then remaining crumbs; press down lightly. Bake for 20 to 25 minutes or until bars are set. Cool completely, then cut into squares to serve.

PER SERVING Calories: 190 | Fat: 6 g | Protein: 5 g | Sodium: 61 mg | Carbohydrates: 39 g | Fiber: 2 g

Brazilian-Style Passion Fruit Pudding

For best results, chill the coconut milk before use, and then use only the thickened top cream—do not include the thin coconut water at the bottom of the can. The acidic quality of the fruit thickens the mixture until it becomes firm.

Vegetarian

INGREDIENTS | SERVES 6

1 (14-ounce) can coconut milk, well chilled

1 (14-ounce) can sweetened condensed milk

1 (16.8-ounce) bottle passion fruit concentrate

2 cups cubed pound cake

1 cup toasted shredded coconut

Fresh fruits such as cut-up strawberries or blueberries as garnish

What Is Passion Fruit?

A tropical fruit native to Brazil, passion fruit has a subtle sweetness and perfume that only enhances its appeal. Its nectar is often blended into a fruit drink and a passion fruit concentrate, which you need for this recipe, is readily available at Hispanic markets. You may also find a frozen concentrate, but it does not produce the same results.

1. Carefully scoop out the thick layer of coconut milk and put it into a bowl. Beat the milk until it thickens and resembles partially whipped heavy cream. Stir in the condensed milk. Fill the condensed milk can with the passion fruit concentrate and pour it into the mixing bowl. Stir well to combine the milks and juice.

2. Line the bottom of a 2-quart dessert bowl with the pound cake. Pour the passion fruit mixture over top and chill until firm. To serve, sprinkle the toasted coconut over the pudding, spoon the mixture into individual bowls, and garnish with fresh fruits as desired.

PER SERVING Calories: 680 | Fat: 32 g | Carbohydrates: 86 g | Protein: 12 g | Sodium: 270 mg | Fiber: 1 g

Ginger Tapioca Pudding

A lively ginger syrup adds a hint of the exotic to this old-fashioned favorite. To make the syrup, use about 2 fresh ginger thinly sliced and cooked with ½ cup brown sugar in 1 cup water. Boil this mixture for about 5 minutes, cool, and strain, discarding the ginger.

INGREDIENTS | **SERVES 4**

½ cup pearl tapioca soaked in 1 cup water for at least 12 hours

1 cup ginger syrup

1½ cups coconut milk

2 eggs, well beaten

6 coconut macaroons, crumbled

What Is Pearl Tapioca?

The old-fashioned tapioca pudding called for using the regular, not instant, pearl tapioca made from the starch of the cassava plant. Larger and harder than the instant tapioca pearls, these require soaking for at least 12 hours, but preferably for up to 24 hours. Otherwise, they never quite soften during cooking. Despite this advance planning, the pudding is really worth the effort.

1. Combine the tapioca, ginger syrup, and coconut milk and pour into a large saucepan. Beat in the eggs and heat over medium-low heat, stirring constantly as the mixture begins to thicken.

2. Meanwhile, sprinkle the crumbled macaroons into the bottom of a 1½-quart dessert dish.

3. When the tapioca pudding has thickened, spoon it into the dessert dish and completely chill until firm.

PER SERVING Calories: 520 | Fat: 25 g | Protein: 6 g | Sodium: 150 mg | Carbohydrates: 73 g | Fiber: 2 g

Banana Mousse

Garnish each serving with 1 or 2 extra banana slices and sprinkle with nutmeg if desired.

Vegetarian, Gluten-free

INGREDIENTS | SERVES 6–8

3 large bananas, mashed

2 cups whipping cream

3 tablespoons powdered sugar

2 tablespoons lemon juice

¼ teaspoon (or to taste) ground nutmeg

1 tablespoon rum, optional

Mousse Is a Must

Mousse is a form of creamy dessert typically made from egg and cream, usually in combination with other flavors such as chocolate or fruit. This recipe, which uses whipped cream, is a bit of a shortcut but no less delicious.

1. Purée the bananas in a blender. Whip the cream at medium-high speed until it forms high peaks. Add the powdered sugar and whip briefly until it forms soft peaks (the mixture should be light and fluffy).

2. Fold the whipped cream into the mashed banana. Carefully stir in the lemon juice, nutmeg, and rum, if using. Spoon into parfait glasses.

PER SERVING Calories: 292 | Fat: 22 g | Protein: 2 g | Sodium: 23 mg | Carbohydrates: 24 g | Fiber: 2.6 g

Summer Fruit Compote

This delicious fruit compote is great on a chilly spring morning or a cool summer evening.

Vegan, Lactose-free, High-fiber, Gluten-free, Low-fat

INGREDIENTS | MAKES 2 CUPS

2 medium bananas

⅓ cup granulated sugar

1 cup water

1 teaspoon peeled and grated fresh ginger

¼ cup lemon juice

4 (5-inch) cinnamon sticks

3 cups dried tropical fruit

1. Peel and slice the bananas.

2. Cook the sugar and water in a saucepan over low heat, stirring to dissolve sugar. Add ginger, lemon juice, and cinnamon sticks. Increase heat to medium and bring to a boil. Reduce heat to low and simmer for 5 minutes. Add dried fruit and bananas. Return to a boil. Reduce heat to low, cover, and simmer until the dried fruit is tender. Remove the cinnamon sticks.

3. Let cool briefly and serve warm, or refrigerate overnight and serve cold.

PER SERVING Calories: 439 | Fat: 0.5 g | Protein: 1.7g | Sodium: 4 g | Carbohydrates: 88 g | Fiber: 5 g

Apple Strawberry Crumble

Even though you'll peel the apples in this recipe, the apple peel is full of fiber, so don't throw it out. Instead, munch on it while the crumble is baking, or chop it up and throw it in a salad.

Low-calorie, Low-fat, High-fiber

INGREDIENTS | SERVES 4

2 cups green apples, peeled and chopped

2 cups strawberries, chopped

¼ cup Egg Beaters

1 mashed ripe banana

1 cup oatmeal

¼ cup Splenda brown sugar

½ teaspoon cinnamon

Fat-free whipped cream to top

1. Combine apples and strawberries and pour into a baking dish. Combine other ingredients except whipped cream and pile on top of the fruit.

2. Bake at 350°F for 10 to 15 minutes, or until golden brown and bubbling. Top with a squirt of fat-free whipped cream.

PER SERVING Calories: 233 | Fat: 2 g | Protein: 5 g | Sodium: 228 mg | Carbohydrates: 47 g | Fiber: 6 g

CHAPTER 11

Brain Food: Good-for-You Snacks

Banana Malted Soy Milk Shake

The bananas are the prime source of fiber in this lovely smoothie. If you like chocolate, make this using chocolate frozen yogurt instead of vanilla.

Vegetarian, High-fiber

INGREDIENTS | SERVES 2

2 bananas

2 tablespoons malt powder

1 cup vanilla frozen yogurt

½ cup soymilk

1 teaspoon honey

Place all ingredients in a blender and blend until smooth.

PER SERVING Calories: 329 | Fat: 4 g | Protein: 9 g | Sodium: 98 mg | Carbohydrates: 67 g | Fiber: 5 g

Celery Peanut Butter Boats

Crisp and spicy, celery is perfect with savory or slightly sweet fillings. Celery adds fiber to anything you pile into it, and its crunch is important in snacks.

Vegetarian, Gluten-free, Low-calorie, Lactose-free

INGREDIENTS | SERVES 4

4 ribs of celery, washed or wiped clean

½ cup crunchy peanut butter

2 tablespoons toasted sesame seeds

1. Fill celery ribs with peanut butter and smooth out the top.

2. Cut the celery on the diagonal into 1" slices.

3. Sprinkle the sesame seeds over the bites and serve.

PER SERVING Calories: 217 | Fat: 18 g | Protein: 9 g | Sodium: 48 mg | Carbohydrates: 9 g | Fiber: 3 g

Red Bean Ice Cream Shake

Red bean paste is a sweetened purée found in Asian groceries. Substitute red bean ice cream for the paste if available. Red bean paste is an excellent source of both protein and fiber. There is also some protein in the ice cream and milk.

Vegetarian, High-fiber

INGREDIENTS | SERVES 2

1 pint vanilla ice cream

1½ cups red bean paste

1 cup milk

Combine everything in a blender and blend until smooth.

PER SERVING Calories: 634 | Fat: 26 g | Protein: 23 g | Sodium: 188 mg | Carbohydrates: 80 g | Fiber: 17 g

Make Your Own

To make your own sweet red beans, which can be puréed in a food processor to make red bean paste, soak 1 cup dried adzuki beans in water overnight. Drain and put the beans in a saucepan with 4 cups water and simmer for 90 minutes. Stir in ½ cup sugar and cook for 10 more minutes, stirring often. Squash the beans with a wooden spoon in the saucepan and stir to thicken. Remove from heat and purée in a food processor for a smoother paste. Chill in the refrigerator before using.

Peanutty Bananas

Try this recipe with almond or cashew butter for variation. Honey may also be substituted for the brown rice syrup.

Vegetarian, High-fiber

INGREDIENTS | SERVES 4

3 bananas
1 cup crunchy peanut butter
¼ cup brown rice syrup
1 cup granola

1. Peel the bananas and cut them into quarters crosswise.

2. Stand the banana pieces cut-sides up on a platter. (Cut the pointed tips off the end pieces so they can stand up.)

3. Mix the peanut butter with the brown rice syrup in a glass bowl and microwave on high for 15 to 20 seconds. Stir together well.

4. Spoon the peanut butter mixture onto the banana pieces.

5. Sprinkle granola over the peanut butter and serve.

PER SERVING Calories: 615 | Fat: 33 g | Protein: 19 g | Sodium: 45 mg | Carbohydrates: 68 g | Fiber: 7 g

Trail Mix

Pack individual servings of this to take with you when you're on campus all day so you have something to snack on if you don't have time to stop for a meal.

Vegetarian, High-fiber

INGREDIENTS | SERVES 8

2 cups dried cherries

2 cups roasted pecans

1 cup M&Ms

2 cups granola

1 cup shelled sunflower seeds

1 cup Pretzel Goldfish

1. Combine everything in a large bowl.

2. Divide into individual portions and store in resealable plastic bags or serve in individual paper cups.

PER SERVING Calories: 647 | Fat: 35 g | Protein: 12 g | Sodium: 46 mg | Carbohydrates: 73 g | Fiber: 9 g

Sweets and Fiber

The more fiber you add to a sweet snack, the easier it is to pass it out of the body. Add nuts for high fiber and protein. Walnuts, almonds, and pecans are readily available. Add some seeds—especially sesame seeds—for more fiber. Flavorful seeds, such as poppy seeds, anise, caraway, and celery seeds, are more an addition to flavor than raw fiber. Add them anyway because every little bit counts.

Almond-Stuffed Dates

Combining almonds and dates is a delicious way to create candylike sweets that are fiber-rich.
If you roast or toast the almonds, they will be crunchier and more satisfying.

Vegetarian, Low-calorie, High-fiber, Lactose-free

INGREDIENTS | SERVES 6

1 cup powdered sugar
12 Medjool dates
½ cup whole almonds

Dates and Nuts

Dates are loaded with dietary fiber and they're sweet to the point of being gooey. If you love sweets, mix them with almonds to scrub out your colon and eat almond-filled high-fiber dates rather than candy.

1. Place the powdered sugar in a bowl.

2. Cut a slit on one side of each date and remove the pit. Replace it with an almond.

3. Roll the dates in the powdered sugar.

PER SERVING Calories: 194 | Fat: 6 g | Protein: 3 g | Sodium: 1 mg | Carbohydrates: 34 g | Fiber: 3 g

Apple Cheddar Rye Rounds

Your fiber here comes from the caraway seeds, the rye flour, and the apples. If you leave the skin on, this snack is even higher in fiber.

Vegetarian, Low-calorie

INGREDIENTS | SERVES 4

8 slices rye bread with caraway seeds
1 tablespoon Dijon mustard
½ cup diced apples, skin on
½ cup shredded Cheddar cheese

1. Preheat broiler and cut 2 circles out of each slice of bread with a small cookie cutter or champagne glass. Discard the crusts.

2. Mix the Dijon mustard, apples, and Cheddar cheese together in a bowl.

3. Spread apple mixture onto each round evenly and place on a foil-lined baking sheet. Broil for 3 to 5 minutes. Let cool before eating.

PER SERVING Calories: 236 | Fat: 7 g | Protein: 9 g | Sodium: 407 mg | Carbohydrates: 34 g | Fiber: 4 g

Caramel Nut Apple Wedges

Another way to serve this is to arrange the undipped apple wedges on a platter and let diners dip their own apples into the caramel and hazelnuts.

Vegetarian, High-fiber

INGREDIENTS | SERVES 6

1 pound of caramels, unwrapped

¼ cup evaporated milk

2 cups chopped hazelnuts

2 red apples

1 Golden Delicious apple

2 Granny Smith apples

Oh, the Sweetness

This recipe includes the best of both worlds: natural sweetness from the apples and artificial sweetness from the candy. Every once in a while you have to give yourself a treat, and this one is especially fun in the fall after a trip to the apple orchard!

1. Melt the caramels and evaporated milk over low heat.

2. Toast the hazelnuts in the oven for 12 minutes at 350°F.

3. Cut the apples into quarters, cut out the cores, and cut the quarters into slices for dipping.

4. Dip the apple wedges into the caramel and then in the hazelnuts. Place the wedges on waxed paper.

5. Refrigerate for 15 minutes or until caramel is set.

PER SERVING Calories: 596 | Fat: 29 g | Protein: 10 g | Sodium: 12 mg | Carbohydrates: 81 g | Fiber: 7 g

Energy Bites

Take these with you when you head to campus for a long day of classes and errands. You'll always have something healthy to snack on.

Low-calorie, Vegetarian

INGREDIENTS | SERVES 12

½ cup honey
½ cup peanut butter
1 cup nonfat dry milk
1 cup uncooked quick-cook rolled oats
½ cup raisins
2 cups crushed corn flakes cereal

Protein Power

These yummy bites are great to have on hand for quick energy. There's a good amount of protein in the peanut butter and milk, and the peanut butter, oats, raisins, and corn flakes give this snack high fiber.

1. Mix the honey and peanut butter together.

2. Add the dry milk, oats, and raisins. Mix together well.

3. Roll the mixture into 2 dozen balls.

4. Roll the balls in the crushed cereal.

5. Cover and refrigerate.

PER SERVING Calories: 191 | Fat: 6 g | Protein: 6 g | Sodium: 78 mg | Carbohydrates: 31 g | Fiber: 2 g

Apricot Oat Cakes

These are like a bowl of oatmeal to go. They're a great alternative to purchased energy bars. You get protein from the egg and yogurt and lots of fiber from the oatmeal and apricots.

Low-fat, High-fiber

INGREDIENTS | SERVES 8

3 cups rolled oats

2 cups flour

¼ teaspoon baking powder

1 egg white

⅓ cup plain yogurt

½ cup sugar

½ cup honey

½ teaspoon vanilla extract

½ cup dried apricots, chopped

1. Preheat oven to 325°F.

2. Pulse the oats in a food processor 10 times, then add the flour and baking powder and pulse to mix.

3. In a bowl, whisk the egg white until frothy, then add the yogurt, sugar, honey, and vanilla. Add the oat mixture and dried apricots to the yogurt mixture. Mix with a wooden spoon.

4. Roll the mixture into 8 balls and flatten them into thick, cylindrical patties.

5. Bake them on a parchment-lined baking sheet for 15 to 20 minutes. Let cool and refrigerate unless eating right away.

PER SERVING Calories: 378 | Fat: 3 g | Protein: 9 g | Sodium: 32 mg | Carbohydrates: 81 g | Fiber: 5 g

Chickpeas with Parmesan Spread

This spread can be served hot or cold. Omit the hot sauce altogether if you have sensitive taste buds.

Low-calorie, Low-fat, Vegetarian

INGREDIENTS | SERVES 2

½ cup canned chickpeas, drained

2 tablespoons freshly grated Parmesan cheese

Few drops hot sauce

1. Mash chickpeas with fork in a small bowl or mix in a blender until smooth.

2. Mix Parmesan cheese with chickpea mixture.

3. Add hot sauce and blend well. Serve with pita bread crisps.

PER SERVING Calories: 100 | Fat: 3 g | Protein: 6 g | Sodium: 109 mg | Carbohydrates: 14 g | Fiber: 4.3 g

Fried Zucchini Sticks

You don't have to deep-fry these zucchini sticks; just sauté them in a bit of oil if you prefer. This makes a great appetizer or snack.

Vegan, Low-calorie

INGREDIENTS | SERVES 4

¾ cup flour

½ teaspoon garlic powder

¾ teaspoon Italian seasoning

¼ teaspoon salt

4 zucchinis, cut into strips

Oil for frying

1. In a large bowl or pan, combine the flour, garlic powder, Italian seasonings, and salt.

2. Lightly toss the zucchini strips with the flour mixture, coating well.

3. Heat oil in a large skillet or frying pan. When oil is hot, gently add zucchini strips to pan. Fry until lightly golden brown on all sides.

PER SERVING Calories: 178 | Fat: 7 g | Protein: 5 g | Sodium: 166 mg | Carbohydrates: 18 g | Fiber: 3 g |

Vegan Tzatziki

Use a vegan soy yogurt to make this classic Greek dip, which is best served very cold. A nondairy sour cream may be used instead of the soy yogurt, if you prefer.

Vegan, Low-calorie, Low-fat, Low-carb, Lactose-free

INGREDIENTS | YIELDS 1½ CUPS

1½ cups vegan soy yogurt, plain or lemon flavored

1 tablespoon olive oil

1 tablespoon lemon juice

4 cloves garlic, minced

2 cucumbers, grated or chopped fine

1 tablespoon chopped fresh mint or fresh dill

1. Whisk together yogurt with olive oil and lemon juice until well combined.

2. Combine with remaining ingredients.

3. Chill for at least 1 hour before serving to allow flavors to mingle. Serve cold.

PER ¼ CUP Calories: 76 | Fat: 3 g | Protein: 2 g | Sodium: 10 mg | Carbohydrates: 10 g | Fiber: 1 g

What Is Tzatziki?

Tzatziki is a Greek appetizer that is also used as a sauce for Greek dishes such as souvlaki and gyros. It is made of strained yogurt (usually sheep's-milk or goat's-milk varieties) with cucumbers, garlic, salt, olive oil, and pepper. Some variations also include lemon juice and parsley or mint.

Simple Scallion Pancakes

Whether you eat them as an accompaniment to a Chinese feast, or just as a snack or appetizer, these salty fried pancakes are a popular street food snack served up hot in East Asia. Plain soy sauce is the perfect dip.

Vegan, Lactose-free, Low-calorie

INGREDIENTS | YIELDS 6 LARGE PANCAKES

2 cups flour
½ teaspoon salt
2½ teaspoons sesame oil
¾ cup hot water
6 scallions, chopped (green parts only)
Oil for frying
Soy sauce for dipping

1. In a large bowl, combine flour and salt. Slowly add 2 teaspoons sesame oil and water, mixing just until a dough forms. You may need a little bit less than ¾ cup water.

2. Knead dough for a few minutes, then let sit for 30 minutes.

3. Divide dough into 6 (2") balls. Roll out each ball on a lightly floured surface. Brush with remaining sesame oil and cover with scallions. Roll up dough and twist to form a ball. Roll out again ¼" thick.

4. Fry each pancake in hot oil 1 to 2 minutes on each side. Slice into squares or wedges and serve with soy sauce.

PER 1 PANCAKE Calories: 232 | Fat: 9 g | Protein: 5 g | Sodium: 198 mg | Carbohydrates: 32 g | Fiber: 2 g

Herbed Potato Chips

Forget those store-bought chips in the shiny bag. These taste better and are better for you!

Low-calorie, Low-carb, Vegetarian

INGREDIENTS | MAKES 16 CUPS

Cold water

Ice cubes

2 lemons, juiced

1 russet potato (about 1 pound)

3 cups canola oil

1 tablespoon minced fresh dill weed

1 tablespoon minced thyme leaves

1 tablespoon salt, or to taste

Yes, You Can Make Chips!

Making your own potato chips is fun. You can sprinkle them with everything from dried herbs and spices to finely grated cheese. Eat them on their own as a snack or as an accompaniment to a healthy sandwich for lunch.

1. Fill a bowl with cold water and add ice cubes and juice from 2 lemons, along with the lemon rinds. Peel potato and cut into thin chips using a food processor, a mandoline, or a vegetable peeler. Each chip should be almost translucent. Place chips into the water mixture as soon as they are formed.

2. In large heavy pan, heat canola oil to 375°F. Working with a handful of potato chips at a time, remove from water and drain on kitchen towels, then pat dry with paper towels. Drop chips into the oil; fry for 3 to 6 minutes, turning with slotted spoon, until chips are light golden brown. Remove and place on paper towels; sprinkle hot chips with a mixture of the herbs and salt. Repeat with remaining chips and salt mixture.

3. Cool completely, then store in airtight container up to 3 days.

PER SERVING Calories: 57 | Fat: 4 g | Protein: 0.6 g | Sodium: 420 mg | Carbohydrates: 4 g | Fiber: 0.37 g

Cheesy Tomato Bruschetta

This flavorful tomato topping can be used in other recipes, too. Fold some into mayonnaise for an appetizer dip, or use it to top broiled chicken or fish.

Low-calorie, Vegetarian

INGREDIENTS | **SERVES 10**

¼ cup tomato paste

2 tablespoons olive oil

1 (14-ounce) can diced Italian tomatoes, drained

3 cloves garlic, minced

1 teaspoon dried basil leaves

1 cup grated Parmesan cheese

16 (½) slices Italian bread

1. Preheat broiler in oven; set oven rack 6" from heat source.

2. In medium bowl, combine tomato paste and olive oil; blend well until smooth. Add remaining ingredients except for bread and mix gently.

3. Place bread slices on broiler pan. Broil bread slices until golden on one side, about 1 to 3 minutes. Turn and broil until light golden brown on second side. Remove from oven and top with tomato mixture. Return to oven and broil for 3 to 5 minutes or until tomato topping is bubbly and begins to brown. Serve immediately.

PER SERVING Calories: 227 | Fat: 7 g | Protein: 1 g | Sodium: 102 mg | Carbohydrates: 31 g | Fiber: 2 g

Tex-Mex Popcorn

Popcorn is a great snack that you can dress up in infinite ways. If Tex-Mex isn't your favorite, use Italian spices or try an Asian touch.

Low-calorie, Low-carb, Vegetarian

INGREDIENTS | MAKES 8 CUPS

8 cups air-popped popcorn
½ cup butter
1 jalapeño pepper, minced
4 cloves garlic, minced
1 tablespoon chili powder
1 teaspoon cumin
1 teaspoon salt
⅛ teaspoon cayenne pepper
½ cup grated Cotija cheese

How to Pop Popcorn

You can pop popcorn with just a pan and a stove burner. Add a tablespoon of oil to the pan. You will need about ½ cup of popcorn kernels to make 10 cups of popped corn. Place the pan over high heat and add the popcorn. Gently shake the pan until the popcorn starts to pop, then put the cover on and keep shaking until the popping slows to 1 pop every 2 seconds.

1. Preheat oven to 300°F. In large bowl, place popcorn. In small saucepan, heat butter over medium heat until melted. Stir in jalapeño; cook and stir for 1 minute. Then add garlic; cook and stir for 2 minutes longer until fragrant. Remove from heat and add chili powder and cumin. Drizzle over popcorn and toss to coat.

2. Sprinkle salt, cayenne pepper, and Cotija cheese over popcorn and toss to coat. Spread on large cookie sheet. Bake for 20 to 25 minutes, stirring once during baking time, until popcorn is glazed. Cool on paper towels. Store in airtight container at room temperature.

PER SERVING Calories 165 | Fat: 14 g | Protein: 3.7 g | Sodium: 121 mg | Carbohydrates: 8 g | Fiber: 1.5 g

Gingerbread Fruit Dip

This dip is wonderful served with fresh fruits like apple and pear slices, banana slices, and strawberries.

Low-calorie, Low-carb, Vegetarian

INGREDIENTS | SERVES 12

1 (8-ounce) package cream cheese, softened

½ cup low-fat sour cream

⅓ cup brown sugar

¼ cup maple syrup or light molasses

2 tablespoons chopped candied ginger

½ teaspoon ground ginger

½ teaspoon cinnamon

¼ teaspoon nutmeg

1. In medium bowl, beat cream cheese until light and fluffy. Gradually add sour cream, beating until smooth. Add sugar and beat well. Gradually add molasses and beat until smooth. Stir in remaining ingredients.

2. Cover and chill for at least 3 hours before serving with fresh fruit.

PER SERVING Calories: 126 | Fat: 8 g | Protein: 1.8 g | Sodium: 63 mg | Carbohydrates: 12 g | Fiber: 0 g

Candied Ginger

Candied ginger is also known as crystallized ginger. It is made of pieces of ginger root simmered in a sugar syrup, then rolled in sugar. You can make your own by combining ¾ cup sugar with ¾ cup water and bringing to a simmer. Add ½ cup peeled and chopped fresh ginger root; simmer for 25 minutes. Drain, dry, then roll in sugar to coat.

Cinnamon Curry Fruit Dip

The sweet tartness of peaches combines beautifully with curry powder.
This special dip can be served as a snack or a dessert.

Low-calorie, Low-carb, Vegetarian

INGREDIENTS | SERVES 8

1 peach
1 teaspoon curry powder
½ teaspoon cinnamon
¼ cup brown sugar
½ cup low-fat sour cream
1 (3-ounce) package cream cheese, softened

1. Peel peach and remove stone; cut peach into slices. Place in food processor or blender along with curry powder, cinnamon, brown sugar, sour cream, and cream cheese and blend until smooth.

2. Place in refrigerator and chill for at least 4 hours before serving. Serve with fruit and bread.

PER SERVING Calories: 88 | Fat: 6 g | Protein: 2.1 g | Sodium: 42 mg | Carbohydrates: 9 g | Fiber: 1 g

Apple Jell-O Cups

You can use cranberry or lemon Jell-O instead of lime; any flavor will taste fantastic.

Vegetarian, Low-calorie, Low-fat

INGREDIENTS | SERVES 2

1 (3-ounce) package sugar-free lime Jell-O
1 apple
2 tablespoons light Cool Whip topping

1. Make Jell-O according to directions and refrigerate.

2. Peel and chop apple into small pieces.

3. When Jell-O is slightly thickened, remove, and add chopped apple. Refrigerate again until firm.

4. Serve each cup of Jell-O topped with 1 tablespoon whipped topping.

PER SERVING Calories: 235 | Fat: 1 g | Protein: 18 g | Sodium: 150 mg | Carbohydrates: 16 g | Fiber: 1.5 g

CHAPTER 12

Pass the Nachos:
College Grub Made Healthy

Simple Pita Chips

Change the flavor of your pita chips by adding a variety of toppings such as garlic and herbs, chili pepper, cinnamon, or Parmesan cheese.

Low-calorie, Low-fat, Vegetarian, Lactose-free

INGREDIENTS | SERVES 4

2 whole-wheat pitas

¼ teaspoon garlic powder

Cut each pita into 8 wedges. Place wedges on cookie sheet and sprinkle with garlic powder. Bake at 350°F for 10 to 15 minutes or until lightly brown and crisp.

PER SERVING Calories: 86 | Fat: 1 g | Protein: 3 g | Sodium: 170 mg | Carbohydrates: 18 g | Fiber: 2 g

Homemade Guacamole

Avocados are a unique fruit because they are naturally high in fat. Since you need some fat in your diet, guacamole makes a really healthy choice.

Low-calorie, Low-carb, Vegetarian, Gluten-free

INGREDIENTS | SERVES 4

2 ripe avocados, peeled and seeded

½ cup tomatoes, diced

½ teaspoon fresh garlic, minced

½ teaspoon salt

1 teaspoon green chili, finely minced

1 teaspoon freshly squeezed lemon juice

½ cup fat-free sour cream

Mix all ingredients to desired texture.

PER SERVING Calories: 187 | Fat: 15 g | Protein: 4 g | Sodium: 300 mg | Carbohydrates: 12 g | Fiber: 3 g

Baked Tortilla Chips

Instead of stocking up with bags of oily chips and crackers, keep corn tortillas in the fridge and bake up an exact amount of chips whenever the need arises.

Low-calorie, Low-fat, High-fiber

INGREDIENTS | SERVES 10

10 fat-free corn tortillas
Salt to taste

Try Different Varieties

You know how tortilla chips come in all kinds of flavors these days? So can your homemade chips! The trick is in selecting different kinds of tortillas. For example, try whole-wheat tortillas for a healthy option, or roasted red pepper tortillas for some extra color and flavor.

1. Preheat oven to 400°F. Cover 2 cookie sheets with nonstick spray. Cut each tortilla into 6 wedges. Scatter wedges onto cookie sheets.

2. Spray wedges with nonstick cooking spray and sprinkle with salt. Bake for 12 minutes.

PER SERVING Calories: 52 | Fat: 0 g | Protein: 2 g | Sodium: 156 mg | Carbohydrates: 11 g | Fiber: 5 g

Not-So-Sinful Potato Skins

Tough-skinned items like potatoes should be scrubbed with a vegetable brush under cool running water. Once clean, pat them dry with paper towels.

Low-calorie, Low-fat, Vegetarian

INGREDIENTS | SERVES 6

6 medium baking potatoes, washed
½ teaspoon salt
⅛ teaspoon black pepper
½ cup fat-free shredded Cheddar cheese
¼ cup green onions, sliced
½ cup fat-free sour cream

1. Cut potatoes in half and scoop out 90 percent of the pulp. Coat a large cookie sheet with nonstick spray.

2. Place potato halves on sheet and sprinkle with salt and pepper. Bake potatoes at 475°F for 10 to 15 minutes or until crispy.

3. Sprinkle potatoes with cheese and return to oven for 2 minutes. Sprinkle potatoes with onions and serve with a dollop of sour cream.

PER SERVING Calories: 173 | Fat: 0 g | Protein: 8 g | Sodium: 271 mg | Carbohydrates: 36 g | Fiber: 3 g

Fresh and Spicy Salsa

Combining fresh and roasted tomatoes adds a great depth of flavor to this easy salsa recipe.

Low-calorie, Low-fat, Low-carb, Vegetarian, Lactose-free

INGREDIENTS | MAKES 3 CUPS

3 pounds tomatoes
4 cloves garlic, minced
2 tablespoons olive oil
½ teaspoon salt
1 jalapeño pepper
1 green bell pepper, chopped
½ cup chopped red onion
2 tablespoons lemon juice
⅛ teaspoon cayenne pepper

Salsa Is Simple

Why buy prepared salsa at the store when you can make your own from scratch? Making salsa at home allows you to save money and customize according to your tastes. In the mood for a hearty bean salsa? Throw in some black or pinto beans. In the mood for a fresher garden salsa? Add in some fresh corn. The possibilities are endless.

1. Preheat oven to 400°F. Cut 3 tomatoes in half; place cut-side up on cookie sheet. Top each tomato with some garlic. Drizzle with olive oil and sprinkle with salt. Roast for 15 to 25 minutes or until tomatoes have some brown spots. Remove from oven and cool.

2. Chop remaining tomatoes and place in bowl. Seed and mince jalapeño and add to chopped tomatoes along with green bell pepper and red onion.

3. Chop cooled roasted tomatoes and add to salsa. Sprinkle with lemon juice and cayenne pepper and stir gently. Cover and chill for 1 to 2 hours before serving.

PER SERVING Calories: 48 | Fat 3 g | Protein: 4 g | Sodium: 45 mg | Carbohydrates: 6 g | Fiber: 4 g

Black Bean Veggie Dip

This colorful dip can be served with tortilla chips or fresh vegetables cut into strips.

Low-calorie, High-fiber, Vegetarian

INGREDIENTS | SERVES 6

1 (15-ounce) can black beans, rinsed and drained

1 tablespoon chili powder

1 teaspoon cumin

¼ teaspoon cayenne pepper

½ cup yogurt cheese

½ cup chopped fresh basil leaves

1 red bell pepper, diced

1 green bell pepper, diced

1 tomato, diced

1 avocado, diced

2 tablespoons grated Cotija cheese

1. Place rinsed and drained black beans in a medium bowl; add chili powder, cumin, and pepper and mash until smooth. Spread on a serving plate.

2. In a small bowl, combine yogurt and basil leaves. Spread over the beans. Top with the vegetables and cheese. Serve immediately.

PER SERVING Calories: 161 | Fat: 6 g | Protein: 21 g | Sodium: 366 mg | Carbohydrates: 34 g | Fiber: 10 g

Cotija Cheese

Cotija cheese is a hard grating cheese similar to Parmesan or Romano, but less expensive and with more flavor. You can find it in ethnic grocery stores, especially Mexican and Latino markets, and sometimes in the regular grocery store in the dairy aisle. It's a good substitute for other hard grating cheeses because you can use less.

Black Bean Nachos with Corn Tomato Salsa

Black beans, cornmeal tortilla chips, tomatoes, and corn all boost the fiber content, making this recipe a better choice than nacho chips with plain salsa.

High-fiber, Vegetarian

INGREDIENTS | SERVES 4

4 cups corn tortilla chips
1 cup cooked black beans
½ cup sour cream
2 cups shredded cheddar cheese
½ cup corn kernels
1 ripe tomato, diced
2 tablespoons chopped fresh cilantro
¼ cup diced red onion
1 tablespoon diced jalapeño pepper
¼ cup fresh lime juice
½ cup guacamole
2 tablespoons sliced black olives
1 tablespoon sliced green onions

1. Preheat the oven to 350°F.

2. Scatter the tortilla chips on an ovenproof platter and set aside.

3. Mash the black beans with half of the sour cream and put spoonfuls of the bean mixture all over the tortilla chips. Sprinkle the cheddar cheese over the tortilla chips and bake until the cheese melts, about 10 minutes.

4. Combine the corn kernels, tomato, cilantro, red onion, jalapeño pepper, and lime juice in a bowl. Remove the nachos from the oven and top them with the corn salsa, guacamole, olives, green onions, and the remaining sour cream. Serve immediately.

PER SERVING Calories: 582 | Fat: 38 g | Protein: 23 g | Sodium: 402 mg | Carbohydrates: 41 g | Fiber: 8 g

Spicy Chicken Nachos

Bar food lovers rejoice! Skip the nacho dip while you're out and enjoy it when you're home. This recipe will satisfy that craving and then some!

Low-carb, Low-calorie, Low-fat

INGREDIENTS | **SERVES 6**

4 cups Baked Tortilla Chips (page 199)

3 cups precooked grilled chicken breast, cut into small pieces

1 cup shredded low-fat Cheddar cheese

1½ cups tomatoes, diced

¼ cup jalapeño peppers, sliced

½ cup fat-free sour cream

1 cup salsa

1. Layer chips, chicken, and cheese in a large baking dish. Bake at 400°F for 5 minutes. Remove to a large serving dish. Sprinkle tomatoes over hot nachos.

2. Serve with peppers, sour cream, and salsa on the side.

PER SERVING Calories: 226 | Fat: 3 g | Protein: 35 g | Sodium: 401 mg | Carbohydrates: 13 g | Fiber: 2 g

Preparing Tomatoes

Core your tomatoes before cutting or dicing. Then season them with freshly ground black pepper and let them soak in the pepper for about 20 minutes. This gives the tomato the most pungent summer taste.

Low-Fat Mexican Layered Dip

Always show up to a party with a healthy dish in hand. If the host has only provided unhealthy choices, you'll at least have one thing to enjoy.

Low-calorie, Low-fat, Vegetarian

INGREDIENTS | SERVES 8

1 (15-ounce) can fat-free refried beans

½ packet taco seasoning

1 (8-ounce) package fat-free cream cheese

½ cup salsa

2 cups romaine lettuce, shredded

1 cup shredded fat-free Cheddar cheese

¾ cup green onions, sliced

1 cup tomatoes, diced

4 cups Baked Tortilla Chips (page 199)

1. Mix refried beans and taco seasoning, then spread onto the bottom of a large shallow serving dish.

2. Cover the beans with cream cheese, salsa, lettuce, cheddar, onions, and tomatoes. Refrigerate at least 1 hour before serving.

3. Serve with Baked Tortilla Chips.

PER SERVING Calories: 129 | Fat: 1 g | Protein: 12 g | Sodium: 684 mg | Carbohydrates: 18 g | Fiber: 3g

Look Familiar?

Chances are you've seen this dish before: at a party or at your local Mexican restaurant. It's definitely a great one for parties, but it's also delicious as a snack for you and a few friends. Quick and easy, this light and tasty dip will have your friends coming back for more!

Jalapeño Tortilla Roll-Ups

You can get very creative with this recipe and add anything you might want to roll up with the jalapeños.

Low-calorie, Vegetarian

INGREDIENTS | **SERVES 6**

1 cup nonfat cream cheese
1 (8-ounce) can chopped jalapeños
4 scallions, chopped
1 clove garlic, minced
1 teaspoon salt
1 teaspoon chili powder
1 teaspoon paprika
6 flour tortillas

1. Cream the nonfat cream cheese in a medium bowl. Mix in the jalapeños, scallions, and garlic.

2. Add the salt, chili powder, and paprika. Evenly spread the mixture onto tortillas. Roll up the tortillas and wrap individually in clear plastic wrap.

3. Refrigerate for a few hours until cold; slice and serve.

PER SERVING Calories: 208 | Fat: 5 g | Protein: 10 g | Sodium: 754 mg | Carbohydrates: 31 g | Fiber: 1 g

Nutty Chicken Fingers

These chicken fingers will have you feeling like a kid again—in a good way. They make a great snack or light dinner.

Low-calorie, Low-carb

INGREDIENTS | **SERVES 8**

¾ cup crushed cornflake crumbs
¼ cup finely chopped pecans
2 tablespoons chopped flat-leaf parsley
¼ teaspoon garlic salt
¼ teaspoon pepper
4 boneless, skinless chicken breasts
3 tablespoons 1% milk

1. Preheat oven to 400°F. In shallow dish, combine crumbs, pecans, parsley, garlic salt, and pepper and mix well.

2. Cut chicken into strips about 3" long and ½" wide. Dip the chicken in the milk, then roll in the crumb mixture to coat. Place in a 15" × 10" jelly roll pan.

3. Bake until chicken is tender, about 5 to 7 minutes. Serve at once with a dipping sauce.

PER SERVING Calories: 117 | Fat: 4 g | Protein: 26 g | Sodium: 78 mg | Carbohydrates: 11 g | Fiber: 3 g

Cajun Chicken Strips

Serve these tender little strips of chicken with any sauce you like.

Low-calorie, Low-carb

INGREDIENTS | SERVES 6

2 cloves garlic, minced

¾ cup dried bread crumbs

¼ cup grated Parmesan cheese

1 tablespoon dried parsley flakes

½ teaspoon paprika

½ teaspoon dried oregano leaves

⅛ teaspoon pepper

1½ pounds boneless, skinless chicken breasts

1 cup buttermilk

It's All in the Seasonings

The seasonings, from parsley to paprika, are what really make this dish come alive. Always keep a collection of basic spices, such as oregano, parsley, thyme, and garlic powder, on hand for recipes like these. You'll be glad you did!

1. Preheat oven to 425°F. Spray a cookie sheet with nonstick baking spray containing flour; set aside.

2. In shallow dish, combine garlic, bread crumbs, cheese, parsley, paprika, oregano, and pepper and mix well.

3. Cut chicken into ½" × 3" strips. Combine with buttermilk on plate, toss to coat, and let stand for 10 minutes.

4. Dip chicken into bread crumb mixture, then place in single layer on prepared cookie sheet. Bake for 5 minutes, then carefully turn with a spatula and bake for 5 to 6 minutes longer until chicken is thoroughly cooked. Serve immediately.

PER SERVING Calories: 224 | Fat: 4 g | Protein: 26 g | Sodium: 271 mg | Carbohydrates: 10 g | Fiber: 0.5 g

Easy, Low-Fat Cheese Fries

Choose the lowest-fat version of French fries you can find. Jazz this recipe up a bit with a little cayenne pepper, chili powder, or a variety of different fat-free cheeses.

Low-calorie, Vegetarian

INGREDIENTS | SERVES 4

12 ounces crinkle-cut frozen French fried potatoes

½ cup fat-free shredded Cheddar cheese

Salt to taste

4 tablespoons ketchup

4 tablespoons fat-free sour cream

1. Bake fries on a nonstick baking sheet at 450°F for 15 to 20 minutes, flipping fries once. Remove fries from oven and sprinkle with cheese.

2. Bake for 3 more minutes or until cheese has melted. Dress with salt, ketchup, or sour cream as desired.

PER SERVING Calories: 176 | Fat: 4 g | Protein: 8 g | Sodium: 130 mg | Carbohydrates: 27 g | Fiber: 2 g

Do It Healthier at Home

This is just one more example of how creating a dish at home is often healthier than ordering it out. The cheese fries you get at a fast-food restaurant are usually made with that artificial orange cheese sauce. While it may be tasty, it's also full of chemicals and fat and likely won't leave you feeling good after you've eaten it. This recipe, which is made with real fat-free cheese, is a much better option!

Smoked Salmon Quesadilla

Salmon is easily found in most grocery stores in vacuum-packed pouches and cans. Salmon is a great source of calcium and omega-3 and omega-6 fatty acids.

INGREDIENTS | SERVES 4

⅓ cup fat-free cream cheese
¼ cup white onions, finely chopped
¼ teaspoon fresh garlic, minced
12 ounces smoked salmon, chopped
⅛ teaspoon ground pepper
4 (8) whole-wheat tortillas

1. Mix all ingredients except tortillas. Spread salmon mixture over half of each tortilla.

2. Fold tortilla over and cook in nonstick skillet over medium heat for 2 minutes on each side. Cut each quesadilla into 3" wedges and serve.

PER SERVING Calories: 262 | Fat: 6 g | Protein: 22 g | Sodium: 1,149 mg | Carbohydrates: 28 g | Fiber: 2 g

Whole-Wheat Biscuits

You can make breakfast sandwiches from these hearty biscuits for a boost in fiber to start your day.

Vegetarian

INGREDIENTS | SERVES 8

1½ cups all-purpose flour
1½ cups whole-wheat flour
4½ teaspoons baking powder
1½ teaspoons salt
1 tablespoon sugar
6 tablespoons cold butter
1¼ cups buttermilk

1. Preheat oven to 400°F.

2. Combine flours, baking powder, salt, and sugar in a mixing bowl. Cut butter into small pieces and mix into dry ingredients with a pastry cutter or your fingers. Add buttermilk and mix with a wooden spoon.

3. Roll dough on a floured board to 1" thickness. Cut circles with a 2" to 3" round cookie cutter. Place rounds on a baking sheet and bake for 12 minutes.

PER SERVING Calories: 262 | Fat: 9 g | Protein: 7 g | Sodium: 503 mg | Carbohydrates: 38 g | Fiber: 3 g

Broccoli Calzones

These are little turnovers baked with a filling of broccoli and cheese. Serve them as appetizers or snacks. If you use frozen spinach instead of broccoli, be sure to thaw it completely and then squeeze all of the moisture out of it.

INGREDIENTS | SERVES 4

16 frozen dinner rolls, unbaked dough
2 cups chopped cooked broccoli
¼ cup diced ham
1 cup grated Cheddar cheese
½ cup grated Parmesan cheese

1. Spray a sheet of plastic wrap with vegetable oil. Lay the frozen dinner roll dough out on a plastic-lined baking sheet and cover with the plastic wrap. Let thaw in the refrigerator overnight.

2. Mix the broccoli, ham, and cheeses together in a bowl. Press each roll flat and put a spoonful of the broccoli mixture in the center of each one.

3. Fold each dough circle in half over the filling and press down to make a half-circle. Use a fork to crimp the edges.

4. Preheat the oven to 375°F.

5. Bake the calzones for 15 to 20 minutes and serve warm.

PER SERVING Calories: 509 | Fat: 20 g | Protein: 30 g | Sodium: 320 mg | Carbohydrates: 66 g | Fiber: 3 g

Easy Homemade Pizza Sauce

Homemade pizza sauce is delicious, and it's nice to be able to control what goes on your pizza!

Vegetarian, Low-calorie, Low-fat

INGREDIENTS | MAKES 1½ CUPS

1 tablespoon olive oil

½ cup chopped onion

3 tablespoons tomato paste

1 cup tomato purée

1 tablespoon Dijon mustard

½ teaspoon salt

¼ teaspoon crushed red pepper flakes

1 teaspoon dried basil leaves

1 teaspoon dried thyme leaves

1 teaspoon dried oregano leaves

¼ teaspoon pepper

1. In a small saucepan, combine olive oil and onion; cook and stir until tender, about 5 minutes.

2. Add all remaining ingredients and cook, stirring frequently, over low heat until thickened, about 15 minutes. Use as directed in a pizza recipe, or store, covered, in refrigerator up to 5 days.

PER SERVING Calories: 31 | Fat: 2 g | Protein: 2 g | Sodium: 321 mg | Carbohydrates: 24 g | Fiber: 3 g

Canned Tomato Products

While the rule of thumb is to try to use fresh rather than canned vegetables in recipes, the rule bends a little in the case of tomatoes. Because tomato sauce needs a variety of ingredients in order to achieve the right flavor and consistency, you need a number of different items, such as tomato paste, crushed tomatoes, and tomato purée. Every recipe is different, but plan on visiting the canned tomato aisle in your grocery store when sauce is on the agenda.

Classic French Bread Pizza

French bread makes an excellent crust for pizza. You can buy the frozen kind or, if you're feeling ambitious, you can make your own!

Vegetarian

INGREDIENTS | SERVES 8

1 loaf French bread

3 tablespoons olive oil, divided

1 onion, chopped

1 green bell pepper, chopped

1 red bell pepper, chopped

3 garlic cloves, minced

2 teaspoons dried basil leaves

1 teaspoon dried oregano leaves

2 cups Easy Homemade Pizza Sauce (page 210)

3 tomatoes, sliced

½ cup sliced black olives

2 cups shredded carrots

1 cup shredded part-skim mozzarella cheese

½ cup grated Parmesan cheese

1. Preheat oven to 450°F. Slice the bread in half lengthwise. Drizzle cut sides of both halves with 2 tablespoons oil and place on a baking sheet.

2. In a large skillet, heat the remaining 1 tablespoon oil over medium heat. Add onion, bell peppers, garlic, basil, and oregano and cook for 5 minutes, or until tender. Remove from heat.

3. Spoon 1 cup pizza sauce on each piece of bread. Top evenly with the onion-pepper mixture, tomatoes, and black olives. Then sprinkle evenly with the carrots, mozzarella cheese, and Parmesan cheese.

4. Bake for 14 to 18 minutes or until cheese is melted and bubbly and the bread is lightly browned. Cut each loaf into 4" pieces to serve.

PER SERVING Calories: 402 | Fat: 12 g | Protein: 2 g | Sodium: 793 mg | Carbohydrates: 30 g | Fiber: 2 g

Why Shredded Carrots?

Shredded carrots are a surprise ingredient on this pizza, and they also sneak their way into many recipes for spaghetti sauce. Not only is it a good way to work in a vegetable, but it also helps thicken the sauce and adds a slight sweetness. If you want them to melt into the sauce, it's best to shred the carrots yourself; preshredded carrots can be dry.

California French Bread Pizza

Romano cheese is similar to Parmesan cheese, but it's often saltier and tangier. Pecorino Romano is made from sheep's milk, while Caprino Romano is made from goat's milk.

Vegetarian

INGREDIENTS | SERVES 8

1 loaf French bread

3 tablespoons olive oil

2 onions, chopped

4 cloves garlic, minced

2 green bell peppers, chopped

2 (4-ounce) jars sliced mushrooms, drained

1½ cups Easy Homemade Pizza Sauce (page 210)

½ cup sliced green olives

1 cup shredded part-skim mozzarella cheese

3 tablespoons grated Romano cheese

1. Preheat oven to 425°F. Slice the bread in half lengthwise. Drizzle cut sides of both halves with 2 tablespoons oil and place on a baking sheet.

2. In a medium saucepan, cook 1 tablespoon olive oil, onions, and garlic over medium heat until crisp-tender, about 5 minutes.

3. In bowl, combine onion, garlic, bell pepper, and mushrooms with pizza sauce. Spread sauce mixture over the bread halves and sprinkle with olives and cheeses.

4. Bake until cheese is slightly browned and bubbly and topping is hot, about 20 to 30 minutes. To serve, slice each half into 4" pieces.

PER SERVING Calories: 328 | Fat: 4 g | Protein: 2 g | Sodium: 580 mg | Carbohydrates: 30 g | Fiber: 2 g

Rolled Cheese Biscuits

*These cheese biscuits are great on their own as a snack or
alongside an entrée with lots of sauce for sopping.*

Low-calorie, Vegetarian

INGREDIENTS | MAKES 20 BISCUITS

2 cups flour

½ cup Cotija cheese

3 teaspoons baking powder

½ teaspoon salt

½ teaspoon cream of tartar

1 tablespoon sugar

6 tablespoons butter

⅔ cup milk

1 cup grated sharp Cheddar cheese

Bountiful Biscuits

Biscuits are a great food to make ahead of
time and freeze. Just keep them in Ziploc
bags in your freezer, and when you're ready
to use some, reheat them in the oven or
toaster oven. Make a big batch on the
weekend so you'll have delicious homemade biscuits to keep you going throughout the week!

1. Preheat oven to 400°F. In large bowl, combine flour, Cotija cheese, baking powder, salt, cream of tartar, and sugar and mix well. Cut in butter until particles are fine. Stir in milk until a dough forms. On lightly floured surface, knead dough about 8 times.

2. Roll dough to ¼" thickness (about 10" × 15" rectangle) and sprinkle with Cheddar cheese. Tightly roll up dough, starting with shorter side, and pinch edges to seal. Cut into ½" slices and place on parchment paper–lined cookie sheets. Bake for 12 to 17 minutes or until biscuits are golden brown. Serve warm.

PER SERVING Calories: 1167 | Fat: 6 g | Protein: 3 g | Sodium: 245 mg | Carbohydrates: 16 g | Fiber: 0.38 g

Whole-Wheat Biscuit Pizzas

If you have premade Whole-Wheat Biscuits (page 208) you can use them to make your pizzas more quickly. The whole wheat in the biscuits adds fiber and B vitamins to the dish.

Vegetarian, High-fiber

INGREDIENTS | SERVES 6

12 unbaked Whole Wheat Biscuits (page 208)

¼ cup pizza sauce

½ cup shredded mozzarella cheese

¼ cup sliced black olives

¼ cup diced green peppers

Get Creative with Pizza

You know why pizza is so much fun? Because it comes in all shapes and sizes! It can be thick or thin, round or square, and it can even come in personal size, like these individual biscuit pizzas. These are great to make one at a time for a quick snack on the go, or in a big batch for a bunch of friends.

1. Preheat oven to 375°F.

2. Lay the individual biscuits out on a sheet pan and press them down to make flat rounds.

3. Spoon pizza sauce over the rounds and sprinkle them with mozzarella cheese.

4. Top the pizzas with black olives and green peppers.

5. Bake for 15 to 20 minutes. Serve immediately.

PER SERVING Calories: 489 | Fat: 21 g | Protein: 16 g | Sodium: 405 mg | Carbohydrates: 62 g | Fiber: 10 g

Cake Doughnuts

These cake doughnuts are a great treat to bring to a party. Your friends won't believe you made doughnuts from scratch!

Low-calorie

INGREDIENTS | MAKES 18 DOUGHNUTS

3 eggs

¾ cup sugar

¼ cup brown sugar

1 cup buttermilk

1 teaspoon vanilla

¼ cup butter, melted

3 to 3½ cups flour

¼ teaspoon salt

1 teaspoon baking powder

1 teaspoon baking soda

½ teaspoon ground nutmeg

3 cups corn oil

Healthy Doughnuts?

While these doughnuts do have ingredients like eggs and butter in them, they're still going to be a lot healthier than any you buy from a doughnut shop. Try dipping these in cinnamon-sugar while they're still hot!

1. In bowl, beat eggs until light. Gradually add sugars, beating until light and fluffy. Add buttermilk, vanilla, and melted butter and mix well. In sifter, combine 3 cups flour, salt, baking powder, baking soda, and nutmeg, and sift over batter; stir in. You may need to add more flour to make a soft dough.

2. On floured surface, roll out dough ⅓" thick. Cut with doughnut cutters. In large skillet, heat oil to 375°F (use a cooking thermometer for best results). Carefully add four doughnuts; fry on both sides, turning once, until golden brown, about 3 to 4 minutes for each side. Repeat with remaining dough. Fry doughnut holes for 1 to 2 minutes on each side.

PER SERVING Calories: 193 | Fat: 7 g | Protein: 2.2 g | Sodium: 141 mg | Carbohydrates: 28 g | Fiber: 0 g

Hummus Tomato Pita Pizza

This is a nacho-style cold pizza. It combines the base of a hummus plate with the ingredients of a Greek salad served on top. Substituting a whole-wheat pita for a regular one boosts the fiber.

Vegetarian, High-fiber

INGREDIENTS | SERVES 2

½ cup hummus
1 pita round
1 small tomato, diced
1 tablespoon diced red onion
1 tablespoon diced cucumber
2 ounces feta cheese
6 pitted ripe olives
1 tablespoon olive oil

1. Spread the hummus around on the pita bread, leaving a small border around the edges.

2. Scatter the tomato, red onion, and cucumber over the hummus.

3. Crumble the feta cheese over the pizza. Scatter the olives over the cheese.

4. Drizzle the olive oil over the pizza.

5. Cut the pizza into wedges and serve.

PER SERVING Calories: 371 | Fat: 23 g | Protein: 13 g | Sodium: 560 mg | Carbohydrates: 32 g | Fiber: 7 g

CHAPTER 13

Keep Warm: Fall and Winter Recipes

Baked Apples Stuffed with Nuts and Raisins

For breakfast or dessert, baked apples are a delightful, spicy, and warm treat in the colder months.

Vegetarian, Low-calorie

INGREDIENTS | SERVES 2

2 large apples, such as Macintosh, Rome, or Granny Smith

2 teaspoons brown sugar

½ teaspoon cinnamon

2 teaspoons chopped walnuts

2 teaspoons raisins

1 teaspoon butter

Try It à la Mode

The spices in these baked, stuffed apples and the tartness of the apples are both complemented nicely by dairy. You can serve these with a little cream poured over the top or a scoop of vanilla ice cream on the side for added richness.

1. Preheat the oven to 350°F. Using a corer, remove the center portions of the apples, being careful not to cut through the bottom of the apple.

2. Form a cup with a double layer of aluminum foil, going ⅓ of the way up the apple. This will stabilize the apple when baking.

3. Mix together the brown sugar, cinnamon, walnuts, and raisins and stuff the mixture into the apples. Top each apple with 1 teaspoon of butter. Put 1 tablespoon of water into each of the aluminum foil cups.

4. Bake for 25 minutes, or until the apples are soft when pricked with a fork.

PER SERVING Calories: 181 | Fat: 8 g | Protein: 1 g | Sodium: 22 mg | Carbohydrates: 28 g | Fiber: 3 g

Sweet Potato Pie Pancakes

Enjoy this dish in early November to get excited about Thanksgiving dinner or a fall harvest celebration.

Low-calorie, Low-fat

INGREDIENTS | SERVES 6

½ cup whole-wheat flour

¼ cup quick-cooking oatmeal

1 tablespoon Splenda

½ teaspoon baking powder

⅓ teaspoon baking soda

⅛ cup egg white substitute

1 cup skim milk

1½ cups canned sweet potatoes

2 tablespoons pecans, chopped

½ teaspoon cinnamon

1 teaspoon Splenda brown sugar

½ teaspoon vanilla extract

1. In a bowl, mix all dry ingredients together. In a separate bowl, mix all wet ingredients together. Gently fold dry ingredients into wet ingredients.

2. Coat skillet or griddle with nonstick spray. Pour ⅓ cup batter per pancake onto skillet.

3. Cook on medium-high heat until pancake develops bubbles on top. Flip the pancake and brown on the other side.

PER SERVING Calories: 122 | Fat: 1 g | Protein: 4 g | Sodium: 160 mg | Carbohydrates: 26 g | Fiber: 3 g

Banana-Nut Stuffed French Toast

This delicious recipe imparts fiber through whole grain, fruits, and nuts. You can vary the French toast with different kinds of nuts and fruits.

High-fiber

INGREDIENTS | SERVES 4

2 bananas

6 eggs

1½ cups milk

1 teaspoon vanilla

1 tablespoon brown sugar

½ teaspoon cinnamon

8 slices day-old whole-wheat bread

2 teaspoons canola oil

1 cup chopped walnuts or pecans

Handful of fresh raspberries

Powdered sugar

Stuff It!

Stuffed foods are all the rage, from stuffed-crust pizza to stuffed French toast. You'll probably find a recipe similar to this one on the brunch menus at some restaurants, but guaranteed it won't be as satisfying as the one you make yourself!

1. Peel and slice the bananas. Whisk together eggs, milk, vanilla, brown sugar, and cinnamon in a bowl.

2. Dip 4 slices of bread in the batter and immediately fry in canola oil over medium heat.

3. Divide the banana slices and nuts evenly among the 4 slices of cooking bread. Dip the remaining four slices of bread into the batter and put them on top of the bananas to create four sandwiches.

4. Add remaining canola oil to the pan, flip the sandwiches over, and fry over medium heat until golden.

5. Halve the French toast diagonally and arrange slices on a platter. Scatter the raspberries over the French toast triangles and sprinkle them with powdered sugar.

PER SERVING Calories: 588 | Fat: 34 g | Protein: 22 g | Sodium: 260 mg | Carbohydrates: 55 g | Fiber: 9 g

Oatmeal Raisin Scones

These luscious scones pack a whopping punch of fiber from oats, wheat germ, and raisins. Try using Irish oatmeal for these scones, but soak it first. Steel-cut oats have the most fiber and instant oats have the least.

INGREDIENTS | SERVES 6

1½ cups rolled oats

½ cup all-purpose flour

2 tablespoons wheat germ

3 tablespoons sugar

½ teaspoon salt

1⅛ teaspoons baking powder

6 tablespoons cold, unsalted butter, cut in pieces

2 eggs

⅔ cup buttermilk

½ teaspoon vanilla

1 cup raisins

1 egg white

2 tablespoons raw sugar

Eat Your Oats

Oats are one of the best sources for soluble fiber, which is important in regulating cholesterol in the bloodstream. Oats also lose only the outer husk during the milling process so they are more nutritious than refined wheat.

1. Preheat oven to 400°F. Line a baking pan with parchment paper or spray lightly with oil. Grind half of the oatmeal into flour in a food processor.

2. Combine remaining oats, oat flour, all-purpose flour, wheat germ, sugar, salt, baking powder, and butter in a food processor with a metal blade. Process until mixture resembles cornmeal.

3. In a large bowl whisk together eggs, buttermilk, and vanilla. Stir in raisins with a spatula or wooden spoon.

4. Add dry ingredients and fold in with spatula. Drop scones in rounds onto prepared baking sheet.

5. Brush scones with egg white and sprinkle with raw sugar. Bake for 15 minutes.

PER SERVING Calories: 373 | Fat: 15 g | Protein: 9 g | Sodium: 243 mg | Carbohydrates: 54 g | Fiber: 4 g

Toad in a Hole

In Britain, Toad in a Hole involves baking sausages and Yorkshire pudding in a large pan with bacon fat drippings and flour, but this recipe—a Pennsylvania Dutch favorite—is far simpler and far less fattening.

Low-calorie, Low-fat, Low-carb

INGREDIENTS | **SERVES 2**

1 slice bread, any kind
Nonfat cooking spray
1 egg
Salt and pepper, to taste

Flipping Toads

As it cooks, the egg adheres to the bread. This makes it super simple to flip the bread in the pan without worrying about dislodging the egg. Be sure to flip your eggs after they've had time to set. Otherwise, you risk getting runny egg all over the place, which won't affect taste but will leave you with a mess.

1. Use a circular cookie cutter to cut a hole in the center of a slice of bread.

2. Place on a warm skillet, sprayed lightly with nonfat cooking spray.

3. Crack the egg and put it in the hole in the bread.

4. Fry and flip to desired consistency.

5. Season with salt and pepper to taste.

PER SERVING Calories: 72 | Fat: 3 g | Protein: 5 g | Sodium: 151 mg | Carbohydrates: 7 g | Fiber: 3 g

Fall Minestrone Soup

Minestrone is the Italian name for a thick and hearty soup that often consists of legumes, veggies, rice, or pasta. The ingredients in this soup change with the season. Whichever vegetable is growing at the time gets used!

Low-calorie, Low-fat, High-fiber, Vegetarian

INGREDIENTS | **SERVES 6**

½ cup yellow onions, chopped

1 clove fresh garlic, minced

½ teaspoon all-purpose seasoning

1 cup frozen peas

1 cup squash, sliced

1 cup green beans

1 cup carrots, sliced

2 cups white beans, cooked

1 cup chickpeas, cooked

1 cup frozen spinach

½ cup whole-wheat pasta

1 teaspoon oregano

¼ teaspoon black pepper

1 chicken bouillon cube

3 cups water

1. Combine all ingredients in a large saucepan. Cook on medium-high heat for 15 minutes.

2. Reduce heat to low, simmer for another 10 minutes, then serve.

PER SERVING Calories: 210 | Fat: 1 g | Protein: 13 g | Sodium: 209 mg | Carbohydrates: 39 g | Fiber: 9 g

Winter Vegetable Soup

Warm up with this aromatic soup!

Low-calorie, High-fiber, Vegetarian

INGREDIENTS | SERVES 6

2 cups frozen mixed vegetables

2 cups zucchini, sliced

2 cups squash, sliced

1 cup yellow onions, diced

4 cups vegetable broth

2 cups diced tomatoes

1 teaspoon olive oil

1 teaspoon fresh minced garlic

½ teaspoon all-purpose seasoning

1 teaspoon fresh basil

1. Combine all ingredients in a large saucepan. Cook on medium heat for 15 minutes.

2. Reduce heat to low, simmer for another 10 minutes, then serve.

PER SERVING Calories: 191 | Fat: 4 g | Protein: 8 g | Sodium: 1,141 mg | Carbohydrates: 34 g | Fiber: 7 g

Substitute to Your Heart's Content

In recipes like this one, it's easy to substitute certain ingredients for others without upsetting the balance. For example, substitute chicken broth for the vegetable broth if you prefer. Go with the low-sodium version of either for the healthiest option.

Spicy Turkey Chili with Chocolate

The combination of smoky chipotle chilies and sweet chocolate adds a deep, rich flavor to this chili.

High-fiber

INGREDIENTS | SERVES 6

2 cups lean ground turkey

½ cup bell peppers, diced

½ cup white onions, diced

1 clove fresh garlic, minced

½ teaspoon all-purpose seasoning

2 tablespoons Splenda brown sugar

1 teaspoon chipotle peppers, finely chopped

1 teaspoon cumin

3 cups pinto beans, cooked

1 cup tomatoes, diced

½ teaspoon black pepper

1 cup chicken broth

1 tablespoon cocoa powder

¼ cup sugar-free chocolate syrup

1. Coat a large saucepan with nonstick spray. On medium-high heat, brown ground turkey with bell peppers, onions, garlic, and all-purpose seasoning, for 10 minutes.

2. Add remaining ingredients to saucepan, reduce heat to low, and simmer for 15 minutes.

Chocolate in Chili?

Cocoa powder or unsweetened chocolate adds depth of flavor and richness to soups and sauces. Although most consumers associate chocolate with sweet confections, it isn't unusual to find it as an ingredient in savory dishes from Mexico and Central and South America. In fact, the national dish of Mexico, Turkey Mole, is built on a thick, chocolate-laced sauce. Chocolate or cocoa powder is especially good in vegetarian black bean dishes.

PER SERVING Calories: 313 | Fat: 7 g | Protein: 25 g | Sodium: 198 mg | Carbohydrates: 39 g | Fiber: 9 g

Savory Stuffed Mushrooms

Stuffed mushrooms are a classic appetizer, but they also make a perfect snack! This version is full of flavor and color.

Low-calorie, Low-carb

INGREDIENTS | SERVES 6

12 large mushrooms
1 tablespoon olive oil
1 onion, minced
½ cup minced green bell pepper
2 cloves garlic, minced
½ cup crushed Saltine crackers
2 tablespoons grated Parmesan cheese
1 tablespoon minced flat-leaf parsley
½ teaspoon dried oregano leaves
⅛ teaspoon pepper
⅓ cup fat-free chicken broth

1. Preheat oven to 350°F. Wipe mushrooms with damp paper towels and remove stems. Mince stems and combine in small saucepan with olive oil, onion, green bell pepper, and garlic. Cook and stir until tender, about 5 to 6 minutes.

2. Remove pan from heat and add cracker crumbs, cheese, parsley, oregano, and pepper.

3. Spoon mixture into mushroom caps, rounding the tops. Place in large baking dish and pour chicken broth around mushrooms.

4. Bake, uncovered, until mushrooms are tender and filling is hot, about 18 to 22 minutes. Serve immediately.

PER SERVING Calories: 84 | Fat: 4 g | Protein: 1 g | Sodium: 77 mg | Carbohydrates: 13 g | Fiber: 1.5 g

Risotto with Winter Squash

Sweet and tender squash combines wonderfully with sage, onion, and leeks in this creamy risotto. This could be the main dish for a vegetarian dinner.

Vegetarian

INGREDIENTS | SERVES 6

4 cups fat-free vegetable broth

1 tablespoon olive oil

3 cups butternut squash, cubed

1 onion, chopped

3 cloves garlic, minced

1 cup chopped leeks

1 teaspoon dried sage leaves

½ teaspoon salt

⅛ teaspoon white pepper

1½ cups Arborio rice

¼ cup grated Parmesan cheese

1 tablespoon butter

¼ cup chopped flat-leaf parsley

1. Place broth in medium saucepan; place over low heat. In a large saucepan, heat oil over medium heat. Add squash; cook and stir until squash begins to brown, about 6 to 7 minutes. Add onion, garlic, and leek; cook and stir for 4 to 5 minutes longer until onion is translucent.

2. Stir in sage, salt, pepper, and rice; cook and stir for 3 minutes longer. Slowly add warm broth, ½ cup at a time, stirring frequently. When rice is al dente and squash is tender, add the cheese, butter, and parsley, cover, and remove from heat.

3. Let stand for 5 minutes, then stir and serve immediately.

PER SERVING Calories: 296 | Fat: 6 g | Protein: 4 g | Sodium: 419 mg | Carbohydrates: 25 g | Fiber: 2 g

Rich Risotto

Risotto is a traditional Italian rice dish and one of the most common ways of cooking rice in Italy. There are many different risotto recipes with different ingredients, but they all use Arborio rice, which is first cooked briefly in butter or olive oil. Then, liquid, usually broth, is added in increments until the rice is fully cooked.

Vegetables in Béchamel Sauce

A simple white sauce is a quick and easy way to lend flavor to canned vegetables.

Vegetarian, Low-calorie, Low-carb

INGREDIENTS | SERVES 4

2 (14-ounce) cans French green beans
1½ tablespoons butter
1 tablespoon all-purpose flour
¼ cup milk
¼ teaspoon (or to taste) ground nutmeg
Salt and pepper to taste

1. Heat the green beans on medium in a saucepan. Reserve ¼ cup of juice from the cooked beans to use in the sauce. Keep the green beans warm on low heat while preparing the sauce.

2. Melt the butter in a small saucepan over low heat. Stir in the flour. Cook on low heat for 3 minutes, continually stirring.

3. Gradually whisk in the milk and the reserved green bean juice. Bring to a boil, continually whisking until thickened. Stir in the nutmeg, salt, and pepper. Pour over the green beans and serve.

PER SERVING Calories: 82 | Fat: 4.6 g | Protein: 2.7 g | Sodium: 60 mg | Carbohydrates: 9.2 g | Fiber: 3 g

Poached Chicken with Pears and Herbs

Pears go very well with all poultry. Try this for a quick dinner or double the recipe for company.

Low-carb, Gluten-free

INGREDIENTS | SERVES 2

1 ripe pear, peeled, cored, and cut in chunks

2 shallots, minced

½ cup dry white wine

1 teaspoon rosemary, dried, or 1 tablespoon fresh

1 teaspoon thyme, dried, or 1 tablespoon fresh

2½ pounds chicken breasts, boneless and skinless

Salt and pepper to taste

Prepare the poaching liquid by mixing the first 5 ingredients and bringing to a boil in a saucepan. Season the chicken with salt and pepper and add to the pan. Simmer slowly for 10 minutes. Serve with pears on top of each piece.

PER SERVING Calories: 307 | Fat: 9 g | Protein: 41 g | Sodium: 2 mg | Carbohydrates: 15 g | Fiber: 2 g

Praise for Pears

You've probably noticed that a lot of the recipes in this book include pears, from baked pears to pears in salad. The reason is that pears are a tasty and versatile fruit that comes in many, many varieties, from Anjou (a great all-purpose pear) to Bartlett (creamy and sweet). Try as many as you can and choose your favorites.

Fried Chicken with Cornmeal Crust

Fried chicken doesn't have to come in a bucket. Make your own at home and see how it compares.

Low-carb

INGREDIENTS | SERVES 4

4 (4-ounce) half-breasts chicken boneless and skinless

½ cup buttermilk

½ cup coarse cornmeal

1 teaspoon baking powder

½ teaspoon salt

Freshly ground pepper to taste

½ inch canola or other oil in a deep pan for frying

1. Soak the chicken in buttermilk for 15 minutes. Mix cornmeal, baking powder, salt, and pepper on a piece of waxed paper and coat the chicken with the mixture.

2. In a large frying pan, heat the oil to 350°F. Fry for 8 to 10 minutes per side. Drain on paper towels.

Cornmeal Crust

Coarsely grated cornmeal makes an excellent crust for fried chicken. There are people who use corn muffin mix as the coating for their chicken, but it's more wholesome to make your own crust.

PER SERVING Calories: 265 | Fat: 9 g | Protein: 42 g | Sodium: 87 mg | Carbohydrates: 9 g | Fiber: 1 g

Mini Spinach Casserole with Brown Rice and Ham

This is a hearty, delicious meal for a cold fall or winter day. It also makes great leftovers!

INGREDIENTS | SERVES 2

2 cups fresh baby spinach

½ cup low-fat ricotta cheese

Salt and pepper to taste

1 cup brown rice, cooked

¼ cup Italian dressing

1 ounce Virginia ham, chopped

1. Purée the spinach and ricotta in the blender. Preheat oven to 300°F.

2. Mix all ingredients together in a 9" pie pan and bake for 20 minutes.

PER SERVING Calories: 342 | Fat: 19 g | Protein: 16 g | Sodium: 593 mg | Carbohydrates: 32 g | Fiber: 1 g

Buttermilk Biscuits

There is no kneading or rolling dough in this easy-to-make biscuit recipe. For best results, stick with real buttermilk; biscuits made with milk that has been soured by adding lemon juice or cream of tartar won't have the same flavor.

Low-calorie, Low-fat

INGREDIENTS | **MAKES 24 BISCUITS**

1 teaspoon baking powder
½ teaspoon baking soda
1 teaspoon salt
2 cups all-purpose flour
¼ cup shortening
About 1¼ cups buttermilk

Buttermilk

Originally, buttermilk was the liquid left behind after churning butter out of cream. It also refers to the range of fermented milk drinks common in warm climates where fresh milk would spoil quickly. The tartness of buttermilk is due to the presence of acid in the milk.

1. Preheat oven to 450°F.

2. Stir the baking powder, baking soda, and salt into the flour, blending thoroughly.

3. Use a knife to cut the shortening into the flour.

4. Quickly stir 1 cup buttermilk into the flour mixture. If necessary, add as much of the remaining ¼ cup of buttermilk as needed. The dough should be just moist, and not too wet. Do not overmix the dough.

5. Drop a heaping tablespoon of dough onto an ungreased baking sheet. Continue with the remaining dough. Bake the biscuits for 9 to 12 minutes, until they are golden brown. Let cool briefly on a wire rack before serving.

PER SERVING Calories: 62 | Fat: 2.3 g | Protein: 1.5 g | Sodium: 183 mg | Carbohydrates: 15 g | Fiber: 0 g

Classic Oatmeal Cookies

Add a cup of raisins or ½ cup of pecans for extra crunch if you like.

Low-calorie

INGREDIENTS | **MAKES 24 COOKIES**

1 cup sugar
¼ cup margarine, softened
2 eggs
¾ cup unsweetened applesauce
1 teaspoon vanilla
2 cups flour
½ teaspoon baking soda
¼ teaspoon salt
1 cup uncooked oats

1. Preheat oven to 375°F. Prepare baking sheets with light cooking spray. Set aside.

2. Beat the sugar and margarine in a large bowl with a hand mixer.

3. Add the eggs, applesauce, and vanilla, mixing well.

4. Combine flour, baking soda, and salt in a medium bowl.

5. Add flour mixture to sugar mixture. Beat well.

6. Stir in the oats and mix well.

7. Drop dough into mounds on baking sheets, about 2" apart. Bake 15 minutes, or until cookies are golden brown.

PER SERVING Calories: 218 | Fat: 5 g | Protein: 4 g | Sodium: 130 mg | Carbohydrates: 39 g | Fiber: 1.2 g

Sugar Cookies

If you like sugar cookies with extra flavor, add orange or almond extract to kick these classic cookies up a notch.

Low-calorie

INGREDIENTS | MAKES 20 COOKIES

1 cup flour
½ cup whole-wheat flour
¾ cup sugar
¼ teaspoon salt
1 teaspoon baking powder
3 tablespoons canola oil
1 egg
2 tablespoons skim milk
2 teaspoons vanilla

Make Cut-Outs

Another fun way to make sugar cookies is to roll out the dough on a floured surface and use cookie cutters to make shaped cookies. Use holiday-themed cutters for the holidays, or use alphabet-shaped ones to spell out someone's name or a message.

1. Preheat oven to 350°F.

2. Mix all dry ingredients in a large bowl.

3. Mix all liquid ingredients in a medium bowl; add to dry ingredients and mix thoroughly.

4. Spray baking sheets with light spray.

5. Drop cookie dough balls about 2" apart on baking sheet.

6. Bake 8 to 10 minutes or until slightly browned on edges.

PER SERVING Calories: 172 | Fat: 5 g | Protein: 3 g | Sodium: 131 mg | Carbohydrates: 29 g | Fiber: 0.5 g

Mascarpone Pudding

The secret to this dessert lies in slowly cooking the rice until the grains are tender. Ricotta cheese can be substituted for the mascarpone.

Vegetarian

INGREDIENTS | **SERVES 6–8**

1½ cups milk

1 cup long-grain rice

½ teaspoon ground cinnamon

1 teaspoon vanilla extract

¾ cup heavy cream

3 tablespoons granulated sugar

1 cup mascarpone

16–20 whole, unblanched almonds

1. In a medium-sized saucepan, add the milk to the rice. Stir in the cinnamon. Bring to a boil, uncovered, over medium heat. Cover, reduce heat to low, and simmer until cooked through, stirring occasionally.

2. Stir the vanilla extract into the heavy cream. Add to the rice, stirring. Continue cooking on low heat until the rice is tender. Remove from the heat.

3. Stir in the sugar and mascarpone. Spoon into dessert dishes and chill. Garnish with almonds.

PER SERVING Calories: 262 | Fat: 13 g | Protein: 8 g | Sodium: 71 mg | Carbohydrates: 28 g | Fiber: 1 g

Oven-Baked Scrod

Scrod—the name for a type of white fish such as cod or haddock—can stand up to almost any kind of cooking, from fried for fish and chips to this delicious recipe.

Low-calorie

INGREDIENTS | SERVES 2

⅔ pound scrod filet

Salt and pepper to taste

1 tablespoon lemon juice

2 tablespoons parsley

1 large tomato, thinly sliced

2 tablespoons fine bread crumbs

1 tablespoon olive oil

1. Preheat the oven to 350°F. Place the fish on an ovenproof pan prepared with nonstick spray.

2. Sprinkle the fish with salt, pepper, lemon juice, and parsley. Arrange the tomato slices on top and sprinkle with bread crumbs. Drizzle olive oil over the top.

3. Bake for 20 to 25 minutes, or until the fish is sizzling and the bread crumbs are brown.

PER SERVING Calories: 207 | Fat: 5 g | Protein: 31 g | Sodium: 75 mg | Carbohydrates: 16 g | Fiber: 1 g

CHAPTER 14

Stay Cool:
Spring and Summer Recipes

Simple Orange Smoothie

To add some bulk to this smoothie, add a small orange to the mixture after blending so you have some sweet orange chunks in the smoothie.

Low-calorie, Low-fat, Vegetarian

INGREDIENTS | SERVES 1

1 cup orange juice
½ cup nonfat yogurt
½ cup skim milk

Combine all ingredients in a blender until smooth. Pour into a tall glass.

PER SERVING Calories: 221 | Fat: 0 g | Protein: 12 g | Sodium: 140 mg | Carbohydrates: 41 g | Fiber: 0 g

Fruit Medley Smoothie

This smoothie is a great option if you're looking to boost your antioxidants.

Vegetarian, High-fiber, Low-fat, Gluten-free

INGREDIENTS | SERVES 1

¼ cup blueberries
¼ cup fresh strawberries
1 large peach, sliced
1 cup raspberries
½ cup nonfat yogurt
½ cup skim milk

Combine all ingredients in a blender until smooth. Pour into a tall glass.

Have a Fruit Frenzy

This isn't called a medley smoothie for nothing. Experiment with all different kinds of fruit in this recipe, from mango to pineapple to kiwi. Chances are, most combos will taste great. Oh, and make sure you keep the seeds in fruits like raspberries and kiwi. They contain an extra dose of fiber.

PER SERVING Calories: 272 | Fat: 2 g | Protein: 14 g | Sodium: 160 mg | Carbohydrates: 55 g | Fiber: 14 g

Pineapple Coconut Smoothie

This smoothie will transplant you to the Caribbean in minutes. Garnish with a cherry and it's pure bliss.

Vegetarian, Low-fat, Gluten-free

INGREDIENTS | SERVES 1

1 cup canned unsweetened pineapple chunks
1 cup coconut water
½ cup nonfat yogurt
½ cup skim milk

Combine all ingredients in a blender until smooth. Pour into a tall glass.

Coconut Water

Coconut water is found in young coconuts. It can be drunk straight from the coconut. Contrary to popular belief, coconut milk is not the liquid found inside a whole coconut. It is made from mixing water with shredded coconut. This mixture is strained through cheesecloth to filter out the coconut pieces.

PER SERVING Calories: 307 | Fat: 1 g | Protein: 14 g | Sodium: 411 mg | Carbohydrates: 63 g | Fiber: 4.2 g

Grilled Caramelized Pineapple

This is a perfect dessert that is quick and easy to make whenever you are grilling. You can get fresh pineapple, peeled, cored, and cut in fat circles.

Vegetarian, Low-fat, Low-calorie, Low-carb, Lactose-free

INGREDIENTS | SERVES 4

4 thick slices pineapple, about 1 each
Juice of ½ lime
4 teaspoons brown sugar

1. Brush both sides of the pineapple slices with lime juice and sprinkle with brown sugar.

2. Place sugar-coated pineapple slices on a hot grill; turn after 3 minutes. Grill another 3 minutes.

3. When the pineapples are done, you should have a nice brown caramel color. Top with lemon sorbet and a drizzle of melted dark chocolate if you want to gild the lily.

PER SERVING Calories: 29 | Fat: 0 g | Protein: 2.4 g | Sodium: 4.3 mg | Carbohydrates: 13 g | Fiber: 2.6 g

Melon Pineapple Salad

This fresh salad can be made with almost any fruit that's in season. Use a different flavor of yogurt if you'd like.

Vegetarian, Low-calorie, Low-fat

INGREDIENTS | SERVES 12

1 cantaloupe

1 honeydew melon

1 ripe pineapple

¼ cup honey

½ cup lemon yogurt

¼ cup pineapple-orange juice

2 tablespoons chopped mint

Bring It with You

Fruit salads like this one are easy to pack in a plastic container and take with you to class, to the park, or anywhere. Having a healthy snack on hand will help you resist the urge to buy less-healthy food while you're out. Just don't forget to bring a fork or spoon!

1. Cut melons in half, remove seeds, and cut into balls with a melon baller, or cut into cubes. Remove leaves from pineapple and cut off skin. Remove center core and slice. Combine fruits in large serving bowl.

2. In small bowl, combine remaining ingredients and mix well. Pour over fruits and toss to coat. Cover and chill for at least 4 hours before serving.

PER SERVING Calories: 108 | Fat: 1 g | Protein: 1.1 g | Sodium: 16 mg | Carbohydrates 27 g | Fiber: 1 g

Cranberry Peach Gelatin Salad

Old-fashioned molded salads are great for parties because they must be made ahead of time. And leftovers are delicious for breakfast!

Low-calorie, Vegetarian, Lactose-free

INGREDIENTS | SERVES 10

2 (3-ounce) packages peach-flavored gelatin

2 cups boiling water

¼ cup orange juice

1 (8-ounce) can crushed pineapple, drained

1 (16-ounce) can whole berry cranberry sauce

1 (15-ounce) can peach slices, drained and chopped

½ cup chopped walnuts

1. In large bowl, combine gelatin and boiling water; stir until gelatin is completely dissolved. Add remaining ingredients and mix well.

2. Pour into 2-quart mold or glass baking dish and chill until firm. Cut into squares to serve.

PER SERVING Calories: 233 | Fat: 4 g | Protein: 2.7 g | Sodium: 18 mg | Carbohydrates: 48 g | Fiber: 1.7 g

Gelatin Salads

There are a few tricks to making gelatin salads. First, be sure to completely dissolve the gelatin in the boiling liquid in the first step. Spoon up a small amount and make sure you can't see any grains of sugar or gelatin. And never use fresh or frozen pineapple, kiwi, or guava in gelatin salads; they will keep it from setting.

Tangy Carrot and Tomato Salad

This colorful salad is perfect with a grilled steak for a summer dinner.
Serve it with some grilled cheese bread for the finishing touch.

Vegetarian, Low-calorie, Low-fat

INGREDIENTS | SERVES 8

1 (16-ounce) package baby carrots
1 pint grape tomatoes
1 green bell pepper, chopped
½ cup sugar
¼ cup apple-cider vinegar
⅓ cup olive oil
1 teaspoon Worcestershire sauce
2 tablespoons Dijon mustard
8 cups mixed lettuces

Cooked Versus Uncooked Carrots

Cooking carrots helps break down the cell structure and fiber in the vegetable and makes the nutrients—especially beta carotene, a precursor to vitamin A—more available to your body. The cooked vegetable is also sweeter than it is when raw, because sugars are readily available to interact with taste buds on your tongue.

1. In medium saucepan, place carrots; cover with cold water. Bring to a boil over high heat; reduce heat to medium and simmer for 4 to 7 minutes until carrots are tender when pierced with fork. Immediately drain and cover with cold water. Drain again and combine with tomatoes and bell pepper in serving bowl.

2. In small bowl, combine sugar, vinegar, olive oil, Worcestershire sauce, and mustard and mix well until blended. Pour over carrot mixture; cover and refrigerate for 1 hour. When ready to eat, toss with lettuces and serve.

PER SERVING Calories: 170 | Fat: 10 g | Protein: 1.5 g | Sodium: 65 mg | Carbohydrates: 21 g | Fiber: 3 g

Scallion Tabbouleh

Bulgur, or cracked wheat, is a nutritious and tasty side dish that's chewy and nutty. It is high in fiber, which fills you up and keeps you satisfied hours after lunch.

Vegetarian, Low-calorie, Low-fat, Low-carb

INGREDIENTS | SERVES 8

1 cup bulgur

2 cups boiling water

½ cup chopped flat-leaf parsley

⅓ cup raisins

⅓ cup dried currants

½ cup chopped green onion

¼ cup lime juice

1 tablespoon olive oil

½ teaspoon salt

⅛ teaspoon pepper

Currants

Currants are small berry-like fruits that are most commonly found in red and black varieties. The tart flavor of the red currant is slightly stronger than the black. Because of their strong flavor, currants are usually cooked, dried, or made into jellies, as opposed to being eaten fresh on their own.

1. In a medium bowl, combine bulgur and boiling water. Cover and let stand for 20 minutes, or according to package directions, until tender.

2. Drain to remove excess moisture, if necessary, then transfer to a serving bowl. Add parsley, raisins, currants, and green onion; toss to mix well. In a small bowl, stir together lime juice, oil, salt, and pepper. Add to the bulgur mixture, toss well, and serve.

3. Mixture can be heated in the microwave, if desired. Microwave on 50 percent power for 2 to 3 minutes, remove, and stir. Continue microwaving on 50 percent power for 1-minute intervals until mixture is steaming. Let stand for 5 minutes, then serve.

PER SERVING Calories: 130 | Fat: 2 g | Protein: 1.3 g | Sodium: 162 mg | Carbohydrates: 14 g | Fiber: 2 g

Classic Shrimp Cocktail

Serve this shrimp with a squeeze of lemon juice for flavor and with cocktail sauce in a cup on the side for dipping.

Low-calorie, Low-fat, Low-carb

INGREDIENTS | SERVES 4

2 quarts water

½ teaspoon salt

1 teaspoon lemon juice

1 pound raw colossal shrimp, peeled and deveined

Cocktail sauce for dipping

Combine water, salt, and lemon juice in a saucepan and bring to a boil. Add shrimp and cook uncovered for 3 minutes or until shrimp turn pink. Drain and rinse shrimp. Serve with cocktail sauce.

PER SERVING Calories: 121 | Fat: 2 g | Protein: 23 g | Sodium: 449 mg | Carbohydrates: 1 g | Fiber: 0 g

Citrus Green Beans

Tender and crisp green beans are perked up with lemon and orange juice in this simple side dish.

Low-calorie, Low-fat, Low-carb, Vegetarian

INGREDIENTS | SERVES 6

1½ pounds fresh green beans

3 tablespoons butter

3 cloves garlic, minced

2 tablespoons lemon juice

¼ cup orange juice

1 teaspoon grated orange zest

1 teaspoon salt

⅛ teaspoon white pepper

1. Bring a large pot of salted water to a boil. Trim green beans and rinse off. Add to water and bring back to a simmer. Cook for 3 minutes, then drain.

2. In large skillet, melt butter and add garlic. Cook over medium heat until garlic is fragrant, about 2 minutes. Then add green beans; cook and stir for 3 to 5 minutes or until beans are crisp-tender. Stir in lemon juice, orange juice, orange zest, salt, and pepper, and heat through.

PER SERVING Calories: 94 | Fat: 6 g | Protein: 1 g | Sodium: 449 mg | Carbohydrates: 10 g | Fiber: 1.2 g

Summer Asparagus

Asparagus combined with fresh vegetables is a wonderful and easy side dish that pairs beautifully with any main dish recipe.

High-fiber, Low-carb, Low-calories, Vegetarian, Gluten-free

INGREDIENTS | SERVES 4

1 pound asparagus spears
2 tablespoons butter
¼ cup chopped green onion
½ cup chopped tomato
1 avocado, peeled and chopped

Ain't Asparagus Great?

Asparagus is low in calories, contains no cholesterol, and is very low in sodium. It is also a good source of folic acid, potassium, and dietary fiber. Need another reason to eat it? It tastes delicious!

1. Wash asparagus spears and snap off ends. Place in boiling salted water; cook for 3 to 4 minutes or until just crisp-tender. Drain in a colander and arrange on serving plate.

2. Meanwhile, in small saucepan combine butter with green onion; cook and stir over medium heat until crisp-tender, about 3 minutes. Remove from heat and stir in tomato and avocado. Pour over asparagus and serve.

PER SERVING Calories: 152 | Fat: 13 g | Protein: 3.4 g | Sodium: 66 mg | Carbohydrates: 9 g | Fiber: 5.4 g

Apricot Rice

Apricot nectar and dried apricots add flavor to plain white rice in this easy pilaf recipe. Serve it with grilled chicken breasts and a spinach salad for a delicious meal.

Vegetarian

INGREDIENTS | SERVES 6

1 tablespoon olive oil

2 shallots, finely chopped

3 cloves garlic, minced

1½ cups long-grain white rice

½ cup finely chopped dried apricots

2 cups apricot nectar

1 cup water

1 teaspoon salt

⅛ teaspoon cayenne pepper

2 tablespoons butter

1. In heavy saucepan, combine olive oil, shallots, and garlic. Cook and stir over medium heat until vegetables are tender, about 4 minutes. Stir in rice; cook and stir for 2 minutes longer. Add apricots along with remaining ingredients except butter. Bring to a boil, then reduce heat, cover, and simmer for 20 to 25 minutes or until rice is tender and liquid is absorbed.

2. Add butter, cover, and remove from heat. Let stand for 5 minutes. Then stir until butter is combined and serve.

PER SERVING Calories: 303 | Fat: 6 g | Protein: 5.3 g | Sodium: 417 mg | Carbohydrates: 57 g | Fiber: 4.3 g

German-Style Potato Salad

This recipe is exceptionally flavorful and tasty and is wonderful when served with barbecued meats.

Vegan, Gluten-free, Lactose-free

INGREDIENTS | SERVES 4

2 large Idaho, russet, or Yukon gold potatoes
¼ cup cider vinegar
¼ cup vegetable oil
1 teaspoon salt
1 teaspoon pepper
1 teaspoon sugar
1 teaspoon Hungarian sweet paprika
1 red onion, chopped
2 scallions, chopped
½ cup fresh parsley, chopped

1. Peel potatoes and cut into ½" slices.

2. Boil the potatoes in salted water to cover, 10 to 15 minutes, or until just softened.

3. Mix the rest of the ingredients in a large bowl. Drain potatoes and add to the dressing immediately. Toss gently to coat. Serve hot or cold.

PER SERVING Calories: 257 | Fat: 14 g | Protein: 4 g | Sodium: 587 mg | Carbohydrates: 32 g | Fiber: 1.5 g

Picnic Time

As with any cold potato or macaroni salad, this dish is a great option to bring to your next picnic or barbecue. And unlike salads that include dairy or mayonnaise, this one will last a little longer out on the picnic table.

Ham and Fig Panini

If you can't find fresh figs, thin apple slices can be substituted. This rich sandwich is exotic and delicious.

INGREDIENTS | SERVES 6

1 loaf Italian bread
2 tablespoons butter, softened
3 tablespoons apricot preserves
6 (1-ounce) slices ham
6 (1-ounce) slices Gruyère cheese
3 fresh figs, thinly sliced

1. Cut loaf in half lengthwise and cut into 6 sections. In small bowl, combine butter and apricot preserves and mix well. Spread mixture on cut sides of all bread pieces.

2. Layer ham, cheese, and fig slices on half of bread pieces; cover with remaining bread pieces. Prepare and preheat panini grill or indoor grill. Spray grill with nonstick cooking spray. Cook 2 sandwiches at a time on the grill, pressing down to flatten sandwiches. Cut in half and serve immediately.

Fresh Figs

Did you know that the fig is actually a flower folded in on itself? Figs are a nutritious "fruit," high in antioxidants, iron, fiber, and calcium. They ripen fully on the tree, so are usually available fresh only in late summer and fall. You can substitute dried figs for fresh figs in most recipes; just slice them thin and use.

PER SERVING Calories: 469 | Fat: 18 g | Protein: 15 g | Sodium: 1081 mg | Carbohydrates: 54 g | Fiber: 2.6 g

Grilled Fruit and Cheese Sandwiches

You may never have had fruit with cheese on a sandwich before, but it is delicious! The spread in this recipe can be refrigerated for up to 4 days.

Vegetarian

INGREDIENTS | SERVES 16

2 firm pears, peeled and cored

1 tablespoon lemon juice

1 (8-ounce) can pineapple rings

1 (8-ounce) package cream cheese, softened

2 tablespoons heavy cream

1 cup grated Havarti cheese

1 cup grated Gouda cheese

32 slices oatmeal bread

6 tablespoons butter, softened

All about Pears

Pears have a slightly gritty texture because they contain stone cells, or cells with a thick wall. If the pears are ripened off the tree, they will contain fewer stone cells. If pears are cooked in a recipe, you can use fruit that isn't quite ripe. The best pears for cooking include the green Anjou and the reddish-brown Bosc.

1. Slice pears into ½" thick slices; sprinkle with lemon juice. Drain pineapple rings and discard juice; place on paper towels to drain further. Prepare and preheat indoor dual-contact grill. Place pear slices on grill; close and grill for 2 to 3 minutes or just until pears develop grill marks. Remove from grill and add pineapple rings to grill. Close grill and cook for 3 to 5 minutes or until pineapple develops grill marks.

2. Let fruit cool for 10 minutes, then coarsely chop. In medium bowl, beat cream cheese with cream until light and fluffy. Stir in Havarti and Gouda and mix well. Stir in fruit; cover, and refrigerate for at least 2 hours before serving.

3. To make sandwiches, place about ¼ cup fruit spread in between bread slices. Butter outsides of sandwiches. Grill until bread is toasted and cheese melts, about 3 to 5 minutes on each side.

PER SERVING Calories: 331 | Fat: 19 g | Protein: 11 g | Sodium: 563 g | Carbohydrates: 31 g | Fiber: 2.6 g

Garden Quesadillas

Quesadillas are simply made from two tortillas with a filling, toasted on a griddle until crisp.

Vegetarian

INGREDIENTS | SERVES 4–6

2 tablespoons olive oil

1 onion, chopped

1 red bell pepper, chopped

½ cup chopped mushrooms

1 cup Fresh and Spicy Salsa (page 200)

8 whole-wheat tortillas

1 cup baby spinach leaves

1 cup shredded pepper jack cheese

1. In medium skillet, heat 1 tablespoon olive oil over medium heat. Add onion; cook and stir until crisp-tender, about 4 minutes. Add bell pepper and mushrooms; cook and stir for 2 to 4 minutes longer until tender. Drain and combine in medium bowl with salsa.

2. Arrange tortillas on work surface. Top half of the tortillas with some of the baby spinach leaves and spoon onion mixture on top. Top with cheese, then remaining tortillas and press down gently.

3. Heat griddle or skillet over medium heat. Brush with remaining olive oil, then grill quesadillas, turning once and pressing down occasionally with spatula, until cheese melts and tortillas are toasted. Cut into quarters and serve immediately.

PER SERVING Calories: 297 | Fat: 16 g | Protein: 11 g | Sodium: 562 mg | Carbohydrates: 29 g | Fiber: 3.7 g

Cilantro Chicken Tacos

By making your own taco shells at home, you significantly decrease the amount of fat in your taco meal.

INGREDIENTS | SERVES 6

2 cups corn or canola oil

6 (6") flour or whole-wheat tortillas

1 tablespoon olive oil

1 onion, chopped

3 boneless, skinless chicken breasts

1 green bell pepper, chopped

1 jalapeño pepper, minced

1 cup Fresh and Spicy Salsa (page 200)

⅓ cup chopped fresh cilantro

½ cup sour cream

1 cup chopped plum tomatoes

1 cup shredded lettuce

1 cup shredded jalapeño Monterey jack cheese

Cilantro and Coriander: Cousins

Two of the most widely used and loved herbs and spices in the world are derived from the same plant, *Coriandrum sativum*. The leaves of this plant are frequently referred to as cilantro, while the seeds are most commonly called coriander. Depending on the cuisine, the entire plant is used for the various flavors and aromas.

1. Pour corn or canola oil into a large deep saucepan and place over medium-high heat. Heat until oil temperature reaches 375°F. One at a time, fold tortillas in half and slip into the oil. Hold the taco shape with tongs as the tortilla fries, turning once during frying. Fry for 2 to 4 minutes on each side until the tortilla browns and puffs. Carefully remove from the oil, draining excess oil over the pot, and place on paper towels to drain. Repeat with remaining tortillas.

2. In large skillet, heat olive oil over medium heat. Add onion; cook and stir for 3 minutes. Meanwhile, cut chicken into 1" pieces. Add to skillet; cook and stir for 4 minutes longer. Add bell pepper and jalapeño; cook and stir for 1 minute longer.

3. Stir salsa and cilantro into chicken mixture; remove from heat. Make tacos with the cooled shells, chicken mixture, sour cream, plum tomatoes, lettuce, and shredded cheese.

PER SERVING Calories: 394 | Fat: 24 g | Sodium: 532 mg | Protein: 21 g | Carbohydrates: 25 g | Fiber: 2.3 g

Pasta with Wilted Spinach and Bacon

Wilted spinach salad takes on a new twist when served as a hot pasta dish. This super-quick recipe is delicious.

Low-calorie

INGREDIENTS | SERVES 6

6 slices bacon
4 cloves garlic, minced
1 pound spaghetti pasta
3 eggs, beaten
¼ cup heavy cream, divided
½ cup grated Parmesan cheese
2 tablespoons sugar
2 tablespoons white vinegar
1 tablespoon apple-cider vinegar
¼ teaspoon salt
¼ teaspoon pepper
4 cups chopped spinach

1. Bring a large pot of salted water to a boil. Meanwhile, in large skillet, cook bacon until crisp. Remove bacon from skillet and drain on paper towels; crumble and set aside. Remove all but 3 tablespoons bacon drippings from skillet. Add garlic to hot skillet and remove from heat.

2. Add pasta to water and cook according to package directions. Meanwhile, beat eggs, cream, and ¼ cup Parmesan cheese in small bowl. When pasta is done, drain and return to pot. Add egg mixture; toss for 2 minutes and remove from heat.

3. Working quickly, place skillet with bacon drippings over medium-high heat. Add sugar, vinegars, salt, and pepper and bring to a boil. Add spinach; toss until spinach starts to wilt.

4. Add all of spinach mixture to the pasta mixture. Toss over low heat for 2 minutes or until mixture is hot and spinach is wilted. Serve immediately with remaining ¼ cup Parmesan cheese.

PER SERVING Calories: 240 | Fat: 17 g | Protein: 12 g | Sodium: 335 mg | Carbohydrates: 27 g | Fiber: 2 g

Tex-Mex Fettuccine

*This simple fettuccine dish is spicy, creamy, and flavorful. Serve it with
a crisp green salad and a fruit salad for a cooling contrast.*

High-fiber

INGREDIENTS | **SERVES 4**

½ pound pork sausage

1 onion, chopped

3 cloves garlic, minced

1 jalapeño pepper, minced

1 green bell pepper, chopped

1 (14-ounce) can diced tomatoes, undrained

12 ounces fettuccine pasta

2 tablespoons flour

½ cup light cream

⅓ cup grated Cotija cheese

What Is *Tex-Mex*?

Tex-Mex is an abbreviation of *Texan-Mexican,* a term used to describe a regional American cuisine that blends foods available in the United States with the culinary creations of Mexico. The cuisine is commonly found in Texas as well as other southwestern border states.

1. Bring a large pot of salted water to a boil. Meanwhile, cook pork sausage along with onion and garlic over medium heat, stirring until sausage is brown and vegetables are tender. Drain well. Add jalapeño, bell pepper, and tomatoes; bring to a simmer.

2. Cook pasta according to package directions until al dente. When pasta is almost done, combine flour and cream in a small bowl and beat well. Add to tomato mixture; bring to a boil and simmer for 3 minutes.

3. Drain pasta and add to saucepan with sauce. Toss for 2 minutes, then sprinkle with cheese and serve.

PER SERVING Calories: 703 | Fat: 19 g | Protein: 23 g | Sodium: 777 g | Carbohydrates: 46 g | Fiber: 5.2 g

Quick and Easy Crab Cakes

Crab is such a luxurious meat; it's a good choice for an appetizer because you use less of it. Serve these little cakes with cocktail sauce and lemon wedges.

Low-calorie

INGREDIENTS | SERVES 6

12 soda crackers, crushed

1 egg, lightly beaten

3 tablespoons plain yogurt

1 teaspoon Worcestershire sauce

1 tablespoon lemon juice

1½ teaspoons Old Bay seasoning

¼ teaspoon crushed red pepper flakes

1 pound lump crabmeat

1 tablespoon olive oil

1. In a large bowl, combine cracker crumbs, egg, yogurt, Worcestershire sauce, lemon juice, seasoning, and red pepper flakes and mix well.

2. Add the crabmeat and gently fold mixture together. Form into 6 patties.

3. Heat olive oil in large nonstick skillet over medium heat. Add the patties and cook, turning once, until patties are brown and crisp and hot, about 10 to 15 minutes. Serve immediately.

PER SERVING Calories: 193 | Fat: 6.6 g | Protein: 14 g | Sodium: 883 mg | Carbohydrates: 18 g | Fiber: 0.7 g

What Is a Crab Cake?

Don't get the wrong idea. This isn't the type of cake you give to someone on their birthday. Crab cakes are an American dish composed of crabmeat and various other ingredients, such as bread crumbs, milk, eggs, onions, and seasonings. Crab cakes are traditionally associated with the area surrounding the Chesapeake Bay, in particular the state of Maryland and the city of Baltimore.

Bean and Corn Tartlets

These little tartlets are cute and bite-sized. Place them on a serving tray and garnish with chopped chives or cilantro.

Low-calorie, Low-fat, Low-carb, Vegetarian

INGREDIENTS | MAKES 32 TARTLETS

¾ cup frozen corn, thawed

1 cup canned black beans, rinsed

¼ cup chopped tomato

1 tablespoon lemon juice

⅛ teaspoon pepper

⅓ cup low-fat sour cream

32 mini frozen phyllo tartlet shells, thawed

1. Drain the corn and black beans very well. Combine with tomato, lemon juice, and pepper in small bowl, then stir in sour cream. Cover and chill until serving time.

2. To serve, spoon 1 tablespoon of the corn mixture into each tartlet shell. Serve immediately.

PER SERVING Calories: 29 | Fat: 0.47 g | Protein: 1.6 g | Sodium: 2.2 mg | Carbohydrates: 4.9 g | Fiber: 1 g

Mini Phyllo Shells

You can find mini phyllo tartlet shells in the freezer section of supermarkets. They are made from phyllo (or filo or fillo) dough and are very crisp. They're already prepared, so all you have to do is let them thaw. They can be filled with just about anything and served as appetizers or dessert.

Lemon Sesame Tuna

Tuna is delicious as an appetizer when it's cut into cubes and marinated in a lemon mixture.

Low-calorie, Low-carb, Low-fat

INGREDIENTS | SERVES 8

2 tablespoons lemon juice

1 tablespoon low-sodium soy sauce

1 tablespoon sesame oil

2 green onions, minced

2 (⅓-pound) tuna filets

¼ cup sesame seeds, toasted

1. In shallow bowl, combine lemon juice, soy sauce, sesame oil, and green onions and mix well. Cut the tuna into 1" cubes and add to the marinade; toss to coat and let stand for 15 minutes.

2. Preheat oven to 400°F. Arrange the fish in a single layer on a baking sheet. Bake until fish is just opaque, about 5 to 7 minutes. Sprinkle with sesame seeds and serve immediately with toothpicks.

PER SERVING Calories: 73 | Fat: 4.8 g | Protein: 6.6 g | Sodium: 78 mg | Carbohydrates: 1.2 g | Fiber: 0.65 g

Raspberry or Strawberry Coulis

Choose the flavor you prefer!

Low-calorie, Low-fat, Vegetarian

INGREDIENTS | MAKES 6 OUNCES

8 ounces strawberries or raspberries, washed and hulled

1 teaspoon lemon juice

Sugar substitute like Splenda to taste (start with one packet)

Blend all ingredients in the blender. Strain and serve.

What Is Coulis?

Haven't you been going to French class? *Coulis* just means "sauce." This fruity variety is delectable over ice cream, sherbet, or sorbet. Make a bunch and save it for when you have a sweet tooth!

PER SERVING Calories: 94 | Fat: 1.8 g | Protein: 1.8 g | Sodium: 1.8 mg | Carbohydrates: 22 g | Fiber: 13 g

Salmon and Broccoli Stir-Fry

*This is a quick and easy supper, in addition to being good
for you. You can blanch the broccoli in advance.*

INGREDIENTS | SERVES 2

½ pound broccoli florets
½ pound salmon filet, skin removed
1 tablespoon canola oil
1 teaspoon Asian sesame oil
1 teaspoon ginger root, minced
2 slices pickled ginger, chopped
1 clove garlic, minced
1 teaspoon hoisin sauce
Optional: 1 cup brown rice
Garnish of 5 scallions, chopped

1. Blanch the broccoli in boiling water for 5 minutes; drain.

2. Toss the broccoli and salmon over medium-high heat with the canola oil and sesame oil. Cook, stirring for 3 to 4 minutes.

3. Add the ginger root, pickled ginger, garlic, and hoisin sauce and serve over rice, garnished with scallions.

PER SERVING Calories: 627 | Fat: 17 g | Sodium: 536 mg | Protein: 33 g | Carbohydrates: 33 g | Fiber: 4 g

Peach Coulis with Ginger

This delicious sauce is perfect over vanilla ice cream. It can also be frozen for future use.

Low-calorie, Low-fat, Low-carb, Vegetarian

INGREDIENTS | MAKES 1 CUP

4 medium-sized ripe peaches
½ cup water
1 teaspoon sugar substitute, or to taste
Juice of ½ lemon

1. Place the peaches in a saucepan with water. Boil for 2 to 3 minutes. Cool; remove pits and skins.

2. Place in the blender with sugar substitute and lemon juice. Blend and serve.

PER 2 OUNCES Calories: 19 | Fat: 1 g | Protein: 0.48 g | Sodium: 0.27 mg | Carbohydrates: 5 g | Fiber: 0.95 g

Strawberry Rhubarb Pudding

This is a wonderful flavor combination for spring and summer. And this pudding is low-fat and low-carb!

Low-calorie, Low-fat

INGREDIENTS | **SERVES 4**

1 envelope unflavored gelatin

¼ cup cold water

1 cup fresh rhubarb, cut in 1" pieces

¼ cup water

½ pint strawberries, washed, hulled, and sliced (half reserved for topping)

½ cup Splenda sugar substitute for baking

2 cups nonfat vanilla yogurt

Rockin' Rhubarb

There are a few different ways to use rhubarb in cooking. One way is to cut up the stalks into 1-inch pieces and boil them in water. Add ½ to ¾ cup of sugar for each pound of rhubarb, then add cinnamon and/or nutmeg to taste. Sometimes a tablespoon of lime juice or lemon juice is added. The sliced stalks are boiled until soft. Alternatively, you can use rhubarb in a recipe, like this one.

1. Place the gelatin and cold water in the jar of the blender.

2. In a saucepan, over medium heat, boil the rhubarb, water, and half the strawberries with the Splenda.

3. Add the hot fruit to the gelatin and pulse to chop and mix the gelatin with the fruit. Cool until room temperature.

4. Swirl the fruit and yogurt together and spoon into glasses or bowls. Add strawberries for topping.

PER SERVING Calories: 224 | Fat: 0.5 g | Sodium: 175 mg | Protein: 7.9 g | Carbohydrates: 48 g | Fiber: 1.7 g

Hawaiian Pineapple Coffeecake

This delicious and easy coffeecake has double the coconut flavor and the sweet tang of pineapple. Serve it warm with some scrambled eggs for a great brunch.

INGREDIENTS | SERVES 18

1½ cups sugar

¼ cup brown sugar

1 teaspoon cinnamon

1 cup coconut

½ cup chopped macadamia nuts

⅓ cup butter, softened

2 eggs

1 (6-ounce) container coconut yogurt

1 (5-ounce) can crushed pineapple, drained

2 tablespoons butter, melted

2½ cups flour

2 teaspoons baking powder

1 teaspoon baking soda

1. Preheat oven to 375°F. Grease a 9" × 13" pan with unsalted butter and set aside. In small bowl, combine ½ cup sugar, ¼ cup brown sugar, cinnamon, coconut, and macadamia nuts and mix well. Mix in ⅓ cup butter until crumbly; set aside.

2. In large bowl, beat eggs with the yogurt until blended. Stir in drained pineapple, 1 cup sugar, and 2 tablespoons melted butter. Add flour, baking powder, and baking soda and mix until just combined. Pour into prepared pan and sprinkle with coconut mixture. Bake for 25 to 35 minutes or until coffeecake is deep golden brown. Cool on wire rack for 30 minutes, then serve.

PER SERVING Calories: 264 | Fat: 12 g | Protein: 3 g | Sodium: 191 mg | Carbohydrates: 36 g | Fiber: 1.3 g

Flaked or Grated Coconut?

It all depends on your taste! Flaked coconut is made of slightly thicker and shorter strands. Grated coconut has longer and thinner strands. And shredded coconut is usually the thinnest of all; it can dry out within a couple of weeks. If it does become dry, you can soak it, or any of these prepared coconut forms, in milk for 30 minutes; squeeze dry and use immediately.

CHAPTER 15

Holidays, Birthdays, and Other Celebrations

Mulled Spiced Cider

This is a classic holiday drink. Serve nice and hot on a chilly fall day or winter's night.

Low-calorie, Low-fat, Vegetarian

INGREDIENTS | MAKES 1 QUART

28 ounces cider

Juice of 1 lemon

1 orange, sliced thinly and seeded

10 whole cloves

2 cinnamon sticks

½ teaspoon allspice, not ground

Mix all ingredients together, heat, and serve.

PER 4 OUNCES Calories: 112 | Fat: 0 g | Protein: 0 g | Sodium: 64 mg | Carbohydrates: 30 g | Fiber: 1 g

Chestnut Purée

This is a wonderful accompaniment to holiday meats like turkey, game hens, or duck. If you use chestnuts from a can or a jar, you will save a great deal of time.

Vegetarian, Low-calorie, Low-fat

INGREDIENTS | MAKES 1 CUP

8 ounces chestnuts, shelled

Salt and pepper to taste

Pinch nutmeg

½ cup whole milk or light cream

Purée all ingredients in a blender or food processor. Warm over low heat and serve.

Charming Chestnuts

While your R.A. probably wouldn't want you roasting these over an open fire, you can still enjoy this classic holiday food while at college. Chestnuts contain very little fat and no gluten, and they're the only nut that has any vitamin C, so they're a great choice for a snack or for use in a recipe.

PER 2 TABLESPOONS Calories: 79 | Fat: 2 g | Protein: 2 g | Sodium: 48 mg | Carbohydrates: 16 g | Fiber: 0 g

Sweet Potato Apple Purée

Now this is a dish for the holidays! Serve it by itself or as a sauce for turkey, stuffing, and other Thanksgiving favorites.

Low-calorie, Low-fat, High-fiber, Vegetarian, Gluten-free

INGREDIENTS | SERVES 12

3 pounds sweet potatoes, peeled and cubed

2 Granny Smith apples, peeled and cubed

½ cup apple juice

2 tablespoons butter

½ teaspoon ground nutmeg

1 teaspoon salt

¼ teaspoon white pepper

¼ cup toasted sunflower seeds

1. In a large saucepan, place potatoes and cover with water. Cover saucepan, bring to a boil, reduce the heat to medium-low, and cook until tender, about 15 minutes. Drain.

2. Meanwhile, in a small saucepan, combine the apples with apple juice. Bring to a simmer over medium heat and cook until tender, about 5 minutes.

3. Transfer potatoes and undrained apples to a food processor. Add butter, nutmeg, salt, and pepper and purée until smooth. Sprinkle with sunflower seeds and serve.

PER SERVING Calories: 150 | Fat: 3 g | Protein: 2.5 g | Sodium: 141 mg | Carbohydrates: 35 g | Fiber: 5 g

Spiced Currant Jelly

This is another excellent condiment, good anytime to dress up meat, game, or poultry.

Low-calorie, Low-fat, Vegetarian

INGREDIENTS | MAKES 1 CUP

1 cup currant jelly
4 whole cloves
½ slice orange with peel, seeded and chopped
½ cinnamon stick

Put all ingredients in a saucepan. Warm over low heat and simmer for 3 minutes. Pour into a bowl and serve.

Not for Your Peanut Butter Sandwich

Currant jelly can be used in the traditional way (on sandwiches, toast, muffins, and so on), but this particular recipe is better when paired with meat and Thanksgiving side dishes. The cloves and cinnamon give it a distinctive holiday flair.

PER 2 TABLESPOONS Calories: 102 | Fat: 0 g | Protein: 0 g | Sodium: 42 mg | Carbohydrates: 26 g | Fiber: 4.6 g

Caramelized Onions

Studies show that onions can significantly cut the risk of blood clots. They contain sulfides, which are known to lower blood pressure and blood lipids.

Low-calorie, Low-fat, Low-carb, Vegan, Lactose-free

INGREDIENTS | SERVES 6

3 yellow onions, peeled and sliced
½ teaspoon all-purpose seasoning

1. Coat a skillet with nonstick spray. Add onion slices and all-purpose seasoning to the skillet.

2. Cook on medium-high heat for 10 minutes, stirring often. Onions are done when they are tender and brown.

PER SERVING Calories: 21 | Fat: 0 g | Protein: 1 g | Sodium: 22 mg | Carbohydrates: 5 g | Fiber: 1 g

Crunchy Eggplant

These can be served hot or cold. Served cold they taste like eggplant potato chips.

Low-calorie, Low-fat, Low-carb, High-fiber

INGREDIENTS | SERVES 3

3 egg whites, whipped

1 teaspoon salt

1 teaspoon pepper

1 teaspoon paprika

1 clove garlic, minced

1 eggplant, sliced

4 tablespoons Parmesan cheese

1. Preheat oven to 350°F.

2. Mix egg whites, salt, pepper, paprika, and garlic in a small bowl.

3. Dredge eggplant slices through this mixture, coating evenly on all sides.

4. Place slices on baking sheet. Sprinkle with Parmesan cheese. Bake for 30 minutes or until crispy.

PER SERVING Calories: 97 | Fat: 2 g | Protein: 8 g | Sodium: 970 mg | Carbohydrates: 12 g | Fiber: 5.6 g

Eggplant History Lesson

The Latin name for eggplant means "mad apple." There was a time when Europeans believed that the eggplant caused you to go insane if you ate it. It was Thomas Jefferson who introduced the eggplant to the United States after he took a trip to France and fell in love with the taste.

Coriander Carrots

Carrots make a wonderful side dish, and these are especially fragrant and flavorful.

Low-calorie, Low-fat, Vegetarian, Gluten-free

INGREDIENTS | SERVES 6

1 tablespoon olive oil
1 onion, chopped
1 cup water
1 bay leaf
½ teaspoon salt
1½ pounds carrots, thickly sliced
¼ cup dried currants
1 tablespoon butter
2 teaspoons ground coriander
2 tablespoons lemon juice
3 tablespoons minced flat-leaf parsley

Serve 'Em Up Right
Coriander and bay leaf add a nice spicy touch to tender carrots. Serve this carrot dish with grilled chicken or rice dishes or as a side for your Thanksgiving meal.

1. Heat oil in large saucepan over medium heat. Add onion; cook and stir until crisp-tender, about 4 minutes. Add water, bay leaf, salt, carrots, and currants and bring to a simmer.

2. Cover pan, reduce heat to low, and simmer for 10 to 15 minutes or until carrots are tender when tested with a fork.

3. Drain carrots, removing bay leaf, and return saucepan to heat. Add butter, coriander, lemon juice, and parsley; cook and stir over low heat for 2 to 3 minutes or until carrots are glazed. Serve immediately.

PER SERVING Calories: 95 | Fat: 3 g | Protein: 1.6 g | Sodium: 254 mg | Carbohydrates: 16 g | Fiber: 4 g

Roasted Zucchini and Squash

Both yellow squash and zucchini are summer squashes. Unlike winter squashes, these can be eaten raw.

Vegan, Lactose-free, Low-calorie, Low-fat, Low-carb

INGREDIENTS | SERVES 6

3 zucchini
3 yellow squash
½ teaspoon all-purpose seasoning

1. Slice vegetables lengthwise into thin strips. Coat a cookie sheet with nonstick spray. Lay veggie strips on cookie sheet, being careful not to crowd them.

2. Sprinkle with all-purpose seasoning. Bake in 375°F oven for 16 minutes, flipping once.

PER SERVING Calories: 33 | Fat: 0 g | Protein: 2 g | Sodium: 25 mg | Carbohydrates: 7 g | Fiber: 3 g

Holiday Squash and Green Beans

Did you know that green beans are helpful in maintaining bone density? They're a super source of vitamins C and K.

Low-calorie, Low-fat, Low-carb, Vegetarian, Lactose-free

INGREDIENTS | SERVES 6

6 cups multicolored squash, sliced
2 cups green beans
½ teaspoon all-purpose seasoning
Salt and pepper to taste

Heat a large skillet on the stove at medium heat. Toss ingredients in skillet and cook until veggies are tender and browning. Add salt and pepper to taste.

PER SERVING Calories: 34 | Fat: 0 g | Protein: 2 g | Sodium: 25 mg | Carbohydrates: 8 g | Fiber: 3 g

Stuffed Sweet Potatoes

Store sweet potatoes in a cool dry place; they do not need to be refrigerated.

Vegetarian, Low-calorie, Low-fat

INGREDIENTS | SERVES 4

2 large sweet potatoes

½ cup canned syrup-free crushed pineapples, drained

¼ teaspoon vanilla extract

¼ teaspoon ground cinnamon

1 teaspoon firmly packed Splenda brown sugar

1. Pierce sweet potatoes with sharp knife and bake 25 minutes at 400°F. Cut potatoes in half lengthwise. Scoop out 80 percent of potato pulp.

2. In a large bowl, combine potato pulp with remaining ingredients. Stir mixture with a fork until well blended. Divide mixture and place back into potato skins.

3. Bake potatoes in a pan at 350°F for 15 minutes.

Stellar Sweet Potatoes

Sweet potatoes are packed with potassium, vitamin A, and vitamin C. Cut a few holes in one, zap it in the microwave, and enjoy for lunch. No need to be fancy; this potato is divine all on its own.

PER SERVING Calories: 85 | Fat: 0 g | Protein: 1 g | Sodium: 9 mg | Carbohydrates: 20 g | Fiber: 2 g

Sweet Potato Puff

This is a Southern specialty that usually involves a lot of sugar, but this recipe substitutes Splenda. You can use virtually any nut to top it, but pecans work well with the sweet flavors.

Low-calorie

INGREDIENTS | SERVES 8

3 cups cooked sweet potatoes, chopped into little cubes

4 egg whites

¼ cup Splenda

1 teaspoon vanilla

½ cup orange juice

2 tablespoons flour

1 teaspoon salt

½ cup chopped pecans

1. Preheat oven to 350°F. Lightly spray a casserole or baking dish.

2. Place all ingredients in a blender or food processor and purée. Transfer to a baking dish. Sprinkle chopped pecans on top. Bake about 30 minutes and serve.

PER SERVING Calories: 145 | Fat: 6 g | Protein: 4 g | Sodium: 328 mg | Carbohydrates: 21 g | Fiber: 3 g

Serving Sweet Potato Puffs

To serve, use an ice cream scoop to scoop out each puff so it's a nice, puffy ball on your plate. You can also top with more sprinkled pecans, and it's also great served atop a bed of green beans.

Buttermilk Mashed Potatoes

Mashed potatoes don't have to be full of fat. Buttermilk adds a creamy richness to this classic dish.

Low-calorie, Low-fat, Vegetarian, Gluten-free

INGREDIENTS | SERVES 12

3 pounds potatoes, peeled and quartered

2 tablespoons butter

1 onion, chopped

1½ cups buttermilk

⅛ teaspoon nutmeg

½ teaspoon salt

⅛ teaspoon white pepper

Must Have Mashed

Every Thanksgiving meal must have a big, steaming bowl of creamy mashed potatoes. Don't think that just because you're in college you can't enjoy this holiday staple. Make a big batch and eat them as leftovers for the next few days after the holiday—after your stomach shrinks back to its original size that is.

1. Place potatoes in a large pot with water to cover. Bring to a boil, cover, reduce the heat to medium, and cook until tender, about 20 minutes.

2. Meanwhile, in small saucepan melt butter over medium heat. Cook onion, stirring occasionally, until tender, about 7 minutes.

3. When potatoes are done, drain, return to the hot pot, add onion mixture, and mash until smooth. Gradually add the buttermilk, stirring constantly. Stir in nutmeg, salt, and pepper. Serve immediately.

PER SERVING Calories: 106 | Fat: 2 g | Protein: 3.1 g | Sodium: 49 mg | Carbohydrates: 17 g | Fiber: 2.9 g

Simple Corn Stuffing

Stuffing can be piled on top of a dish instead of being stuffed into meat. This dish is exceptional, a remembrance of the first Thanksgiving and the Native Americans' gift of corn to the starving Pilgrims.

Vegetarian

INGREDIENTS | MAKES 4 CUPS

¼ pound butter or margarine

1 sweet medium-sized onion, chopped

4 celery stalks with leaves, chopped

20 juniper berries, bruised

1 cup chicken, vegetable, or beef stock (depending on what you're stuffing)

1 teaspoon thyme, dried, or 1 tablespoon fresh

1 teaspoon savory, dried, or 1 tablespoon fresh

1 teaspoon sage, dried, or 1 tablespoon fresh

½ cup fresh parsley, chopped

2 cups cornbread stuffing, from a package

2 cups frozen corn niblets

1 cup 2% milk

1. Melt the butter or margarine in a pan over medium heat. Sauté the onions, celery, and juniper berries for 5 to 7 minutes.

2. Add the broth, herbs, and spices. Mix well and add the cornbread stuffing, corn, and milk. Use with any holiday entrée!

PER 1 CUP Calories: 460 | Fat: 26 g | Protein: 8 g | Sodium: 322 mg | Carbohydrates: 48 g | Fiber: 2.6 g

Zucchini Casserole

This casserole not only serves as a delicious side dish, it is filling enough to serve as an entire vegetarian entrée. As an entrée it should provide 3 servings.

Low-calorie, Low-fat

INGREDIENTS | SERVES 6

1 clove fresh garlic, minced

1 teaspoon olive oil

4 large zucchini, sliced

1 cup white mushrooms, sliced

1 (15-ounce) can Italian-style stewed tomatoes

½ cup Italian-style bread crumbs

¼ cup shredded low-fat Parmesan cheese

¼ cup shredded low-fat mozzarella cheese

Gotta Have Garlic

So many recipes call for garlic that it's a good idea to have a few helpful tools on hand. One is a garlic press. They're inexpensive and can be found at most home goods stores. Another is a food processor. One of these handy gadgets will make the work of chopping or mincing garlic a snap.

1. Coat a 9" × 13" baking dish with nonstick spray.

2. Place garlic and olive oil in a large skillet and sauté for 6 minutes on medium heat.

3. Add zucchini to skillet and sauté for 5 minutes. Add mushrooms to skillet and sauté for 5 minutes. Remove from burner, add tomatoes, and stir.

4. Pour veggies into the baking dish. Cover veggies with bread crumbs. Sprinkle both cheeses over bread crumbs.

5. Bake at 350°F for 15 minutes or until cheese melts and sauce boils.

PER SERVING Calories: 111 | Fat: 2 g | Protein: 7 g | Sodium: 486 mg | Carbohydrates: 17 g | Fiber: 3 g

Baked Sweet Potato Fries

Tired of the same old sweet potatoes at Thanksgiving? Give these sweet, crispy fries a try!

Vegetarian, Low-calorie, Low-fat, Gluten-free, Lactose-free

INGREDIENTS | SERVES 6

2 pounds peeled sweet potatoes

2 teaspoons ground cinnamon

1 tablespoon olive oil

1. Preheat oven to 450°F. Cut potatoes into matchsticks, about ½" thick. Toss potatoes, cinnamon, and olive oil in a bowl.

2. Coat a large cookie sheet with nonstick spray. Bake for 25 to 30 minutes or until potatoes are fairly crispy.

PER SERVING Calories: 136 | Fat: 3 g | Protein: 2 g | Sodium: 14 mg | Carbohydrates: 27 g | Fiber: 4 g

Festive Turkey Salad

This is a great use for your leftover Thanksgiving turkey! Make sure to warm up the turkey just a little before mixing it into the salad.

High-fiber

INGREDIENTS | SERVES 4

3 cups chopped cooked turkey

1 cup chopped celery

1 cup chopped granny apple

1 (10-ounce) can mandarin oranges, drained

½ cup chopped macadamia nuts

1 teaspoon curry powder

¾ cup fat-free mayonnaise

6 large lettuce leaves

1. Mix turkey with celery, apple, oranges, and nuts. Add curry powder and mayonnaise.

2. Serve on lettuce leaves.

PER SERVING Calories: 440 | Fat: 23 g | Protein: 35 g | Sodium: 2128 mg | Carbohydrates: 27 g | Fiber: 6.1 g

Lettuce-Wrapped Turkey
with Cranberry Mayonnaise and Apples

This is a terrific way to use up Thanksgiving leftovers in a healthy way.

Low-carb

INGREDIENTS | SERVES 1

2 large romaine lettuce leaves

2 teaspoons low-fat mayonnaise

1 teaspoon cranberry sauce, jelled

1 teaspoon prepared horseradish

¼ pound deli or leftover turkey, diced

½ stalk celery, chopped fine

1 slice onion, chopped fine

½ tart apple, cored and chopped fine

1 tablespoon walnuts, toasted and chopped

1. Lay the lettuce leaves on a work surface. In a small bowl, mix together the mayonnaise, cranberry sauce, and horseradish.

2. Place the diced turkey on top of the lettuce leaves. Mix the celery, onion, apple, and walnuts with the cranberry mayonnaise. Spread on the turkey and roll up the wrap.

PER SERVING Calories: 325 | Fat: 15 g | Protein: 32 g | Sodium: 1201 mg | Carbohydrates: 15 g | Fiber: 3.5 g

Flavored Mayonnaise

To add extra pizzazz to your salads, sandwiches, and wraps, try making your own varieties of flavored mayonnaise. Adding curry to mayonnaise makes a great spread for chicken salad, and adding fresh herbs, such as dill and parsley, makes a great spread for a garden salad wrap.

Baked Gingerbread Pancakes

Never heard of baked pancakes? Give these a try and see what you think.

Low-calorie, Low-fat

INGREDIENTS | SERVES 4

½ cup fat-free milk

½ cup flour

½ cup unsweetened applesauce

1 cup Egg Beaters

1 tablespoon dark molasses

2 tablespoons Splenda

½ teaspoon ground ginger

½ teaspoon ground cinnamon

¼ teaspoon salt

1 cup nonfat vanilla yogurt

1. Preheat oven to 425°F. Coat a circular cake pan with butter-flavored cooking spray.

2. Stir all ingredients except yogurt in a medium bowl and whisk until batter is smooth.

3. Pour batter onto cake pan and bake until it puffs up, about 15 minutes.

4. Cut into 4 slices like a pizza and serve.

5. Top each slice with about ¼ cup of the yogurt

PER SERVING Calories: 188 | Fat: <1 g | Protein: 13 g | Sodium: 315 mg | Carbohydrates: 33 g | Fiber: 1 g

Be Warned

This puffy cake-like mixture will deflate as soon as you remove it from the oven. Do not be alarmed, it's supposed to do that. You can use any flavor of nonfat yogurt if you want to alter the taste slightly.

Holiday Gingerbread

Sprinkle this cake lightly with a little powdered sugar before serving.

Low-calorie

INGREDIENTS | SERVES 10

⅓ cup sugar

¼ cup margarine

½ cup molasses

1 egg

1½ cups flour

1 teaspoon ground ginger

½ teaspoon baking soda

¼ teaspoon ground nutmeg

⅛ teaspoon ground cloves

⅛ teaspoon salt

⅔ cup fat-free milk

Sweet Ginger

Queen Elizabeth I may have invented the gingerbread man, but Chinese cooks have been putting ginger's subtle flavor to use since ancient times. Many people serve gingerbread to soothe an upset stomach or nausea, and nothing beats a comforting cup of ginger tea when you're feeling run down.

1. In a large bowl, mix the sugar and margarine with an electric mixer until well blended.

2. Add the molasses and egg. Mix well.

3. Mix the flour, ginger, baking soda, nutmeg, cloves, and salt in a large bowl.

4. Add the flour mixture to sugar mixture.

5. Add the milk and mix well.

6. Lightly spray a square baking pan.

7. Pour batter into the pan.

8. Bake for about 30 minutes or until done.

PER SERVING Calories: 196 | Fat: 5 g | Protein: 3 g | Sodium: 167 mg | Carbohydrates: 34 g | Fiber: 0.23 g

Ginger Cookies

Ginger cookies are done when the tops start to crack in the oven.
Once you see the cracking, pull them out and let them harden.

Low-calorie

INGREDIENTS | **MAKES 20 COOKIES**

1¼ cups flour
2 teaspoons ground ginger
¼ cup packed brown sugar
¼ teaspoon vanilla
¼ cup molasses
3 tablespoons margarine, melted
¼ cup unsweetened applesauce
1 egg white, lightly beaten

Chill That Dough

Cookie dough is usually chilled before use to make it easier to handle. But chilling dough has other advantages. It lets you use a bit less flour, which results in a more tender cookie. And it lets the gluten in the flour relax, so the dough is easier to handle and rolls without springing back.

1. Sift flour and ginger in a large bowl, then stir in sugar.

2. Mix the vanilla, molasses, margarine, applesauce, and egg white in a medium bowl.

3. Add wet ingredients to the dry and stir until well blended.

4. Place dough in freezer until firm.

5. Preheat oven to 350°F.

6. Shape firm dough into balls and drop onto a baking sheet.

7. Bake 12 minutes and let cool.

PER SERVING Calories: 138 | Fat: 4 g | Protein: 2 g | Sodium: 130 mg | Carbohydrates: 24 g | Fiber: 0.53 g

Classic Cupcakes

These basic cupcakes make a great surprise for a friend who's celebrating her birthday while away at college.

Low-calorie, Low-fat

INGREDIENTS | SERVES 12

1 cup self-rising flour
½ cup nonfat dried milk powder
1 (3.4-ounce) box sugar-free chocolate Jell-O pudding mix
1 tablespoon unsweetened cocoa
½ cup Splenda
1 teaspoon vanilla
½ cup applesauce
¼ teaspoon baking soda
4 egg whites
Pinch of salt

Checking for Doneness

To see if your cupcakes are done, insert a clean toothpick into the center of a cupcake. The toothpick should come out clean. You can also tell by gently pressing on the top of the cupcake with a spoon; if the cupcake bounces back with spring, the batch is done.

1. Preheat oven to 350°F.

2. Mix flour, milk powder, Jell-O mix, cocoa, and Splenda in a medium bowl.

3. In a separate bowl, blend the vanilla, applesauce, and baking soda.

4. In a small bowl, beat the egg whites and salt until stiff.

5. Add the flour mixture to the egg whites, beating with an electric mixer.

6. Add the applesauce and beat until blended.

7. Line a muffin tin with paper cupcake wrappers and fill each ¾ of the way with batter.

8. Bake for 20 minutes.

PER SERVING Calories: 121 | Fat: <1 g | Protein: 6 g | Sodium: 374 mg | Carbohydrates: 23 g | Fiber: 0.87 g

Butterscotch Cupcakes

Use butterscotch ice cream topping as the frosting for these cupcakes, about 1 tablespoon per cupcake.

Low-calorie, Low-fat

INGREDIENTS | **SERVES 16**

½ cup cake flour
¾ cup powdered sugar
5 egg whites
⅛ teaspoon salt
1 teaspoon heavy cream
½ cup butterscotch ice cream topping
¼ cup granulated sugar
½ teaspoon vanilla

1. Preheat oven to 350°F. Line muffin tins with cupcake liners and set aside.

2. In a large bowl, sift the cake flour and powdered sugar twice.

3. In a medium bowl, beat the egg whites and salt with an electric mixer until frothy.

4. Add heavy cream and butterscotch until soft peaks form.

5. Add sugar and continue beating.

6. Fold in flour mixture gradually until blended.

7. Add vanilla. Mix thoroughly.

8. Spoon batter into muffin cups.

9. Bake for 20 minutes or until cupcake tops are browned.

PER SERVING Calories: 82 | Fat: <1 g | Protein: 2 g | Sodium: 75 mg | Carbohydrates: 19 g | Fiber: 0 g

Triple-Chocolate Cupcakes

A cross between a brownie and a muffin, these gooey cupcakes have an intense chocolate flavor heightened by the cocoa powder. You should use 3½"-round muffin tins.

Vegetarian

**INGREDIENTS | MAKES ABOUT 16 (3")
CUPCAKES**

4 ounces unsweetened chocolate squares

½ pound (2 sticks) unsalted butter

6 large eggs

1 cup granulated sugar

¾ cup cake flour

1½ teaspoons baking powder

2 teaspoons vanilla extract

1 tablespoon cocoa powder

Pinch salt

1 cup mini chocolate morsels

You Deserve It!

While staying healthy in college is important, it's also important to treat yourself every once in a while. College life can be stressful, and a little chocolate goes a long way toward making you feel better. Enjoy these cupcakes with friends. Celebrate!

1. Preheat the oven to 350°F. Spray nonstick muffin cups with nonstick cooking spray. Melt the chocolate and butter together over low heat. When melted, cool to room temperature.

2. Meanwhile, beat the eggs with the sugar until the mixture turns a pale lemon-yellow. Spoon the cooled chocolate mixture into the sugar-egg mixture and stir until combined. Stir in the cake flour, baking powder, vanilla extract, cocoa powder, and salt and beat for about 30 seconds. Stir in the chocolate morsels. Spoon the mixture into the cups until each is about ⅔ full.

3. Bake 15 to 18 minutes or until a toothpick inserted in the center comes out clean and the cupcakes feel firm. Cool completely.

PER SERVING Calories: 290 | Fat: 20 g | Protein: 4 g | Sodium: 75 mg | Carbohydrates: 27 g | Fiber: 2 g

Thanksgiving Pizza

This unique spin on pizza is quick, sweet, and delicious. The skin on the potato is the most nutritious part, so leave it on; it enhances the texture as well.

Low-calorie, Low-fat

INGREDIENTS | SERVES 2

1 medium sweet potato

1 whole-wheat pita

Dash of salt

1 tablespoon fat-free turkey gravy

2 ounces roasted turkey breast, cut in small chunks

1. Bake sweet potato with skin on in microwave for 10 to 12 minutes, or until soft. On a plate, mash potato with fork.

2. Place pita on a plate and smear sweet potato to cover it. Dash with salt. Top potato with gravy, followed by turkey.

3. Cook at 350°F for 6 to 8 minutes or microwave for 45 to 60 seconds.

PER SERVING Calories: 205 | Fat: 3 g | Protein: 12 g | Sodium: 223 mg | Carbohydrates: 34 g | Fiber: 4 g

Glossary of Basic Cooking Terms

Active dry yeast

This is a small plant that has been preserved by drying. When rehydrated, the yeast activates and begins producing carbon dioxide and alcohols.

Al dente

A term used in Italian cooking that refers to the texture of cooked pasta. When cooked "al dente," the pasta is tender, but still firm in the middle. The term literally means "to the tooth."

Bake

To cook in dry heat, usually in an oven, until proteins denature, starches gelatinize, and water evaporates to form a structure.

Beat

To combine two mixtures and to incorporate air by manipulating with a spoon or an electric mixer until fluffy.

Blanch

Blanching is a means of cooking food by immersing it in boiling water. After blanching, the cooked food is immediately placed in cold water to stop the cooking process. Always drain blanched foods thoroughly before adding to a dish.

Butter

A natural fat obtained by churning heavy cream to consolidate and remove some of the butterfat.

Calorie

A unit of measurement in nutrition, a calorie is the amount of energy needed to raise the temperature of 1 gram of water by 1 degree Celsius. The number of calories in a food is measured by chemically analyzing the food.

Cholesterol

Cholesterol is not a fat, but a sterol, an alcohol and fatty acid, a soft, waxy substance used by your body to make hormones. Your body makes cholesterol and you eat foods containing cholesterol. Only animal fats have cholesterol.

Chop

Chopping consists of cutting food into small pieces. While chopped food doesn't need to be perfectly uniform, the pieces should be roughly the same size.

Confectioner's sugar

This sugar is finely ground and mixed with cornstarch to prevent lumping; it is used mostly in icings and frostings. It is also known as powdered sugar and 10X sugar.

Corn oil

An oil obtained from the germ of the corn kernel. It has a high smoke point and contains a small amount of artificial trans fat.

Cornmeal

Coarsely ground corn, used to make polenta, also to coat foods to make a crisp crust.

Cornstarch

Very finely ground powder made from the starch in the endosperm of corn; used as a thickener.

Deep-fry

To fry in a large amount of oil or melted shortening, lard, or butter so the food is completely covered. In this dry-heat method of cooking, about 10 percent of the fat is absorbed into the food.

Dice

Dicing consists of cutting food into small cubes, usually ¼ inch in size or less. Unlike chopping, the food should be cut into even-sized pieces.

Dissolve

To immerse a solid in a liquid and heat or manipulate to form a solution in which none of the solid remains.

Drain

Draining consists of drawing off the liquid from a food. Either a colander (a perforated bowl made of metal or plastic) or paper towels can be used to drain food.

Dredge

To dip a food into another mixture, usually made of flour, bread crumbs, or cheese, to completely coat.

Edamame

The Japanese word for edible soybeans, a green pea encased in a pod.

Emulsify

To combine an oil and a liquid, either through manipulation or the addition of another ingredient, so they remain suspended in each other.

Fatty acids

A fatty acid is a long chain of carbon molecules bonded to each other and to hydrogen molecules, attached to an alcohol or glycerol molecule. They are short-chain, medium-chain, and long-chain, always with an even number of carbon molecules.

Flaky

A word describing food texture, usually a pie crust or crust on meat, which breaks apart into flat layers.

Flaxseed

This small, oil-rich seed is used primarily to make linseed oil, but is also a valuable source of nutrients like calcium, iron, and omega-3 fatty acids.

Fry

To cook food in hot oil, a dry heat environment.

Gluten

A protein in flour made by combining glutenin and gliadin with a liquid and physical manipulation.

Golden

The color of food when it is browned or quickly sautéed.

HDL

High-density lipoproteins, the "good" type of cholesterol that carries fat away from the bloodstream.

Herbs

The aromatic leafy part of an edible plant; herbs include basil, parsley, chives, thyme, tarragon, oregano, and mint.

Hummus

A combination of puréed chickpeas with garlic, lemon juice, and usually tahini; used as an appetizer or sandwich spread.

Hydrogenation

The process of adding hydrogen molecules to carbon chains in fats and fatty acids.

Italian salad dressing

A dressing made of olive oil and vinegar or lemon juice, combined into an emulsion, usually with herbs like basil, oregano, and thyme.

Jelly

A congealed mixture made from fruit juice, sugar, and pectin.

Julienne

To julienne food (also called matchstick cutting) consists of cutting it into very thin strips about 1½ to 2 inches long, with a width and thickness of about ⅛ inch. Both meat and vegetables can be julienned.

Kebab

Meats, fruits, and/or vegetables threaded onto skewers, usually barbecued over a wood or coal fire.

Kidney bean

A legume, either white or dark red, used for making chili and soups.

Knead

To manipulate a dough, usually a bread dough, to help develop the gluten in the flour so the bread has the proper texture.

Lard

The fat from pork, used to fry foods and as a substitute for margarine or butter.

LDL

Low-density lipoproteins, the "bad" cholesterol, which carries fat from the liver and intestines to the bloodstream.

Lecithin

A fatty substance that is a natural emulsifier, found in eggs and legumes.

Lipid

Lipids are organic molecules insoluble in water, consisting of a chain of hydrophobic carbon and hydrogen molecules and an alcohol or glycerol molecule. They include fats, oil, waxes, steroids, and cholesterol.

Long-chain fatty acids

These fatty acids have twelve to twenty-four carbon molecules bonded to hydrogen molecules and to a glycerol molecule.

Margarine

A fat made by hydrogenating polyunsaturated oils, colored with yellow food coloring to resemble butter.

Marinate

To coat foods in an acidic liquid or dry mixture to help break down protein bonds and tenderize the food.

Mayonnaise

An emulsification of egg yolks, lemon juice or vinegar, and oil, blended into a thick white creamy dressing.

Meat thermometer

A thermometer specially labeled to read the internal temperature of meat.

Medium-chain fatty acids

These fatty acids have six to twelve carbon molecules bonded to each other and to hydrogen molecules. Coconut and palm oils contain these fatty acids which are used in infant formulas.

Mince

Mincing consists of cutting food into very small pieces. In general, minced food is cut into smaller pieces than chopped food.

Monounsaturated oil

A fatty acid that has two carbons double-bonded to each other, missing two hydrogen molecules. These very stable oils are good for frying but can have low smoke points. Examples include olive, almond, avocado, canola, and peanut oils.

Mortar and pestle

A mortar is a bowl-shaped tool, sometimes made of stone or marble, and a pestle is the round instrument used to grind ingredients in the mortar.

Mouthfeel

A food science term that describes the action of food in the mouth; descriptors range from gummy to dry to slippery to smooth to chewy to tender.

Nuts

The edible fruit of some trees, consisting of a kernel in a hard shell. Most edible nuts are actually seeds and are a good course of monounsaturated fats.

Omega-3 fatty acids

A polyunsaturated fat named for the position of the first double bond. The body cannot make omega-3 fatty acids; they must be consumed.

Omega-6 fatty acids

A polyunsaturated fat named for the position of the first double bond. Too much of this fatty acid in the body can cause heart disease. Like HDL with LDL cholesterol, it works in concert with omega-3 fatty acids.

Organic food

Food that has been grown and processed without pesticides, herbicides, insecticides, fertilizers, artificial coloring, artificial flavoring, or additives.

Pan-fry

To quickly fry in a small amount of oil in a saucepan or skillet.

Polyunsaturated oil

A fatty acid that has more than two carbon molecules double-bonded to each other; it is missing at least four hydrogen molecules. Examples include corn, soybean, safflower, and sunflower oils.

Processed food

Any food that has been manipulated by chemicals or otherwise treated, such as frozen food, canned food, enriched foods, and dehydrated foods.

Rancid

Fats can become rancid over time and through exposure to oxygen. The fats oxidize, or break down, and free radicals form, which then exacerbate the process. Rancid fats smell and taste unpleasant.

Reduction

Quickly boiling or simmering liquid to evaporate the water and concentrate the flavor.

Risotto

An Italian rice dish made by slowly cooking rice in broth, stirring to help release starch that thickens the mixture.

Roast

To cook food at relatively high heat in an oven. This is a dry-cooking method, usually used for vegetables and meats.

Roux

A mixture of flour and oil or fat, cooked until the starches in the flour can absorb liquid. It is used to thicken sauces, from white sauce to gumbo.

Saturated fat

A fatty acid that has no double-bonded carbons but has all the carbons bonded to hydrogen molecules. Butter, coconut oil, and palm oil are all high in saturated fats.

Sauté

To quickly cook food in a small amount of fat over relatively high heat.

Sear

Searing meat consists of quickly browning it over high heat before finishing cooking it by another method. Searing meat browns the surface and seals in the juices.

Season

To change the flavor of food by adding ingredients like salt, pepper, herbs, and spices.

Short-chain fatty acid

A fat that contains two to six carbon molecules; examples include lauric and octanoic acids.

Shortening

A partially hydrogenated oil that is solid at room temperature, used to make everything from frostings to cakes to pastries and breads.

Shred

Shredding food consists of cutting it into thin strips that are usually thicker than a julienne cut. Meat, poultry, cabbage, lettuce, and cheese can all be shredded.

Simmer

Simmering food consists of cooking it in liquid at a temperature just below the boiling point.

Smoke point

The temperature at which fats begin to break down under heat. The higher the smoke point, the more stable the fat will be while frying and cooking. Butter's smoke point is 350°F, olive oil's 375°F, and refined oils' around 440°F.

Spices

Aromatic seasonings from seeds, bark, roots, and stems of edible plants. Spices include cinnamon, cumin, turmeric, ginger, and pepper, among others.

Trans

Latin word means "across," referring to the positioning of the hydrogen molecules on the carbon chain of a fatty acid.

Trans fat

A specific form of fatty acid where hydrogen molecules are positioned across from each other, in the "trans" position, as opposed to the "cis" position.

Tropical oils

Oils from plants grown in the tropic regions; the most common are coconut oil and palm oil. These oils are usually fully saturated and are solid at room temperature.

Unsalted butter

Sometimes known as "sweet butter," this is butter that contains no salt or sodium chloride. It's used for greasing pans, since salt in butter will make batter or dough stick.

Unsaturated fat

Fatty acids that have two or more carbon molecules double-bonded to each other; an unsaturated fat is missing at least two hydrogen molecules.

Vanilla

The highly aromatic seeds contained in a long pod, or fruit, of the vanilla plant, a member of the orchid family.

Vegetable oil

Oils made by pressing or chemically extracting lipids from a vegetable source, whether seeds, nuts, or fruits of a plant.

Vitamins

Vitamins are molecules that are used to promote and facilitate chemical reactions in the body. Most vitamins must be ingested as your body cannot make them.

Index

Find out Everything on Anything
at everything.com!

The new **Everything.com** has answers to your questions on just about everything! Based on the bestselling Everything book series, the **Everything.com** community provides a unique connection between members and experts in a variety of fields. Since 1996, Everything experts have helped millions of readers learn something new in an easy-to-understand, accessible, and fun way. And now Everything advice and know-how is available online.

At **Everything.com** you can explore thousands of articles on hundreds of topics—from starting your own business and personal finance to health-care advice and help with parenting, cooking, learning a new language, and more. And you also can:

- **Share advice**
- **Rate articles**
- **Submit articles**
- **Sign up for our Everything.com newsletters to stay informed of the latest articles, areas of interest, exciting sweepstakes, and more!**

Visit **Everything.com** where you'll find the broadest range and most authoritative content available online!

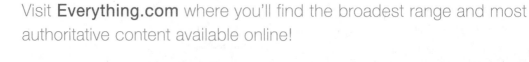